CAMBRIDGE COMMONWEALTH SERIES
General Editor: Professor E. T. Stokes

MACKINNON AND EAST AFRICA 1878–1895
A STUDY IN THE 'NEW IMPERIALISM'

CAMBRIDGE COMMONWEALTH SERIES

Toward 'Uhuru' in Tanzania: G. ANDREW MAGUIRE
Developing the Third World: the experience of the nineteen sixties: RONALD ROBINSON (ED)
Mackinnon and East Africa 1878–1895: a study in the 'New Imperialism': JOHN S. GALBRAITH

These monographs are published by the Syndics of the Cambridge University Press in association with the Managers of the Cambridge University Smuts Memorial Fund for the Advancement of Commonwealth Studies.

MACKINNON AND EAST AFRICA 1878-1895

A Study in the 'New Imperialism'

JOHN S. GALBRAITH

CAMBRIDGE
at the University Press 1972

Published by the Syndics of the Cambridge University Press
Bentley House, 200 Euston Road, London NW1 2DB
American Branch: 32 East 57th Street, New York, N.Y. 10022

Library of Congress Catalogue Card Number: 70-168895

ISBN: 0 521 08344 3

Printed in Great Britain
by Alden and Mowbray Ltd
at the Alden Press, Oxford

For Jim, John, and Mary

Contents

Illustrations

Preface

This is the story of dreams and dreamers and of an enterprise foredoomed to failure. Sir William Mackinnon and his associates in their east African schemes seemed to repudiate the principles of good business and even of good sense. The Imperial British East Africa Company was marked for early death from its inception. On these conclusions most historians who have written about the Company agree. They differ as to the basic cause of the Company's failure. Some have maintained that the Company failed because of lack of governmental support. Others attribute its demise to the ineffectuality of Mackinnon, its creator. Either interpretation can be supported with facts; neither is an adequate explanation.

In this essay I attempt to explain the motives of the Company's founders and the interrelationships of Mackinnon and other directors with the Imperial government during the brief period of the Company's existence. Since Mackinnon was the prime force behind the Company, I shall devote considerable attention to his involvement in east Africa before the Company came into being.

This history of the British East Africa Company is the beginning of what I hope will be a general study of the nineteenth-century chartered companies in their relationship to Imperial policy. The selection of this Company was in part fortuitous and in part recognition of the existence of other works. Kennedy Tregonning has written a history of the British North Borneo Company, and John Flint's *Sir George Goldie* provides considerable insight into the development and operation of the Royal Niger Company. I thus decided to deal in detail first with the East Africa and then with the South Africa Company.

Among those to whom I am especially indebted is Marie de Kiewiet Hemphill. Her dissertation on the East Africa Company, which regrettably has not been published, provided me with considerable help, and like many other scholars I have profited greatly by the use of the Mackinnon papers which are available largely through her efforts. I have benefited from the advice of Eric Stokes, Cambridge University; Leonard Thompson, Yale; Robert Collins, University of California, Santa Barbara; and my colleague Edward Alpers of the University of California, Los Angeles. My thanks also to my research assistants Oliver Pollak and Phillip Kennedy. And of course as always I acknowledge the multifarious help provided by my wife.

I wish to thank the following for permission to reproduce maps: Oxford University Press, from Roland Oliver and Gervase Mathew (eds.), *History of East Africa*, vol. I, East African Publishing House and Longmans, Green & Co., from B. A. Ogot and J. A. Kieran, *Zamani*, and H.M. Stationery Office and the Public Record Office. I also thank the British India Steam Navigation Co. Ltd for permission to include the photograph which appears as the frontispiece.

Finally, I express my thanks to Cambridge University for awarding me a Smuts Fellowship which enabled me to do the research on which this book is based and to Professor E. E. Rich and others at St Catharine's College, who made my stay at Cambridge a particularly pleasant one.

JOHN S. GALBRAITH

I

The background

During the 'imperialist' era of the late nineteenth century,[1] Great Britain authorized the creation of four chartered companies and endowed them with extensive political as well as commercial privileges. The first of these, the British North Borneo Company, chartered in 1881, was significant mainly because it was the forerunner; its history is associated with no great events.[2] The African companies, on the other hand, provided much of the energy for British expansion in western, southern, and eastern Africa. The Royal Niger Company came into being as a chartered company in June 1886, but it had been established under the name of the National African Company as a dominant economic force on the lower Niger since 1879.[3] The British South Africa Company, so closely identified with the career of Cecil Rhodes, was chartered in 1889. In each of these cases, the initiative was clearly that of the private entrepreneurs who sought governmental recognition. The Imperial British East Africa Company, chartered in 1888, also was the product of private initiative, but the life of the company from its origin was deeply affected by British foreign policy toward Germany.

Anglo-German relations after 1884, when Bismarck entered Germany in the race for colonies, were greatly influenced by clashes of British and German claims overseas. Whether these issues were pretexts invented by Bismarck to serve German diplomatic objectives in Europe, or represented a genuine conflict of colonial ambitions, the effect on Whitehall was the same. In areas of contending British and German interests, high policy was

---

[1] I use the term in the sense of John A. Hobson rather than that of Lenin. See Eric Stokes, 'Late Nineteenth-Century Colonial Expansion and the Attack on the Theory of Economic Imperialism: A Case of Mistaken Identity?' *Historical Journal* XII, 2 (1969), 285–301.

[2] For a history of this company see Kennedy G. Tregonning, *Under Chartered Company Rule* (Singapore, 1958).

[3] There is no history of the Royal Niger Company, but its life was closely related to that of its founder and chief motivating spirit, Sir George Goldie. See the biography by John E. Flint (London, 1960).

involved. Appraised by the requirements of that policy, the East Africa Company was sometimes considered by the Foreign Office as an instrument and sometimes an obstacle; in either case, commercial interests were affected by political considerations.

As a background to discussion of the interrelationships of Government and Company in east Africa, some reference must be made to the motivations for the expansion of Britain and Europe in the last quarter of the nineteenth century. All generalizations are dangerous, and in this area particularly so, for in the last few years scholars have effectively demolished the old orthodoxy and have produced new and to a considerable extent conflicting interpretations.

Whatever side one takes in this historians' quarrel, there is general agreement that there were certain basic factors. The expansion of the West was made possible by a technology which revolutionized the European industrial system and the means of transport of men and goods and provided military power which enabled Europeans to overawe or defeat societies possessing less advanced weapons. Basic to empire is a disparity of power and that disparity was great between Europe and the rest of the world throughout the nineteenth century. As David Landes has pointed out,[1] it is no coincidence that the Araucanian Indians who successfully resisted the Spanish in the eighteenth century fell before the Chileans in the nineteenth or that the Indians of the American southwest who had remained free from Spanish and Mexican rule, succumbed to the Americans. In both cases, the repeating weapon was irresistible. In the words of Hilaire Belloc,

> Whatever happens we have got
> The Maxim gun, and they have not.

With superior power went an assumption of superior morality and superior rights. Those who possessed that power could dominate those who did not without qualms of conscience that what they did contravened God's laws. 'Civilized' men did not need to rationalize their possession of lands occupied by lesser beings.

The predominance of European power over African societies

---

[1] David S. Landes, 'Some Thoughts on the Nature of Economic Imperialism', *Journal of Economic History* XXI, 4 (December 1961), 511.

should not be overstated. It has been pointed out that the actual capital and manpower expended in east and central Africa was very small, and that African societies were not completely helpless against the intrusion of European power.[1] The Imperial British East Africa Company with resources of less than half a million pounds could not impose effective rule over the vast areas between the east African coast and Buganda.[2] The German East Africa Company went bankrupt in its efforts to control the coast. The German government when it replaced the company with direct rule was unwilling to invest large resources in manpower and money in the 'pacification' of the interior. But it is nevertheless true that where the Europeans chose to exercise their power in east Africa their technological superiority was decisive. Lugard's Maxim gun, as unreliable as it was, made it possible for the British to dominate Buganda, and Captain Hermann von Wissman's troops crushed the Abushiri rising in the German sphere.

Technology clearly made imperialism possible but did it make it inevitable? So far as east Africa was concerned, European mercantile and financial involvement at the time of Germany's entry into the area in the 1880s was insignificant by comparison with the main centers of world trade. No scholar any longer disputes the fact that Africa – exclusive of the south – was a poor field for trade and investment (John A. Hobson himself did not argue the contrary).[3] But the statistics of investment and trade do not adequately measure the strength of economic motivation. A recent work, while conceding that tropical Africa was not commercially of great significance, points out that this fact does not in itself discount the importance of economic motives.[4] This observation is well taken. The strength of the economic drive cannot be measured by statistics of trade and finance. The Spanish who sought

[1] Terence O. Ranger, 'African Reactions to the Imposition of Colonial Rule in East and Central Africa', in L. H. Gann and Peter Duignan (eds.), *Colonialism in Africa, 1870–1960* (Cambridge, 1969), I, 291–6.

[2] A word of explanation is in order regarding the uses of 'Buganda' and 'Uganda' in this essay. The coastal traders from Zanzibar referred to the kingdom of Buganda as Uganda. The British at first used the words interchangeably, but eventually 'Uganda' was used to denote Buganda and surrounding areas which were included in the wider British protectorate. I shall use the words in this latter sense. See D. A. Low, *Buganda in Modern History* (Berkeley, 1971), p. 227.

[3] For a discussion of some critics of Hobson, see Robin W. Winks, *Historiography of the British Empire-Commonwealth* (Durham, N. C., 1966).

[4] D. C. M. Platt, *Finance, Trade, and Politics in British Foreign Policy, 1815–1914* (Oxford, 1968), pp. 256–61.

Eldorado were no less strongly motivated because they did not find it. The gold-seekers of Rhodesia who failed to make their fortune were no less dominated by avarice than were the Midases of the Rand. In an analysis of economic motivation, consequently, consideration must be given to hopes and expectations as well as to realization.

At the beginning of the scramble the potential resources of Africa were largely a matter of speculation, but reports by explorers and other pioneers contributed to excessive expectations. Since Livingstone's famous appeal in 1857 'to open up Africa for commerce and Christianity', a large number of explorers had travelled through the continent, west, north, and east, and most of them had suggested that great profits awaited European enterprise. Samuel Baker, who in the 1860s had had little good to say about the country at the headwaters of the Nile, had changed his emphasis by 1873, and now described east Africa's economic future in glowing terms. *The Times*, commenting on a speech by Baker in December of that year, was infected by his enthusiasm:

It is not long since Central Africa was regarded as nothing better than a region of torrid deserts or pestiferous swamps, and its people as a race hopelessly sunk in the lowest degradation. The veil has since been lifted sufficiently to give us glimpses of elevated and temperate plains, magnificent lakes, and beautiful scenery and a people who, however miserable, seem not incapable of some cultivation. There seems reason to believe that one of the finest parts of the world's surface is lying waste under the shroud of malaria which surrounds it, and under the barbarous anarchy with which it is cursed. The idea dawns upon some of us that some better destiny is yet in store for a region so blessed by nature, and the development of Africa is a step yet to come in the development of the world.[1]

The explorers of the 1870s were propagandists for European involvement in Africa and certainly stimulated the cupidity of capitalists in Britain and Europe. Verney Lovett Cameron, the first European to traverse equatorial Africa from coast to coast, described Africa as a treasure house. In his account of his epic journey, published in 1877 under the title *Across Africa*, Cameron appealed to the avarice of his readers with reference to 'the almost unspeakable richness', 'vast fortunes', and 'incalculable wealth' of tropical Africa.[2] Before the book was published, Cameron had

[1] *The Times*, 9 December 1873.
[2] V. Lovett Cameron, *Across Africa*, quoted in H. Alan C. Cairns, *The Clash of Cultures* (New York, 1965), p. 223.

communicated his hyperbole to interested listeners in Britain and in Europe, among them Leopold II. His tales of the wealth of the Congo led Leopold to employ Stanley to explore the area more intensively. Cameron's message also had great appeal in the British mercantile community. Africa, he told them, provided the outlet for the glut of the British enonomy. He wrote the President of the Royal Geographical Society, Sir Henry Rawlinson, in 1875: 'With a capital of from £1,000,000 to £2,000,000 to begin with, a great company would have Africa open as I say in about three years, if properly worked.'[1]

He suggested that a company organized on the model of the East India Company would be the appropriate agency to develop the riches of central Africa. Evidence of the existence of these riches was not impressive – a copper bracelet here, a gold trinket there, but, remarkably, many supposedly sober businessmen were impressed. The Great Lakes of central Africa were reputed to be the locus of great riches. In addition to Cameron, Horace Waller, Edward Hutchinson, Robert James Mann, and others were active propagandists of the myth of the treasure house of Africa. Central Africa, Waller told his audience in the Society of Arts, must be opened up and become 'the great heart from which commerce must be pumped into the country'.[2]

General Charles E. (Chinese) Gordon, whose experience in the Sudan presumably gave him expertise, confidently asserted that the Upper Nile, including Uganda, could yield great profits for British capitalists. He told Horace Waller in 1877 that during his tenure of two and a half years the area had yielded £100,000 in ivory alone, and that the Khedive had received £90,000 clear profit. With strong backing and expansion into the 'enormously rich' country south of Lakes Albert and Victoria, profits could be vastly increased.[3]

Reports from explorers were supported by some officials on the spot. Sir John Kirk, the great consul-general of Zanzibar, from the 1870s was an ardent promoter of east Africa as an area of great potential profit. The governor of the Gold Coast in 1886 reported

[1] Cameron to Rawlinson, 22 November 1875, in *Proceedings of the Royal Geographical Society* xx (1875–6), 119.
[2] H. Waller, 'Livingstone's Discoveries in Connection with the Resources of East Africa', *Journal of the Society of Arts* XXIII, no. 1, 164 (12 March 1875), 362.
[3] Waller to Mackinnon, 12 January 1877, Mackinnon Papers, School of Oriental and African Studies; same to same, 14 January 1877, in A. Roeykens, *Léopold II et l'Afrique, 1855–1880* (Brussels, 1957), p. 370.

that there was a 'vast amount' of wealth stored in the interior, an 'enormous' quantity of palm oil and kernels, and a smaller supply of rubber, valuable timber, cotton growing wild, and 'doubtless many other useful products'.[1]

Scientific, geographical, and philanthropic societies provided a means for giving publicity to the accounts of the explorers and exerting pressure on governments to support British interests in tropical Africa. Though their numbers were small, many of the members were prominent in business or politics and had entrée to the seats of power.[2]

Buoyant accounts of African riches emanating from apparently authoritative sources certainly were significant in the background of the 'scramble'.[3] These reports circulated not only in Britain but in France, Germany, and other European states. Cameron's and Stanley's reports stimulated Leopold's involvement in the Congo, and tales of the potentialities of the Great Lakes and Uganda contributed to Sir William Mackinnon's interest in the development of east Africa. But these reports of great wealth in western, central, and eastern Africa were little supported with factual data and underestimated the problems of transportation of commodities from the interior to the coast. In the late 1870s the palm oil trade of the Niger suffered from a fall in prices; and there seemed to be no strong incentive for further European commercial activity or for political intervention. The resources of the interior of Africa remained a mystery. The vast herds of elephants which then roamed over much of the continent were a source of ivory which could produce profits provided it could be transported at costs which were economic. But carriage across land was expensive, the primary vehicle of transport being African porters. In 1890 George Mackenzie estimated that it cost £130 per ton to transport goods from the east coast to Lake Victoria.[4] Further, the availability of ivory rapidly declined with the slaughter of the elephants. Sir Charles Dilke, writing in 1890, stated that the Arabs in east

---

[1] Colonial Office to Foreign Office, 5 May 1886, F.O. 84/1785, Public Record Office, hereinafter cited as P.R.O.

[2] For a discussion of these societies see Dorothy O. Helly, ' "Informed" Opinion on Tropical Africa in Great Britain 1860–1890', *African Affairs* LXVIII, no. 272 (July 1969), 195–217.

[3] Exaggerated impressions of the richness of Africa had gained credence long before the 'scramble'. See Philip D. Curtin, *The Image of Africa* (Madison, 1964), *passim*.

[4] Cairns, *The Clash of Cultures*, p. 22.

Africa had killed elephants at such a rate that unless the British East Africa Company imposed restrictions, there would likely be no ivory to be obtained after fifteen or twenty years.[1] Even where elephants were plentiful the returns did not justify the optimism of the enthusiasts. For the first ten years of its existence, Leopold's Congo Free State depended upon ivory as its primary source of revenue. In 1887–8 the income was only one-tenth of the expense. In 1893–4 it rose to one-third, but massive contributions still had to be made by the King and the Belgian government to avert bankruptcy. The Free State would undoubtedly have ended in financial failure had it not been for a windfall which no one had anticipated at the time the Free State was founded, the increasing demand for wild rubber.[2] In the late 1870s also there was knowledge of the existence of copper deposits in the Katanga area, though not of their extent, and of gold workings of ancient vintage in the Matabele country, which might prove, some thought, to be King Solomon's mines. This catalogue of resources, known or suspected, did not document the contention that Africa was worth the attention of European merchants or capitalists. Sir John Pope Hennessy in 1890 wrote an article entitled 'Is Central Africa Worth Having?' and had no difficulty convincing himself that the answer was 'no'.[3] Edward Dicey simultaneously came to the same conclusion in an article with the same title.[4] Harry Johnston made a valiant effort to rebut these detractors of the importance of Africa. He stated that the total trade of the British Empire with British Africa was approximately £25,200,000 annually (excluding £9,000,000 to £10,000,000 annual trade with Egypt).[5] This was an impressive amount, but Pope Hennessy pointed out that Johnston had included in his statistics the value of gold and diamonds from south Africa and that when this was subtracted, the remainder was insignificant.[6]

[1] Charles W. Dilke, *Problems of Greater Britain* (2 vols., London, 1890), II, 170.
[2] Jean Stengers, 'The Congo Free State and the Belgian Congo before 1914', in L. H. Gann and Peter Duignan, *Colonialism in Africa, 1870–1960* (Cambridge, 1969), I, 272.
[3] John Pope Hennessy, 'Is Central Africa Worth Having?' *Nineteenth Century* CLXIII (September 1890), 478–87; also 'The African Bubble', in the same journal, CLXI (July 1890), 1–4.
[4] Edward Dicey, 'Is Central Africa Worth Having?' *Nineteenth Century* CLXIII (September 1890), 488–500.
[5] H. H. Johnston, 'The Value of Africa: A Reply to Sir John Pope Hennessy', *Nineteenth Century* CLXII (August 1890), 175.
[6] John Pope Hennessy, 'Is Central Africa Worth Having?' *Nineteenth Century* CLXIII (September 1890), 478–87.

That inveterate cynic, Labouchère's *Truth*, commented in caustic terms on the hyperbole of the Africanists and their monomania for public and private action to support their enthusiasm:

Whenever any one has made a name in Africa by exploration, like Stanley, or by administration, like Captain Lugard, he loses all sense of proportion, and fancies that the sole business of the British tax-payer is to aid in annexing vast African territories, and that in some mysterious way this long-suffering beast of burthen is to be deemed a criminal if, instead of looking after our own poor and bettering their condition, he does not expend millions in an endeavor to lead the Africans in the right path by shooting them if they stray from it. I am sorry that Africans in their native jungle are given to enslave each other, but why we should take upon ourselves to reform these local habits instead of looking closer at home, I never have understood.[1]

As was not infrequently the case, *Truth* distorted the issue. The appeal of Stanley and Lugard was to 'commerce and Christianity', to the prospect of profit as well as to the evangelical spirit. But economic considerations alone would scarcely have roused businessmen or governments to action in Africa. The steely-eyed, calculating individual who supposedly epitomized the Victorian business man would not have been attracted by a prospectus of the kind the African lobby was able to produce. Frederick Lugard in 1895 told an audience of the Royal Colonial Institute that Africa, 1,400 years before Christ had contributed ivory, apes, and peacocks to the world's wealth, but that now it was making a more substantial contribution. The partition of Africa, he said,

. . . was the natural overflow of the nations of Europe into the waste places of the earth, following the law which has guided and indeed formed the history of the world. In the nineteenth century, moreover, there has been a new propelling influence at work over and above that blind impulse which prompts a certain proportion of the manhood of civilised nations to wander forth into less civilised lands. The impulse to which I allude is to some extent distinct from that which forces the emigration of surplus population from the congested cities of Europe and it is the direct result of the great trade rivalry and commercial warfare which has followed the cheapening of transport — by the introduction of steam. In our own case, the hostile tariff imposed by other nations upon our industries, the competition of foreign-made goods, and the depression of trade, have driven us to seek new markets and new fields for our surplus energy. Settlers driven to seek their fortunes in new colonies, by motives such as these, do

[1] *Truth*, 13 October 1892.

not embark for Africa with the primary object of benefitting the natives, but of benefitting themselves.[1]

Lugard, it will be noted, spoke not so much of the positive importance of Africa as of the mandate of European countries to find new markets in order to survive. Superficially, he thus seemed to be supporting the position usually identified with Marxist-Leninism. But the view that colonies were necessary for prosperity was widely held by Lugard's contemporaries. This conclusion, however, did not imply that those who supported it were prepared to make financial sacrifices themselves. The Manchester Chamber of Commerce and leading industrialists who belonged to it ardently advocated British expansion in east Africa in the mid-1880s, but the resources necessary to carry out their desires were not forthcoming from the Manchester area. Either the Exchequer should provide the money or some public-spirited capitalist, such as Sir William Mackinnon, but Manchester would not advance a sixpence 'unless the money was secure'.[2] The government, on the other hand, was not prepared to take on the financial responsibility, and Parliament would undoubtedly have opposed such a levy of tax funds had it been advocated. The East Africa Company in the early 1890s encountered this parliamentary resistance when it appealed for assistance in building the Uganda railway. Rosebery's reference in 1893 to 'pegging out claims for the future' and Chamberlain's Birmingham speech of 1896 asserting the duty of government to protect and advance commerce were both made after the most active phase of land grabbing had passed and their views did not represent the consensus among their colleagues.

There was unquestionably a strong economic component in late nineteenth-century imperialism; unquestionably also, that influence was not all-important, and it was probably not decisive in directing governmental policy. Obviously, no single-cause explanation will suffice, nor will any composite of explanations apply equally to all areas of British expansion, much less to that of Europe in general. Recent German research suggests that Bismarck's involvement in imperial expansion was a 'pragmatic' decision designed to relieve critical tensions within the German society. He would have preferred, as would Britain, to have relied

[1] F. D. Lugard, 'The Extension of British Influence (and Trade) in Africa', *Proceedings of the Royal Colonial Institute* XXVII (1895–6), 6.
[2] Minute, 'Zanzibar', by Sir Percy Anderson, 14 April 1885, F.O. 84/1737, P.R.O.

B

upon the expansion of commerce in a free-trade world, but reacted to the protectionist policies of European rivals, particularly France, and gave way to those pressure groups who were demanding colonies as a means of preserving present and prospective markets for German goods. In so doing, Bismarck, a German historian has argued, also was able to divert the people of Germany from depression at home and class differences to an anglophobic nationalism which unified the society, maintained the power structure, and kept the 'bonapartist dictator' in power.[1]

Whatever fundamental explanations for imperialism, British, German, or French, may be accepted, it is evident that the partition of Africa cannot be explained in exclusively 'rational' terms, as several writers have pointed out. The contributions of such emotional factors as national pride and of actions with unintended consequences should not be underestimated. The participants themselves often had difficulty in discerning the national advantages to be gained by their actions. Lord Derby as Colonial Secretary admitted to Earl Granville that 'there is something absurd in the scramble for colonies, and I am as little disposed to join in it as you can be'. He added, however, that it was necessary for Britain to extend its existing empire in order to protect what it had.[2] Derby was referring in particular to possible German annexations in southeast Africa adjacent to Natal. But as Gladstone observed in another connection, 'Place the burden where you will, the difficulty will always arise *on the border*'.[3]

British concern to protect the environs of existing colonies seemed to jealous rivals mere rationalization for an effort to interdict most of the unclaimed real estate of the world to other European states. Britain was neither willing to develop these territories itself nor to allow other powers to do so. As the *Kölnische Zeitung* stated in April 1884: 'Africa is a large pudding which the English have been preparing for themselves at other people's expense, and the crust of which is already fit for eating.'[4]

[1] Hans-Ulrich Wehler, 'Bismarck's Imperialism 1862–1890', *Past and Present*, no. 48 (1970), 119–55. The author in this article summarizes the findings of his book, *Bismarck und der Imperialismus* (Cologne, 1969). The author is critical of some of the recent interpretations of British expansion in the 1880s and 1890s.
[2] Derby to Granville, 28 December 1884, PRO 30/29/120, P.R.O.
[3] Cabinet meeting, 10 March 1883, Gladstone Papers, Addtl. MSS 44644, British Museum.
[4] *Kölnische Zeitung*, 22 April 1884, quoted in John Holland Rose, *The Development of European Nations, 1870–1900* (London, 1905), p. 516.

Many years later, in 1905, Thomas H. Sanderson, Permanent Undersecretary at the Foreign Office, took a sympathetic view of German frustrations. Germany, he said, was a young power, ambitious for world influence. But everywhere she had sought to expand she had found 'the British lion in her path'. He added: 'It has sometimes seemed to me that to a foreigner reading our Press the British Empire must appear in the light of some huge giant sprawling over the globe, with gouty fingers and toes stretched in every direction, which cannot be approached without eliciting a scream.'[1]

That was not the mood of the 1880s. Then, British statesmen saw their German and French counterparts as aggressive imperialists whose voracity posed a threat to the free flow of trade and to strategic British interests. The Germans and French had similar convictions regarding the British. Neither side quite comprehended the motives of the other; perhaps neither quite understood their own. But assumptions and speculations about other governments' intentions were a factor in the scramble.

The character of the European impact overseas, however, was not primarily determined by the predilections of prime ministers and foreign secretaries. They rarely initiated policy; rather, they were required to react to rapidly changing events arising from the activities of missionaries, traders, and soldiers over whom they exercised little control. These 'warlike classes' as Lord Ripon called them,[2] posed problems for home governments. An impetuous action of a soldier or a governor might be disavowed or the murder of a missionary ignored for reasons of state, but the action creating the diplomatic environment came principally from men and forces outside the chancelleries of Europe. The government at home frequently had to deal with the consequences. As Granville lamented to the German ambassador after one of Bismarck's numerous outbursts at alleged British aggressiveness overseas, 'It is unavoidable that in places far distant from Europe the action not only of British and German individuals but even of official servants of each state may be such, as unchecked, might lead to unnecessary complications.'[3] Sir William Harcourt in 1885 wrote

---

[1] Zara S. Steiner, *The Foreign Office and Foreign Policy 1898–1914* (Cambridge, 1969), p. 69.
[2] Ripon to Rosebery, 28 February 1895, Ripon Papers, Addtl. MSS 43516, British Museum. Ripon was Colonial Secretary at the time.
[3] Granville to Münster, 16 February 1885, F.O. 244/391, P.R.O.

of the extreme folly of irritating Bismarck on issues involving territories of no conceivable value to Britain. 'We seem most unfortunate,' he complained, 'in our Agents who are getting us into difficulties in every quarter of the globe.'[1]

The apparent vacillations of British imperial policy in the 1880s and 1890s were a product of rapidly changing conditions which necessitated expedient decisions. Gladstone as leader of the opposition in 1876 could state that the security of the Suez Canal rested solely on British maritime superiority in the Mediterranean and that intervention in Egypt would be madness.[2] As prime minister in 1882, he and his cabinet were required to make decisions in response to conditions very different from what he had observed six years earlier. As the responsible head of a cabinet, he acted in a way seemingly contrary to his individual professions. Garnet Wolseley mockingly referred to him as 'that old crocodile' whose noble pronouncements were belied by his actions.[3] In fact, the genuineness of Gladstone's anti-annexationism is beyond doubt, but the problems he confronted did not admit of resolution by moral maxims. The nature of these problems he and his colleagues imperfectly understood, as the correspondence of cabinet members indicates; the consequences they could not foresee at all. Such is the common lot of statesmen in foreign relations.

These comments should not be taken to suggest that the government of a Gladstone or a Salisbury made decisions blindly. On the contrary, major policy was shaped by the most careful analysis of the information available and of the likely consequences to British interests of alternative courses of action. But they were removed in space and time from the areas to which their decisions related.[4] The 'man on the spot' on whom they had to rely to a considerable extent suffered from similar disabilities. He was often unaware of what was taking place in districts remote from his headquarters and was deficient in understanding of the local

---

[1] Note of Harcourt, 29 April 1885, PRO 130/29/145, P.R.O.

[2] Gladstone to Granville, 17 November 1876, PRO 30/29/29A, P.R.O., published in Agatha Ramm (ed.), *The Political Correspondence of Mr. Gladstone and Lord Granville, 1876–1882* (2 vols., London, 1962), I, 20.

[3] Mekki Shibeika, *British Policy in the Sudan, 1882–1902* (London, New York, 1952), p. 303.

[4] For a discussion of the events which influenced 'the official mind', see Ronald Robinson and John Gallagher, *Africa and the Victorians* (London, 1961), ch. 1 and *passim*.

societies with whom he had to deal.[1]

To vary Hobson's famous metaphor, Whitehall acted as a governor of the imperial engine. The energy came from a variety of interest groups and of powerful men who represented them. The Foreign Office responded to these initiatives in terms of their prospective costs in money and in commitments. The study of the Imperial British East Africa Company concerns itself with the interaction of the active force of the 'men on the spot' and their backers at home and the regulating power of the home government.

When the home government was prepared to apply the brakes, the expansionist proclivities of overseas Britons could be frustrated and frequently were. When Captain W. F. Owen declared a protectorate over Mombasa in 1824, his action was promptly disavowed. Various efforts to assert British authority over Delagoa Bay likewise were fruitless because of the opposition of Whitehall. The role of the Foreign Office was essentially negative; it could prevent action; it generally did not initiate it.

In west and south Africa the dynamic of expansion is associated with a forceful personality who dominated the scene. It is significant that there have been biographies of Sir George Goldie and of Cecil Rhodes but no histories of the companies they represented. In this panorama of Empire, the east African sector appears dull by comparison; Sir William Mackinnon still awaits a biographer. Mackinnon is usually portrayed as a hard-headed, canny little Scot whose Calvinism was softened with a dash of humanitarianism – a grey man. Further, he organized the East Africa Company in the last years of his life, and historians have described him as an aging man whose lack of energy doomed his enterprise to failure. Sir John Kirk was a great force, and he has merited the accolades of Sir Reginald Coupland and others who have written about his influence in Zanzibar. But Kirk retired before the Company was chartered, and his relationship to it was that of a senior statesman.

This contrast between the vibrancy of Goldie and Rhodes and the feebleness of Mackinnon has been greatly overdone. Furthermore, Mackinnon cannot be reduced to the composite of 'businessman' cum 'humanitarian'. No 'businessman' dominated by considerations of profit would have embarked upon the schemes he projected in Africa. His own description of his aims is no more helpful as a clue to his involvement. He stated that he and his

[1] For a discussion of this subject in a slightly earlier era, see W. David McIntyre, *The Imperial Frontier in the Tropics, 1865–75* (New York, 1967).

friends proposed 'to take their dividends in philanthropy'.[1] In that assertion he was undoubtedly sincere, but the labels 'philanthropist' or 'humanitarian' tell little about the individual they describe. A man's drives and aspirations cannot be encapsulated in a word. Certainly the humanitarian impulse was alloyed with material considerations; without the support of economic interests the crusade against the slave trade and slavery probably could not have prevailed. Decades before Mackinnon's involvement, Lord Palmerston had indicated that his opposition to the slave trade was not actuated solely by idealism:

My belief is, that if the slave trade could be entirely put down there would be a very great increase of legitimate trade with the coast of Africa; the natives are much in want of commodities with which we can furnish them, and they possess very simple means of paying for them in commodities which we require.[2]

There is nothing essentially un-humanitarian in the view that a humane action can provide economic benefit. Livingstone himself could have endorsed Palmerston's statement. But a wide range of people avowed their purpose to be the civilization of the benighted and the saving of the heathen, and the contrast between profession and practice delighted the cynics. Leopold II's assertions of high-minded devotion to the cause of civilization and Christianity and his performance in the Congo Free State provide a classic text on the odiousness of sanctimonious hypocrisy. When Cardinal Lavigerie in 1890 announced the formation of the 'Armed Brethren of the Sahara' to eliminate the slave trade and to Christianize the heathen, he evoked irreverent responses. One Englishman composed a 'hymn' to be sung at the dedicatory service of the Brethren:

> Take this Banner, and if e'er
> Arabs will not bow in prayer,
> Chant a psalm their shrieks to drown,
> Shrive and Bible in your hands
> Teach the truth through heathen lands
> Preach, convert, baptise, anoint,
> Even at the bayonet's point

[1] E. Carton de Wiart, *Les grandes compagnies coloniales anglaises du XIXe siècle* (Paris, 1899), p. 239.

[2] Henry Reeve (ed.), *The Greville Memoirs* (new impression, 1903), VI, 131–2, cited in Roger T. Anstey, 'Capitalism and Slavery: A Critique', *Economic History Review*, second series, XXI, no. 2 (August 1968), 307–20. This article, which reviews Eric Williams' book, is essential reading for anyone with an interest in nineteenth-century British humanitarianism.

Far and wide, without surcease,
Spread the Gospel's news of peace
Far and wide, in Heaven's name,
Spread the news with steel and flame
....

Brethren! Oh! be not afraid
Heaven your Christian work will aid;
Banish all your doubts and tears,
Rifles cannot fail 'gainst spears.
Take your banner! Onward go!
Christian soldiers, seek your foe,
And the devil to refute,
Do not hesitate to shoot.[1]

The bloody record of avowed evangelists such as Henry
Morton Stanley gave force to the indictment of all idealistic
projects as humbug or hypocrisy. But the movement for opening
up Africa was not a mere cloak for exploitation. The zeal to carry
out the injunction of Livingstone was widely and honestly held in
his native Scotland, in England, and elsewhere. Mackinnon himself
was strongly influenced by this feeling, and there is no reason to
doubt the genuineness of his belief that he was benefiting Africa
as well as Britain by his activities. It does not explain his commitment, but no explanation would be adequate which ignored it.
The exact nature of this moral urge, however, is not so clear.
Mackinnon shared the Anglo-Scottish nineteenth-century conviction of the inevitability and desirability of material progress.
He accepted unquestioningly the superiority of his own moral
standards and the truth of the precepts of his church. He undoubtedly believed that Africans would benefit from British trade,
British institutions, and British religion. But in all his extant
correspondence there is little evidence of interest in Africans as
fellow human beings. Like the explorers who seemed by their
narratives to trek across previously undiscovered wilderness,
Mackinnon gave little thought to the people who inhabited his
area of interest in east Africa except to the extent they could
advance or thwart his schemes. His east Africa was inhabited by a
Sultan with some power to assist, considerable human resources of
labor, some agglomerations of humanity which were threatening,
and few if any black human beings with faces. In that picture of the
African scene he reflected the general view of his British contemporaries. In the 1870s those who had a special concern with east

---

[1] *Truth*, 16 April 1891.

Africa also saw it through their own prisms. Government officials and the missionary societies were predominantly actuated by the object of the extirpation of the slave trade. Their concern was not with understanding African societies but with the relationship of these societies to British interests – first with regard to the slave trade and secondarily to commerce. Their knowledge of the area was principally confined to the coast. The Sultan of Zanzibar was significant because it was hoped that if he were properly managed by British advisers he might be the agency of a beneficent revolution which would eliminate slavery and increase legitimate commerce.

Zanzibar came within the sphere of British interest because of its significance in the Indian Ocean slave trade. Immediately after the passage of the Act of Parliament of 1807, the Royal Navy began patrols on the Atlantic coast, and it was not long before British attention was directed to the east coast and to Zanzibar. After the close of the Napoleonic Wars the anti-slave trade effort in this area was intensified. This campaign concentrated on Said bin Sultan, who until his death ruled over both Oman and Zanzibar and claimed much of the east African coast. By 1840 he had in effect shifted his capital to Zanzibar from Oman.

Said maintained and extended his authority over his dispersed sultanate during his reign of fifty years. He reclaimed to his rule territories along the coast which had drifted away from or repudiated Oman's overlordship. The rebellious Mazrui of Mombasa were reduced to submission and other coastal towns were brought under his rule either by diplomacy or by force. The rule of Oman-Zanzibar became acknowledged from the Juba River on the north to Cape Delgado on the south. He also claimed the Somali coast as far as Cape Guardafui as well as the Comoro Islands and certain islands off the coast of Madagascar. These latter claims were somewhat shadowy; what jurisdiction he exercised was more formal than real.

On the 'Benadir coast' from the Juba River to Warsheikh Zanzibari power was confined to the ports; in the surrounding territories the Somali peoples not only repudiated the pretensions of Zanzibar but were advancing southward in the interior toward the Tana river area where between 1850 and 1865 they collided with a section of the Galla people and ousted them from their pastoral lands. More importantly for the future plans of the Imperial British East Africa Company, the Somali established a monopoly of the trade in ivory down the Juba River. They rejected the efforts of Zanzibar to dominate them as they would later resist similar attempts by Europeans.[1]

During Said's time the caravan trade with the interior expanded greatly. At the beginning of the nineteenth century there was relatively little contact between the coast and the African peoples inland, except in the southern interior. The principal middle-men between the interior and Mombasa, the Kamba, sold ivory to the merchants on the coast either directly or through Nyika traders. But in the 1820s and 1830s Arabs and Swahili from the coast began sending caravans upcountry.[2] There were three principal trade routes. The southernmost from such ports as Kilwa Kivinje, Mikindani, and Lindi traversed the southern region of present-day Tanzania to the region around Lake Nyasa. The principal trade was in slaves and ivory, provided for the most part by Yao dealers. The main route began opposite Zanzibar, from Bagamoyo and Sadani to the territory of the Nyamwezi in the vicinity of Tabora, and then proceeded to Lake Tanganyika and beyond, west to the Congo, north to Buganda and south-west to the area north and west of Lake Nyasa. Although there was some slave-trading associated with this route, the principal commodity was ivory. The northernmost route, from Pangani, Tanga, and Mombasa, proceeded to the Chagga country in the vicinity of Kilimanjaro, then through Masai territory to Lake Victoria. Of the three routes, two terminated on the coast in what would become the German sphere of influence, and the third involved ports on both the British and the German side of the line of demarcation.[3]

Before the 1820s Arab activity into the interior was sporadic, but Said's development of the economy of the coast had effects inland as well. Though he did not, as is sometimes asserted, introduce the cultivation of cloves in Zanzibar and Pemba, he was instrumental in the development of this cash crop as the mainstay of the islands, and the cultivation of cloves greatly expanded the need for slaves who were brought in from the interior. As the elephants near the coast were hunted out, traders had to penetrate further inland to acquire the ivory for European and Asian markets. A more highly

---

[1] D. A. Low, 'The Northern Interior, 1840–1884', in Roland Oliver and Gervase Mathew (eds.), *History of East Africa* (Oxford, 1963), I, 321–2.

[2] F. J. Berg, 'The Coast from the Portuguese Invasion to the Rise of the Zanzibar Sultanate', in B. A. Ogot and J. A. Kieran (eds.), *Zamani* (Nairobi, 1969), pp. 139–40.

[3] Norman B. Bennett, 'The Arab Impact', in *ibid.* pp. 216–18.

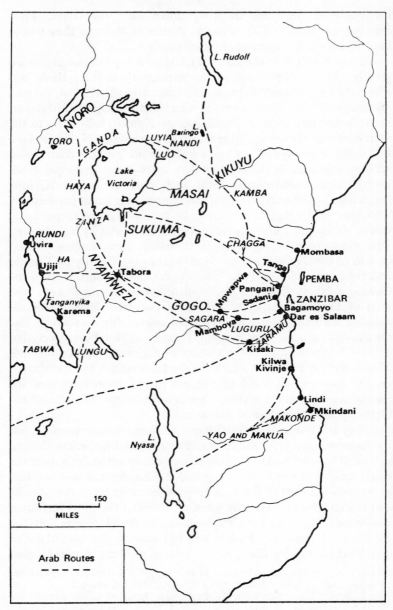

Map 1   Arab routes

developed and more regular system of delivery was required, and this was provided by Arab caravans supplied with capital by Indian merchants on the coast and in Zanzibar. A major settlement was established by the Arabs among the Nyamwezi at Tabora. The Nyamwezi, an association of peoples connected by historically related chiefdoms, were the most important African traders in the interior. Stanley described them as being the 'Scotchmen' of central Africa,[1] and their relationships with the Arabs were not entirely peaceful, for the Arabs were competitors. Some Nyamwezi chiefs, notably Mirambo, carried on almost continuous war with the Arabs of Tabora; others sought to collect tariffs from the Arab caravans, with resulting collisions, but the cooperation of elements of the Nyamwezi was essential for the porterage and provisioning on which the Arab caravans depended.[2]

Large, well-armed caravans carried the influence of the Zanzibar Arabs into the interior, though the relative power of the Arabs as compared to the Africans has often been exaggerated. They possessed greater numbers of fire-arms than the Africans but their military superiority was not such as to overawe those well-organized African societies with whom they came into contact, and as traders they usually preferred to acquire their goods in peace rather than by resort to arms. Arab influence in the interior was affected by such factors as the degree of organization of the African societies and the control by Africans of the food and water on which the caravans depended.[3] The caravans during Said's time traded not only in slaves and ivory but in gum copal and other commodities, and the revenue from 'legitimate commerce' steadily rose during his rule. In the 1820s the total customs receipts of Zanzibar were only about £10,000 per year; at his death they had increased fivefold. In 1859 Zanzibar's exports were valued at £755,666, and its imports, £908,911.[4] Said reserved for himself a monopoly of ivory and copal in the area between the ports of Pangani and Kilwa but with this restriction the trade of the coast was open to all. 'I am nothing but a merchant,' Said is reported to

[1] Andrew Roberts, 'Nyamwezi Trade', in Richard Gray and David Birmingham (eds.), *Pre-Colonial African Trade* (London, 1970), p. 68.
[2] *Ibid.* pp. 39–70.
[3] Norman R. Bennett, 'The Arab Impact', in Ogot and Kieran, *Zamani*, p. 219.
[4] John Gray, 'Zanzibar and the Coastal Belt, 1840–1884', in Oliver and Mathew, *History of East Africa*, I, 219.

have said, and his rule reflected his attention to the importance of a prosperous economy.[1]

The growing commercial importance of Zanzibar and east Africa, particularly after the opening of the Suez Canal, attracted the attention of the British, German, French and American traders, but the European trade with east Africa throughout most of the nineteenth century was small by comparison with that of Indian merchants in Zanzibar and on the coast. Long before Said's time, Indian merchants had been active in Muscat. As Said built up the commerce of Zanzibar and the coast, Indians participated actively in the development as merchants and as financiers. The customs of Zanzibar were farmed by an Indian firm, and by the 1860s, if not earlier, the great bulk of the trade of the coast was in Indian hands. Sir Bartle Frere in 1873 stated that along 'some 6,000 miles of sea coast in Africa and its islands, and nearly the same extent in Asia', Indian financiers and traders had become dominant:

Hardly a loan can be negotiated, or mortgage effected, or a Bill cashed without Indian agency; not an import cargo can be distributed, nor an export cargo collected which . . . does not go through Indian hands. The European or American, the Arab or Sowaheli [sic] may trade and profit, but only as an occasional link in the chain between producer and consumer, of which the Indian trader is the one invariable and most important link of all.[2]

In 1875, there were over 4,000 Indians in Zanzibar and on the coast. Most of them were traders; Sir Bartle Frere after a tour of east Africa and Madagascar stated that he had hardly found 'half a dozen exceptions to the rule that every shopkeeper was an Indian'.[3] Indian merchants also controlled most of the banking business of Zanzibar, and the symbol of their financial predominance was the gradual replacement of Maria Theresa dollars (thalers) as the principal currency by Indian rupees.[4]

Most of these enterpreneurs came from British India, and the establishment of the British Agency in Zanzibar in 1841 under the aegis of the Government of Bombay was largely in response to this

[1] J. Gray, 'Zanzibar and the Coastal Belt', in Oliver and Mathew, *History of East Africa*, I, 223–4.
[2] J. S. Mangat, *A History of the Asians in East Africa* (Oxford, 1969), p. 12.
[3] Frere to Granville, 7 May 1873, F.O. 84/1391, P.R.O., quoted in Mangat, *A History of the Asians in East Africa*, p. 10.
[4] Mangat, *loc. cit.*

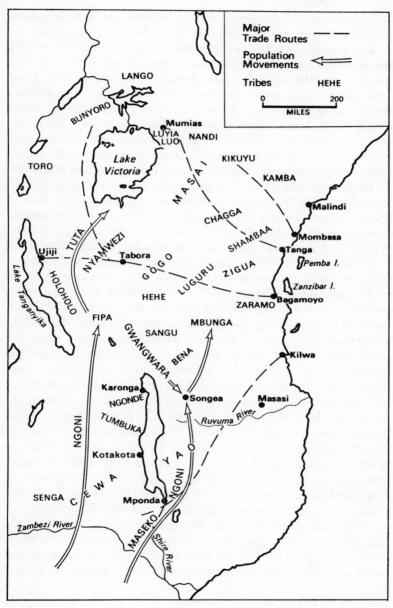

Map 2   Peoples of east Africa

Indian activity. This agency was to become the lever by which British influence was asserted over the Sultanate of Zanzibar.

The state of Zanzibar as organized by Said and perpetuated by his successors was stable against threats from adjacent African peoples. In the coastal towns between Warsheikh and Cape Delgado, local governors supported by small units of mercenary troops ruled with a considerable measure of autonomy. To the north, the Somali acknowledged Zanzibar's suzerainty, but it was tacitly recognized on both sides that this allegiance would not be put to the test by the exercise of Zanzibari authority. The only formidable neighbors of Zanzibar were the Somali and the Galla. In the interior the Masai had a fearsome reputation, and some of them occasionally disturbed trade in the hinterland behind Mombasa and Tanga, but the bulk of the Masai were separated from the coast by the inhospitable thorn-covered desert called the *Nyika*,[1] and the Arabs made no effort to subdue them. Had it not been for the advent of the European powers, this relaxed relationship between the Arabs and the African population of east Africa could undoubtedly have lasted a considerable time. Zanzibar, however, even during Said's time, was already faced with the problem of reconciling itself to European influences. While Said was a boy during the early years of the Napoleonic wars, his father had rejected French overtures and cast his lot with the British, whom he assessed to be more powerful and hence more dangerous.[2] From that time, British influence was paramount with the Sultan. That influence was exerted for the abolition of the slave trade from the accession of Said. At first the pressure was delicate, but it steadily increased. This British intervention was directly contrary to the established morality of the Arabs of Oman-Zanzibar and to what they believed to be their economic interests. Said's measures for the commercial development of Zanzibar indeed increased the demand for slave labor. The cultivation of cloves and copra required an increased labor supply to maintain the plantations and harvest the crops, and the only source available was slaves imported from the continent. Furthermore, goods from the interior were transported principally on the backs of African slaves.[3] Acquiescence in the wishes of British

---

[1] *Nyika* is the Swahili word for wilderness.
[2] John Gray, *History of Zanzibar* (London, 1962), pp. 110–11.
[3] For the slave trade, see E. A. Alpers, *The East African Slave Trade* (Nairobi, 1967).

anti-slavery advisers consequently meant for the Sultan alienation from the Arab community which depended for its prosperity on slaves and the slave traffic, and each concession to the British made him more dependent on them. For Said's successors, it was only by the backing of British power that the Sultan could survive.

During Said's life, British officials were generally circumspect despite the demands of anti-slavery zealots for more resolute action. They secured an agreement with the Sultan in 1822 prohibiting the sale of slaves to Christian states, and authorized British cruisers to seize vessels contravening the agreement, but Said refused to go beyond this restriction which left the trade with Islam unaffected.[1]

Said's successors did not have his powers of resistance. His son Majid, who became ruler of Zanzibar when on Said's death the Sultanates of Zanzibar and Oman were divided, was dependent completely on British protection. An expedition from Oman to overthrow him and reunite the two kingdoms was intercepted by the British, and an internal plot to unseat him and replace him with his brother Barghash was also quelled by the British navy. Barghash during his years in exile had time to ponder the lessons of his unsuccessful coup. He drew the inevitable conclusion that he must cooperate with the British if he were to accede to the throne and thereafter remain as Sultan. At the beginning of his reign in 1870 he indeed made an effort to shake off his dependence on Britain by offering Germany a protectorate over Zanzibar. But the new German Empire was not interested in extra-European adventures, and he received no response from Berlin.[2] Barghash concluded that he had no choice but to accept the predominance of British influence. Thereafter, during the eighteen years of his Sultanate, he was occasionally fractious but never to the point of open defiance. In his first three years in office, he attempted to avoid the full consequence of enforcement of anti-slavery measures. Many of his most prominent subjects and his subordinate officials were investors in the slave trade, and he was anxious not to alienate them. But the British were not to be put off by this policy of *pro forma* enforcement. Not only did they insist on the Sultan's active cooperation but imposed upon him a far more severe

[1] Gray in *History of East Africa*, I, 234.
[2] Reginald Coupland, *The Exploitation of East Africa, 1856–1890* (London, 1939), pp. 94–5.

anti-slave-trade policy. In 1873 a mission headed by Sir Bartle Frere negotiated with Barghash a treaty which prohibited the export of slaves from the Sultan's dominions and closed the public slave markets. To the Sultan's protest that imposition of these measures would alienate him from his people, Frere responded with the threat of a naval blockade. Barghash decided to cooperate with the British.

Frere was not actually present when his ultimatum was given to Barghash. He had left the task of convincing the Sultan in the hands of John Kirk, who carried out his responsibility with due regard for Barghash's sense of dignity. Kirk, the Agency surgeon, had succeeded to the acting consulship two months after Barghash became Sultan, when the consul, H. A. Churchill, was forced to retire because of ill health. Until his departure from Zanzibar sixteen years later, Kirk was the embodiment of British influence in Zanzibar, the personification of the power of the 'man on the spot' to influence and at times to determine Imperial policy. Even after his retirement, Kirk continued to exercise considerable influence on the Foreign Office. Sir Reginald Coupland has asserted that Kirk was the Imperial factor in east Africa during his years in Zanzibar.[1] That is an overstatement, in part a reflection of Kirk's own assessment of his sagacity and power, but the exaggeration is not so great as to be manifestly untrue. Kirk, by a combination of tact, friendly persuasion, firmness and appeals to reason and interest, was usually able to induce Barghash to move in the direction he wished him to go. It was unnecessary for Kirk to remind the Sultan that the consul was backed by the British navy, and Kirk was sensitive enough to avoid except as a last resort, a blatant display of power.

The Sultan's dependence on the British was further increased when at the instance of Kirk and the Foreign Office he employed Lieutenant Lloyd Mathews of the Royal Navy to organize his military force. In 1877 Mathews was given leave from the navy to train a force of 300 local Africans; by 1880 he had under his command 1,300 men; and the next year he retired from the navy to accept a permanent position under the Sultan as commander of the troops with the title of general.[2] The troops were the Sultan's but their loyalty was to Mathews. As Mathews' biographer wrote,

[1] Coupland, *Exploitation of East Africa*, p. ix.
[2] *Ibid.* pp. 242–3.

'For all practical purposes the army was his body guard, devoted to his person and ready to follow wherever he led.'[1] Mathews obviously would not lead them into actions contrary to the policy of the British government as interpreted by Kirk.

The lives of Kirk and Barghash were intertwined for sixteen years. Kirk was the bulwark of Barghash's authority and also the means of weakening it. Kirk respected Barghash's intelligence but could not tolerate his right to exercise it contrary to British policy. Puppets cannot have the power of independent action. The relationship between the two men was thus a strange compound of contradictory elements. Kirk realized that by imposing upon the Sultan British standards of morality he was divorcing Barghash from the Arab aristocracy. That, in Kirk's view, was desirable. The Sultan's Arab advisors he considered to be reactionary, 'effete', 'an incubus' which the Sultan must throw off if Zanzibar were to progress.[2] If Barghash listened to their counsels and resisted Kirk's advice, Zanzibar would have a new Sultan. Barghash to retain his throne chose to accept measures in which he did not believe. Occasionally he burst out in protest. When Frere sought to impose on him the anti-slave-trade treaty of 1873, Barghash cried out, 'A spear is held at each of my eyes, with which shall I choose to be pierced?'[3] But he had no alternative but to give way.

During the Kirk–Barghash era the trade of Zanzibar and the coast increased substantially. The application of measures to control the slave trade after the treaty of 1873 caused severe losses to the slave dealers, but the transition to 'legitimate' trade was effected with remarkably little disorganization of the economy. Kilwa, which had been the principal outlet for slaves, turned to trade in rubber, which had recently become a profitable commodity in the world's markets. In the decade between 1862 and 1872, the average annual value of the trade of Zanzibar and its dependencies had been approximately £1,000,000; by 1879 it had risen to £2,200,000. In 1887 the import and export trade of Zanzibar was as shown in the Table.[4]

---

[1] Robert N. Lyne, *An Apostle of Empire* (London, 1936), p. 48.
[2] Kirk to Mackinnon, private, 5 March 1876, Mackinnon Papers.
[3] L. W. Hollingsworth, *Zanzibar Under the Foreign Office, 1890–1913* (London, 1953), p. 14.
[4] Macdonald to F.O., 19 December 1887, F.O. 84/1854, P.R.O. A dollar (thaler) was worth approximately four shillings and sixpence.

C

		Dollars
Imports, from Bombay and other Indian ports		1,500,000
London		800,000
United States		450,000
Germany		400,000
France		250,000
	Total	3,400,000
Exports, to England		1,500,000
India		2,000,000
United States		700,000
Germany		550,000
France		300,000
	Total	5,050,000

Rubber had become the principal export, followed by cloves and ivory. The tonnage of British shipping increased sevenfold between 1871 and 1879, stimulated by the opening of the Suez Canal. British Indians continued to be the predominant traders of the coast. German and French firms established branches on the island of Zanzibar during the 1870s.[1] But it was the interior of east Africa behind the sweltering coast which seemed to offer the greatest prospects for commercial development. Frederic Holmwood, Kirk's vice consul, described the highlands area and its prospects in these terms:

The salubrious highlands of the interior are generally peopled by finer and more intelligent races possessing an energy which under favorable circumstances would have induced them to make use of the natural resources of their country in foreign trade, but the coast, their only outlet, having been for centuries virtually in the possession of half-civilized treacherous and unscrupulous Semitic adventurers whose evil reputation everywhere preceded them, such tribes have come to avoid all intercourse with strangers from the East, and in many cases they attack everyone crossing their frontier.

There are thus millions of native Africans occupying some of the fairest and most fertile regions of the earth, living in a temperate and even bracing climate, where clothing is one of the first practical necessities, who have therefore habituated themselves to the use of hides and skins, the most inconvenient form of clothing in any tropical country, rather than enter into commercial relations with the people of the coast from whom alone they believe manufactured goods are to be procured.[2]

[1] Gray, 'Zanzibar and the Coastal Belt, 1840–1884', in Oliver and Mathew, *History of East Africa*, I, 241.
[2] Holmwood to Salisbury, 28 May 1888, F.O. 84/1922, P.R.O.

Once this distrust of strangers was dispelled, he maintained, the region offered great prospects for agricultural development, including rubber, copal, grain, oil, seeds and tobacco. Holmwood's opinion was supported by the testimony of most of the missionaries and explorers who visited the interior. With such attractions, east Africa could not be expected to remain for long outside the scope of European commercial activity.

The increasing importance of Zanzibar and east Africa resulted in the decision by the Imperial government in 1883 to transfer the Zanzibar Agency from the control of the Indian government to that of the Foreign Office. In arguing for the transfer, Kirk pointed out that Imperial interests had increased so greatly as a result of the expansion of trade and the opening up of steam and telegraphic communication that it was no longer feasible to consider British interests in Zanzibar as the province of the Indian government. The French, Germans, and Americans had established consulates; the British could do no less.[1]

At about the same time, Barghash presented the British government with an opportunity to reinforce its paramountcy over his dominions. He proposed to name his eldest son as his successor and to designate the Imperial government as guardian of his son and his successors if they came to the throne as minors.[2] Some of the permanent staff of the Foreign Office, in particular T. V. Lister and Clement Hill, saw in the proposal an opportunity to prevent another European state from intruding its political influence into east Africa and thus discriminating against British trade. The Parliamentary Undersecretary, Sir Charles Dilke, also was favorably inclined to the idea. But Lord Tenterden, the Permanent Undersecretary, was more cautious. He pointed out that Barghash's sons were only six and five and a half years old (the elder died while the discussion was going on) and that the regency might be a long one, with Britain being required to protect the young Sultan from all pretenders to the throne.[3] The Foreign Secretary, Earl Granville, concluded that the risks of foreign intervention were not substantial enough to warrant the responsibility. He, therefore, declined with thanks.[4]

[1] Kirk to Granville, 28 November 1881, F.O. 84/1601, P.R.O.
[2] Memorandum by Barghash, 26 August 1881, enclosure in Kirk to Granville, 10 October 1881, F.O. 84/1601, P.R.O.
[3] Notes on Kirk to Granville, 10 October 1881, F.O. 84/1601, P.R.O.
[4] Granville to Barghash 19 June 1882, F.O. 84/1631, P.R.O.

The consequences of this rejection should not be overstated. It has been suggested that if Britain had agreed to Barghash's proposal, 'Zanzibar would have acquired a new political stability, freed from recurrent periods of uncertainty and strife, and the mainland – as far as the Great Lakes, it is safe to say – would have fallen for good or ill to British guardianship'.[1] This statement of a missed golden opportunity does not seem realistic. The mere assertion of British guardianship of a minor Sultan would not have interdicted the entry of other European states into the mainland of east Africa beyond the area of Zanzibar's effective control; it would not have prevented the German challenge which actually developed. The incident is significant primarily for the insight it provides into the assumptions of British policy-makers. In the early 1880s no British official, not even Kirk, was prepared to accept responsibility for the effective government of the east African interior; the attraction of Barghash's proposal to its advocates in the Foreign Office was that it promised to serve British interests at no expense to the Imperial government; its main deficiency to its opponents was that it might involve such expense. A policy of no-risk, no-expense was adequate in the early 1880s; it could not turn back the aggressive German intrusion of 1886.

[1] Coupland, *The Exploitation of East Africa*, pp. 377–8.

2

Mackinnon and east Africa: prologue

Until the 1870s the career of William Mackinnon had been identified with India and the maritime trade relating to it. But early in that decade he became actively interested in the continent of Africa. This shift of attention was logical; east Africa lay across the Indian Ocean, and in his search for new sources of profit it was natural that he would investigate the potentialities of the African coast. It might be assumed that Mackinnon was led into his venture into east Africa by the expansion of his shipping line. This judgment would be true, but it would be utterly misleading. Mackinnon's involvement went far beyond such a mundane, business explanation. It became an intense emotional experience, whether he was buoyed up by hopes or reduced to despair. Africa affected many men in this way, but Mackinnon had seemed an unlikely prospect to succumb to Afro-mania.

Until he was drawn into Africa, Mackinnon seemed to be dominated by the drive for material success. His energies were devoted to that end, his world was that of trade and finance. His rise to eminence in the industrial-financial community of Great Britain was a testament to his devotion to business and to his superior acumen. It is difficult to reconcile the able shipping magnate of these earlier years with the promoter of ill-starred ventures on the continent of Africa whose objects were unrealistic and whose methods were ineffectual. Several explanations have been offered. It has been suggested that years of toil had sapped his strength and that in his late fifties and sixties he underwent a change of character. The disciplined Scot had become feckless, his involvement in his new scheme was spasmodic and unpredictable.[1]

It has been maintained that Mackinnon's Indian experience led him to the erroneous assumption that money could be made as

[1] In her unpublished doctoral dissertation, 'History of the Imperial British East Africa Company' (London, 1955), Marie de Kiewiet Hemphill comments on Mackinnon's apparent change in character. Other writers go beyond her in their description of Mackinnon's apparent loss of business sense.

easily in east Africa as in India.[1] It is also alleged that Mackinnon's management of the East Africa Company left much to be desired. This last contention appears to be true. Mackinnon was willing neither to delegate full responsibility to the board of directors nor to devote his time and energy to supervision himself. Consequently, the operation of the Company was hampered by a constant flow of advice and instructions from his home in Scotland or his retreat in the south of France. Sir John Kirk in 1891 complained that Mackinnon made a lot of work for the board with his 'endless changes' and expressed the wish that Mackinnon would take the business into his own hands and manage it himself. But it is significant that Kirk had no doubt of Mackinnon's ability to do so. The great deficiency of the Company, in Kirk's opinion, lay not so much in its management as in its objects: 'There is too much philanthropy and Imperialism and too little regard to finance in that Company.'[2]

The details of Mackinnon's life seem to support the alleged contrast between his Indian and African years. Mackinnon was born in the village of Campbeltown on the Mull of Kintyre, Argyleshire, in 1823. His formal education was limited to elementary school, which he left to become a clerk in the grocery trade. Campbeltown did not offer much scope for an ambitious young man and he moved to Glasgow, where he soon found employment with a merchant engaged in trade with the Far East and India. In 1847 Mackinnon went to India where he joined a former schoolmate, Robert Mackenzie, then operating a small general store in one of the towns on the Ganges. After Mackinnon became involved the firm prospered. By 1855, under the name of Smith, Mackenzie and Company, it had established headquarters in Calcutta and rapidly became one of the leading mercantile companies in the Indian Ocean area. Mackinnon soon became aware of the opportunities for profit in the carrying trade. Acting on a suggestion from a captain in the Burma trade, in 1856 he founded the Calcutta and Burmah [sic] Steamship Navigation Company which became the British Indian Steamship Navigation Company. Within two decades of his arrival in India Mackinnon had made himself one of the merchant princes of the East and a master of one

---

[1] Douglas Johnson and A. S. Baxendale, 'Uganda and Great Britain,' *University, of Birmingham Historical Journal* VIII, 2 (1962), 162–88.
[2] Kirk to Cawston, 16 December 1891, British South Africa Company Papers, IV Misc., Rhodes House, Oxford.

of the world's great steamship lines. At the time of his death, his shipping company had a fleet of approximately 110 vessels. He became a man of importance, with entrée into the higher reaches of British society and with close acquaintanceship with other powerful men of business.[1]

Mackinnon's success seemed to epitomize the ideals which dominated the Scottish society of his day, in particular its stress on the realization of individual potentiality through hard work. The state school system, unlike that of nineteenth-century England, involved the mass of the population, and young Scots not only learned to read and to count, but to exercise their intellectual powers against those of their fellows. Every institution of society emphasized the virtue of 'doing one's best', and the ministers of the Kirk not only held forth for the virtuous a heavenly eternity but temporal rewards as well. Whether Calvinism produced the Scottish ethos, or the national character attracted Scots to Calvinism, the hardworking God-fearing Scot was no myth. William Mackinnon certainly can be so described. As a devout member of the Free Church of Scotland he felt his religious principles strongly and seems to have applied them in his business and private life. So passionately did he believe in his version of orthodoxy that he refused to accept a Declaratory Act passed in 1892 relaxing the stringency of subscription to the confession, and he provided financial assistance to the small number of congregations, mostly in the Highlands, who rejected this 'dilution' of the faith. *The Times* correctly described him in its obituary as 'a perfect type of the old-fashioned Scotch Presbyterian'.[2] Mackinnon was no 'Sunday Christian'; no shadow of scandal ever touched his name, no suggestion of impropriety or sharp practice. He acted in accordance with God's injunctions as revealed by the Bible and God's favor had been bestowed upon him. His old friend and long-time associate James Hall mirrored Mackinnon when he wrote in a business letter:

It would have been a rare pleasure to have sat face to face once more as of yore, and talked the times of old over again, when we were but 'a small people'. Truly His Goodness and Mercy have followed us, and our hands

[1] For the History of Smith, Mackenzie and Company Ltd, see the volume by that name published by the company in 1938. Brief accounts of Mackinnon's life are contained in the *Dictionary of National Biography* and in his obituary in *The Times*, 23 June 1893.
[2] *The Times*, 23 June 1893.

still join. May we, when the journey here is ended, resume again and sit together in the House of the Lord forever.[1]

The epitome of Scottish Presbyterian virtues which Mackinnon seemed to be should not have been attracted to the great speculative schemes which engrossed his attention in his later years. Either his character changed or the stereotype applied to him inadequately represented him.

Stereotypes are always dangerous; 'national characteristics' are often belied; 'canny' Scots have not infrequently been involved in ventures where canniness was not in evidence. The Darien scheme of the late seventeenth and early eighteenth centuries involved the triumph of national enthusiasm over rationality – even the English of the time regarded the project as lunatic, and the resulting fiasco was foreordained. Scottish investments in the nineteenth-century American west did not document the national reputation for financial shrewdness;[2] indeed the 'canny Scot' is as much of a caricature of the Scottish character as was Sir Harry Lauder. As a wide variety of Englishmen inhabited the Victorian society, so did the contemporary Scots evidence many different, and sometimes contradictory, traits. Mackinnon's canniness was well attested by his business success, but there was an element in his nature, submerged throughout much of his life, which erupted in his last years. The symptoms were Afro-mania, but the fundamental cause was a burning desire for a kind of involvement and recognition which his business career had not achieved. His friends thought of him as dedicated, hardworking, kindly, philanthropic – all complimentary adjectives applying to a good Scottish Presbyterian. But they did not recognize the hunger for power and for fame which he manifested in his African ventures; he undoubtedly did not recognize it in himself. Mackinnon craved identification with great men and with great causes; his employment of his wealth in the development of Africa enabled him to experience excitement which he had never known in his earlier years. This little Scot with a colorless personality was intoxicated by associations with Leopold II, Stanley, Kirk, and the other giants. On his yacht, the *Cornelia*, he participated in the development of grand schemes affecting the future of a continent.

[1] Hall to Mackinnon, 6 February 1873, Mackinnon Papers, School of Oriental and African Studies, University of London.
[2] W. Turrentine Jackson, *The Enterprising Scot* (Edinburgh, 1968), pp. 312–13.

He was a factor to be reckoned with by world statesmen; he was awarded a baronetcy for his distinguished service.[1] Mackinnon thought of the Imperial British East Africa Company as a vehicle for the realization of Imperial objectives; it was also a vehicle for his realization of himself.

He applied himself to his mission of empire-building with the same tenacity and singleness of purpose he had manifested in his business activity, much to the annoyance of such statesmen as Lord Salisbury. Germany was his enemy, for it threatened to thwart his objectives of a great British sphere of influence in east Africa; and he developed an antipathy for Germans which bordered on Germano-phobia. The wider issues of high policy which preoccupied the Foreign Office were alien to Mackinnon; he interpreted their efforts to come to an understanding with Germany as base cowardice, while Salisbury regarded him as a menace.

Before he concentrated his attention on east Africa, Mackinnon had already manifested the tunnel vision which so irritated Salisbury. In 1883 he, the Duke of Marlborough, the Duke of Sutherland, and Admiral Inglefield developed a scheme for a maritime canal through Palestine from the Mediterranean through the Dead Sea into the Gulf of Aqaba. The Palestine Channel Syndicate was organized with an initial capital of £10,000, not an impressive amount for the project in view, but the directors sought the Gladstone government's blessing for their undertaking. In their planning the syndicate had done considerable investigation into technical feasibility, but none into political issues. They apparently had ignored the relevant consideration that the territory through which the canal would pass was under Turkish sovereignty. Lord Granville, the Foreign Secretary, indicated politely that the Turks 'would feel great jealousy in being by-passed' and suggested that they approach a representative of the Turkish government.[2] Lord Northbrook, Secretary of State for India, on reading the correspondence, noted 'this seems to be a chimerical project'.[3]

Viewed from the India Office, this assessment was undoubtedly correct. One canal, which had so recently been the cause of

---

[1] Mackinnon, who had no sons to inherit the title, sought to perpetuate his baronetcy through his nephews, but his application was rejected. See note, 1 July 1889, by Salisbury's secretary, File E, Salisbury Papers.

[2] Granville to Marlborough, private, 12 May, 1883, PRO 30/29/152, P.R.O.

[3] Note by Northbrook, 10 May 1883, on unsigned note, 8 May 1883, F.O., in *ibid.*

British intervention in Egypt, was enough. Mackinnon and his associates had approached as a financial and engineering proposition what the cabinet saw as a vexed political issue. The two perspectives were far apart. In east Africa this distance was also evident. Mackinnon could not understand Salisbury, as Salisbury could not understand him. Their objectives were different; each saw in the other wilfulness and perversity; and each blamed the other for the East Africa Company's ill fortunes.

Mackinnon was associated with governmental policy in Persia at about the same time as he was seeking a charter for his East Africa Company and in a failure which was clearly not personal. For many years, British policy had favored opening of the Karun River to navigation, and Sir Henry Layard in 1841 and 1842 had proposed building a railway to provide access to the central provinces of the Shah. The Foreign Office in 1886 sponsored a Persian railway conference attended also by representatives of the India Office. The two businessmen whom they called upon for expert advice on the possibilities for railway construction were William Mackinnon and George Mackenzie, of Gray, Dawes and Company, who was soon to be associated with Mackinnon in the East Africa Company. These two developed a plan for a narrow gauge line with various branches as a means of opening up Persia, and proposed an international company domiciled in London to carry out the project. The plan was endorsed by the government, but the Shah, who initially had seemed willing to cooperate, had second thoughts and declined to provide financial assistance. Mackinnon and Mackenzie reminded the Foreign Office that they had been involved at the instance of the government and that they could not now be expected to take full financial responsibility for building the railways without even a government guarantee. No guarantee was forthcoming, and the plan collapsed.[1] The Persian railway scheme has significant parallels with Mackinnon's African experience shortly thereafter. In both cases the initiative, at least in part, was governmental; in both, the government was disinclined to assist with the burdens. It should also be noted that Mackinnon was one of two men to whom the government turned for help to build the railways; this is a testament to its judgment of his ability to conceive and execute a large undertaking. Henry Morton Stanley blamed the failure of Mackinnon's East Africa Company

[1] Rose L. Greaves, *Persia and the Defence of India 1884–1892* (London, 1959), pp. 145–8.

on the intrusion of politicians who diverted it from its commercial purpose to the advancement of governmental ends: 'The object of the Company was mainly commercial, and left alone by politicians, Mackinnon was the man to make it remunerative.'[1] Stanley's portrait of Mackinnon was that of a great soul whose noble purpose had been frustrated by Conservative and Liberal governments, but in this characterization he underscored Mackinnon's inability to comprehend the world of Whitehall.

The world of politics was alien to Mackinnon, but he was nevertheless attracted to it. In November 1885 he offered himself as the Liberal candidate for Parliament in his native Argyleshire but was wounded by the heckling to which politicians are subjected in the hustings and avoided exposure to hostile audiences as much as possible.[2] He was defeated. He did not again stand for office, but the experience did not end his involvement in politics; it merely changed the nature of that involvement.

Mackinnon was not only ingenuous with regard to politics; he was remarkably trusting for a man with such impressive business achievements. His relationship with Charles Euan Smith is a case in point. Precisely where and when the two first met is not known; probably it was in India, and it was before 1873, when Mackinnon and Euan Smith were already on an intimate basis. Euan Smith was only seventeen when he entered the Indian Army in the late 1850s. Ten years later he was attached to a special mission to Persia. In 1873 he accompanied Sir Bartle Frere to Zanzibar on a special mission which attempted unsuccessfully to induce the Sultan to sign a treaty prohibiting the export of slaves from the part of the mainland over which he exercised control. Thereafter he served briefly at Zanzibar while Sir John Kirk accompanied the Sultan on a visit to England. He returned to India in 1876 and was appointed assistant resident at Hyderabad; his assignments thereafter included resident appointments at Muscat and at Bhurtpore in the residency of Agra. In 1886 Euan Smith, now a

---

[1] Dorothy Stanley (ed.), *The Autobiography of Sir Henry Morton Stanley* (London, 1909), p. 446.

[2] *The Times*, 23 June 1893. Stanley wrote of the campaign that Mackinnon was 'wise enough to keep clear of places where there is a determined opposition'. He predicted that despite Mackinnon's distaste for the rough and tumble of politics, he would be elected by a substantial margin, in large part because of Mackinnon's reputation for piety and philanthropy. Piety and philanthropy, however, did not prevail. Stanley to Sanford, 10 November 1885, in François Bontinck, *Aux Origines de l'Etat Independant du Congo* (Louvain, 1966), pp. 341–2.

colonel, was appointed consul-general in Zanzibar as successor to Kirk and he was thus in a strategic position to be of assistance to the East Africa Company during the first few years of its operations. The assistance he provided, however, was only that which was required of anyone in his office. He showed the Company no special favor; on the contrary he was highly critical of its management, and his unfavorable reports were a factor in the government's negative judgment.

Euan Smith's lack of bias toward the Company is significant because he was deeply indebted to Mackinnon. During his life in India Euan Smith had acquired a taste for comfortable living which required resources in excess of his income. During his years at Hyderabad he had earned the nickname of 'Tea Party' Smith as a testament to his social activity.[1] He was perpetually in debt, and he early began the practice of relieving his financial embarrassment by applying to Mackinnon for help, which was freely given. These gifts and loans enabled Euan Smith to ward off his creditors for over two decades. In June 1874 Euan Smith was in debt for approximately £10,000, and Mackinnon came to his assistance with a substantial loan.[2] A few months earlier, in gratitude for past favors, the prodigal spender had written his benefactor that 'sometimes I think I would throw up the sponge if I had not you and your kindness at my back'.[3] Well he might, for his needs were substantial. In 1881, for example, he gave Mackinnon a list of his debts which he sought to clear up:

	£
B. Aitchard	1,550
King & Co., Bombay	500
Tatta Suliman	240
University Life Assurance Co.	350
Tradespeople in London and India	282

Total 2,922

If Mackinnon would only remit him that amount, he said, 'it is my deeds and not words that must show you how I appreciate your help'.[4] Mackinnon might have had occasion to reflect on the emptiness of these words when he read Euan Smith's highly

[1] *Pall Mall Gazette*, 27 July 1892.
[2] Euan Smith to Mackinnon, 29 June 1874, Mackinnon Papers.
[3] Euan Smith to Mackinnon, 15 January 1874, Mackinnon Papers.
[4] Euan Smith to Mackinnon, 28 April 1881, Mackinnon Papers.

critical comments on the Company, but though he protested against them,[1] he took no action to retaliate. On the contrary, he continued to give him financial assistance. In 1889 he advanced £2,500, and in 1891, when Euan Smith was about to depart for Morocco, Mackinnon provided several thousand pounds more to clear up his debts.[2]

Apparently Euan Smith also had a standing authorization from Mackinnon to draw on him for funds to cover debts to be repaid over a period of years.[3] Such generosity is so nearly incredible in a relationship between non-relatives as to suggest the possibility of blackmail. But there is no evidence to support such a sinister interpretation. On the contrary, what Mackinnon did for Euan Smith he did for others. H. Austen Lee, a prominent member of Parliament, also sought and received Mackinnon's financial aid to keep him solvent.[4] Mackinnon's generosity in no case seems to have been inspired by the expectation of reciprocal favors. He seems to have been, remarkably, a man who derived pleasure from his ability to help his friends. General Sir Arnold Burrowes Kemball, later to be a member of the board of the East Africa Company, approached Mackinnon in 1882 for a loan of £5,000 to the Duke of Sutherland, whom Kemball represented. Mackinnon gave the loan without even a request for a receipt. Kemball wrote Mackinnon, 'You are indeed a wonderful man. . . . I must either regard this nonchalance as a great compliment to me or as evincing a remarkable confidence in the honesty of your fellow man.'[5] Both assumptions were undoubtedly correct.

Mackinnon's generosity and trust in the honesty of others obviously did not blight his business career. His confidence was almost always justified, and the beneficiaries were usually men in influential positions. His guilelessness, however, did cost him dearly in the amoral world of statecraft.

There is a significant parallel in the lives of Mackinnon and the Dent brothers, Edward and, particularly, Alfred. Like Mackinnon, their fortunes were made in the Far East. At the time when

---

[1] Euan Smith to Currie, private, 22 May 1890, Salisbury Papers, A/80, Christ Church, Oxford.
[2] Euan Smith to Mackinnon, private, 3 November [1891], 17 November 1891, both in Mackinnon Papers.
[3] Euan Smith to Mackinnon, private, 8 August 1892, 13 February 1893, both in Mackinnon Papers.
[4] This correspondence is also in Mackinnon Papers.
[5] Kemball to Mackinnon, 29 September 1882, Mackinnon Papers.

Mackinnon was establishing himself in Calcutta, Alfred Dent was building an important mercantile company with branches in Shanghai and London which had contacts with businessmen in Ceylon, Singapore, China, and India. Through mutual business interests, Mackinnon and the Dents became close friends, with important consequences for the British Empire.

Like Mackinnon, Alfred Dent knew only success in his years as a rising businessman. The combination of hard work and shrewdness in both cases brought handsome dividends. Like Mackinnon, Dent in the 1870s turned his attention to an enterprise which involved important political considerations. When Dent decided to seek a charter for a company to develop North Borneo, Mackinnon was among his most intimate advisers. Dent sent his Scottish friend copies of all the correspondence relating to the charter, and Mackinnon was one of the prominent capitalists who gave support to Dent in his negotiations with the British government.[1] Mackinnon's association with Dent is significant not only because of the coincidence that both founded chartered companies. Both companies, so long as Dent and Mackinnon were directing them, were failures. Mackinnon's company was moribund at his death, and expired two years later. The British North Borneo Company under Dent's control was so unsuccessful that a shareholders' revolt nearly unseated him from a directorship.[2] This parallelism of unvarying success in private companies followed by failure in a chartered company suggests that there may have been factors beyond the business abilities of the principals which were involved in their ill-fortune. The combined functions of government and business vested in the chartered companies imposed a load which made them ineffective in both. The only exception to this generalization was the Royal Niger Company, which for the decade and a half of its life conducted a prosperous business. But there were special features in the Royal Niger Company's revenue privileges which contributed to this success. Its charter gave the Company power to levy customs duties and other charges to pay for administrative expenses, and a generous interpretation of

---

[1] Kennedy G. Tregonning, *Under Chartered Company Rule* (Singapore, 1958), pp. 29–30; John S. Galbraith, 'The Chartering of the British North Borneo Company', *Journal of British Studies* IV, 2 (May 1965), 119.

[2] *Financial News*, 5 July 1893. A motion to appoint W. C. Cowie, Dent's *bête noire*, instead of Dent, was defeated by a vote of 19 to 11. The British North Borneo Company between 1881 and 1893 paid no dividends, except in 1890, when 5% was paid.

'administrative purposes' make it possible for the Company to shift considerable burdens from itself to its competitors.[1]

The personal factor, however, cannot be discounted entirely. There was one common attribute of Mackinnon and Dent which had a relationship to the ill-success of their chartered companies. Both were wealthy men when they promoted these companies; they continued to be wealthy despite the adversity which befell the companies. Mackinnon was able to contribute many thousands of pounds from his private fortune without financial embarrassment; his shipping company and other businesses continued to flourish. When he died his personal estate was valued at £560,563,[2] not perhaps a massive fortune but enough to describe him as a wealthy man. He did not create a chartered company with the expectation of losing money, but neither did he conceive it a means of making profits. As with Cecil Rhodes, he conceived his company as serving a higher object. Rhodes indentified it as the expansion of the British Empire; Mackinnon, the spread of civilization, but both found in these noble ideals their own self-fulfilment.

Mackinnon's romance with Africa drew him inexorably to Leopold II, whose vision of a cooperative project for the development of tropical Africa from ocean to ocean fired Mackinnon's imagination and contributed to the formation of the British East Africa Company. A variety of designations can be applied to Leopold. He has, with justice, been called 'The King Incorporated'.[3] He was also one of the greatest confidence men of his or any other day. And he was certainly possessed of what Stanley called an 'enormous voracity' for territory. With no significant base of power, this remarkable man was able to establish his sovereignty over a huge area of central Africa and to extend his claims from the Congo basin to the upper Nile. His achievement was made possible in part by his shrewd utilization of European power rivalries to his own advantage. Like Cecil John Rhodes, Leopold had great visions; like Rhodes, he devoted his energy ruthlessly to the achievement of his ambitions. But Leopold surpassed Rhodes as a player in the game of power politics. In his achievements he out-Rhodesed Rhodes.

Leopold had dreamed of empire since the mid-1850s, when he

---

[1] John E. Flint, *Sir George Goldie and the Making of Nigeria* (London, 1960), p. 325.
[2] *The Times*, 27 October 1893.
[3] Neal Ascherson, *The King Incorporated* (London, 1963).

was still the Duke of Brabant. He had been fascinated by Rajah James Brooke and indeed tried to buy Sarawak. During the next twenty years he dabbled in a variety of schemes, involving concessions in the Philippines and Mozambique, purchase of a province in Argentina; and, most glamorous of all, an international enterprise in China with the powers of the old East India Company in India.

The imagination of Leopold confounds all rational analysis, but he was not a 'rational' man – he was driven by an imperialist spirit which most of his contemporaries found incomprehensible. As Jean Stengers notes, he was ready to appropriate any territory not claimed by any other European power and even to annex land abandoned by others. When Britain seemed reluctant to accept responsibility for Uganda, Leopold offered to lease the territory. Though the ruler of a small kingdom, he considered himself a world statesman. In 1886 he suggested to Queen Victoria that the Near Eastern question might be resolved if the Prince of Wales would assume the Turkish throne with a daughter of the Tsar as his consort.[1] In 1895 he proposed to Lord Salisbury that Britain evacuate Egypt and receive compensation by annexing China to the Indian Empire. The contrast between the magnitude and range of his schemes and the paucity of his resources might suggest that he was afflicted with some mental disorder had he not been so remarkably successful in the Congo. If he had died in 1875, he would be remembered as a visionary out of touch with reality, an impractical monarch who plunged into wild real estate schemes, all of which came to nothing. Frustrated in other areas of the world, he at last turned to Africa, and after a flirtation with the possibility of acquiring the Transvaal, concentrated his attention on the Congo. Some years later, after he had become master of the Congo Free State, he told a Belgian audience, 'If the Fatherland remains our headquarters the world ought to be our objective. . . . There are no small nations, there are only small minds.'[2] Leopold's was no small mind.

Mackinnon probably became acquainted with Leopold sometime in the early 1870s. Precisely when and under what circum-

[1] Jean Stengers, 'The Congo Free State and the Belgian Congo before 1914', in L. H. Gann and Peter Duignan, *Colonialism in Africa, 1870–1960* (Cambridge, 1969), i, 285–6.
[2] Pierre Daye, *Léopold II* (Paris, 1934), p. 309, quoted in Roger Anstey, *King Leopold's Legacy* (London, 1966), p. 1.

stances the two first met cannot be determined from the available documents, but their intimate association related to the extension of Mackinnon's business activity to the east coast of Africa, which in the early years Leopold considered to be the take-off area for penetration to the Great Lakes. Mackinnon first seems to have considered the commercial possibilities of east Africa in relationship to the operation of his shipping company. In 1872 he secured a contract from the British government for a monthly mail service between Aden and Zanzibar. In the course of his investigation of the possibilities for profits for his shipping line, he came to the conclusion that there were excellent trade prospects on the mainland. This impression was reinforced by information from Euan Smith and from Sir John Kirk. While Euan Smith was in Zanzibar as a member of Frere's mission in 1873 he frequently wrote to Mackinnon about economic conditions on the island and on the mainland. From his visits to various ports as far south as Mozambique, Euan Smith reached the judgment that east Africa offered excellent opportunities for profit – even in 'sleepy and exclusive Mozambique'. There was evidence of increasing commercial activity, which was capable of immense development. True, the trade of the coast was almost exclusively in the hands of British Indian subjects who acted as middlemen in virtually every transaction, but an effectively run British company could make substantial profits in legitimate trade in competition with the Indians and by 'the sudden entry of light into these dark places' could do much to eliminate the slave trade and slavery.[1] At about the same time, Sir John Kirk was communicating to Mackinnon his zeal for commerce as the vehicle of civilization. Mackinnon had apparently consulted Kirk when he was contemplating an Aden–Zanzibar service. The first letter from Kirk to Mackinnon preserved in Mackinnon's papers, however, was in November 1873. Kirk was evidently responding to an inquiry as to the prospects for the extension of steam navigation from Zanzibar to Natal and to Madagascar. The Natal service, he asserted, would not succeed, but a new line from Zanzibar to Madagascar had good prospects even though it would have competition from Messrs O'Swald and Company of Hamburg. The Aden–Zanzibar line, he assured Mackinnon, would 'very soon be an immense success and do more for the country than anything else it was possible for Government

[1] Euan Smith to Mackinnon, 8 March 1873, Mackinnon Papers.

to do'.[1] In January 1874 he hailed Mackinnon as 'the real suppressor of the slave trade'; he would justify all the work of Kirk and Frere to attack the traffic; without Mackinnon's intervention their labors would have been in vain. Fortune would bless Mackinnon, Kirk assured him, 'in ample rewards of a very substantial kind' in the shape of profit for all his outlay.[2] A twentieth-century reader might be tempted to dismiss such rhetoric as hyperbole mixed with cant. Such a judgment would reflect no understanding of the character of Sir John Kirk, who devoted himself with great energy and tenacity to the anti-slavery cause and who believed with Livingstone that commerce was the means of bringing civilization to Africa. Kirk's appeal was perfectly attuned to Mackinnon's character. The two became close friends in the autumn of 1874. Kirk was a guest at Mackinnon's home in Argyll, and there the two talked of Zanzibar, its present and its future. That future, Kirk convinced Mackinnon, must be associated with beneficent British guidance of 'the poor ignorant Sultan'[3] and the expansion of British commerce with Mackinnon as a major instrument. Their conversations were resumed when Kirk accompanied Sultan Barghash to England during the summer of 1875, and the idea of a great African company under the formal sovereignty of Zanzibar began to take form.[4] Early in 1876 Mackinnon's interest was further stimulated by meetings with Horace Waller and others. Waller, like Kirk, was imbued with great optimism as to the possibilities for profits in the interior of east Africa.[5]

He had participated in Livingstone's Zambezi expedition of 1861–2 and thereafter had constituted himself one of the principal spokesmen for commerce and Christianity as the means of eliminating the slave trade in east Africa. Waller was a prominent member of the Committee of the Anti-Slavery Society, a frequent speaker at meetings relating to Africa and a prolific writer both of letters and of articles on the need for greater British involvement in east Africa. His circle of acquaintances included most of the

[1] Kirk to Mackinnon, 19 November 1873, private and confidential, Mackinnon Papers.
[2] Kirk to Mackinnon, 21 January 1874, private, Mackinnon Papers. Kirk was in London at the time.
[3] Kirk to Mackinnon, 16 October 1874, Mackinnon Papers.
[4] A. Roeykens, *Léopold II et l'Afrique, 1855–1880* (Brussels, 1957). Father Roeykens indicates that the Kirk–Mackinnon conversations on the development of east Africa began at this time; but, as I have indicated, this theme in the vaguest of terms was evident in their discussions earlier.
[5] Waller to Mackinnon, 12 January 1877, Mackinnon Papers.

leading figures involved in promoting the opening up of Africa.

Association with Waller and Kirk made Mackinnon highly susceptible to the spell of Leopold, who indeed captivated Kirk as well. There is no record that Mackinnon and Leopold consulted together before the opening of the Brussels Conference in September 1876, but it is likely that they had discussions during Leopold's visit to London in May and June 1876, when the King met with several prominent British philanthropists, including Baroness Burdett-Coutts, and with Sir Henry Rawlinson, a member of the Council of the Royal Geographical Society. At these meetings, Leopold expatiated before a receptive audience on the opportunity for Europe to follow up the discoveries of the great explorers with a concerted effort to extend civilization to Africa. With the encouragement he received, he proceeded with his plans for an international conference which convened in Brussels on 12 September 1876, with delegates from Germany, France, Britain, and other countries. The members of the British delegation, selected in consultation with the Prince of Wales, included two explorers – Verney Lovett Cameron and Colonel J. A. Grant – and eight other prominent men, mostly from the Royal Geographical Society – Sir Rutherford Alcock, President of the Society, Sir Thomas Fowell Buxton, Sir John Kennaway, Frere, Rawlinson, Admiral Sir Leopold Heath, and William Mackinnon.[1] The British delegates seem to have been enraptured by Leopold's call to join in a great humanitarian crusade. Sir Rutherford Alcock proposed a chain of stations from Bagamoyo, opposite the island of Zanzibar, reaching into the center of Africa through Ujiji, on Lake Tanganyika, already famous in Europe for its association with Livingstone and Stanley. Alcock's suggestion was formally endorsed in an expanded form by a subgroup of the conference which included Mackinnon and the other British delegates. They advocated:

The establishment of a continual line of communication between the eastern and western coasts of the continent south of the Equator, with subsidiary lines through the Lake regions which would connect the trunk road with the Nile basin and the lower course of the Congo to the north with the Zambesi country to the south, and would debouch at convenient points on the sea-coast.[2]

[1] Roger Anstey, *Britain and the Congo in the Nineteenth Century* (Oxford, 1962), p. 58; R. S. Thomson, *Fondation de l'État Indépendent du Congo* (Brussels, 1933), p. 42.
[2] Anstey, *Britain and the Congo*, p. 60.

The eastern terminus of this transcontinental route, they agreed, should be on the coast opposite Zanzibar, and steamers should be employed on the Congo and on Lakes Victoria and Tanganyika to promote the development of trade between the Zambezi and the Nile.[1] It is remarkable that a group with such impressive credentials should have gone so far in support of a grandiose project involving huge expenditures without consideration of the possibilities of governmental support. It is even more remarkable that Mackinnon should have identified himself with such a scheme to the extent of being prepared to commit large personal resources to its execution. Before he left Brussels, Mackinnon had decided to devote his money and his energy to a project for opening up the country between the east coast and Lake Nyasa in which he and other British capitalists would cooperate with a Belgian group. While he was a guest at Leopold's palace he wrote Kirk of the project and asked for advice. Kirk's reply stimulated his enthusiasm. Kirk assured Mackinnon that the project would not only be beneficial to civilization but would be likely to provide handsome financial returns. The sponsors could reap great profits from cotton and rubber from the coastal regions, and a route to the Great Lakes would open up the riches of the interior of Africa. The best area of operations, Kirk suggested, would be the district between Lamu and Portuguese-controlled territory. The Somali coast was not safe, since it was peopled by a 'blood thirsty race' who would not permit peaceful commerce, but to the south of Lamu all was quiet. His only stricture was the inadequacy of east African rivers as routes of commerce, except for the Zambezi. That river might be used for the transportation of men and goods to Lake Nyasa when the obstructive Portuguese were dislodged from their hold on the coast. Kirk suggested that Mackinnon select a port under Zanzibar sovereignty which would not be so close to Zanzibar itself as to cause irritation with the Sultan's central government – Dar es Salaam, he indicated, would be ideal. Kirk assured Mackinnon of his full support and that of the Sultan, for whom 'I think I can answer'. Mackinnon must induce the Foreign Office to instruct him to use his influence with the Sultan and all would be well – the necessary concession would be obtained and the work would proceed.[2]

[1] Anstey, *Britain and the Congo*, p. 60.
[2] Kirk to Mackinnon, private, 17 October 1876, Mackinnon Papers.

While Mackinnon and Kirk were corresponding the British delegation to the Brussels Conference had returned home with the intention of establishing a national committee to work under the auspices of the new International African Association, of which the Conference had elected Leopold president. By November their plans were so far advanced that Alcock announced to the Royal Geographical Society the formation of a national committee with the Prince of Wales as its president; at the same time, business-men in the Glasgow area, including Mackinnon, were discussing the formation of a Scottish branch of the English committee, and in November 1876 a meeting in Glasgow, presided over by Sir James Watson, and attended by Frere, supported Mackinnon's project for a road from the east coast to the Great Lakes.[1]

Until December 1876 planning proceeded without consultation with the Foreign Office, or indeed without informing it. On 5 December Alcock told the Permanent Undersecretary, Lord Tenterden, that the Prince of Wales had agreed to accept the presidency of the British national committee if the government approved, and asked for an interview with the Foreign Secretary, Lord Derby. He gave Tenterden an outline of the proposed plan for the British committee to construct a road from the east coast to Lake Tanganyika and thence to Lake Nyasa. Tenterden's response came as a shock. Rather than expressing support for noble ends, he asked about means. Who was to protect the road-builders and the traders to follow? Alcock could only reply that the sponsors had not yet worked out the details but that they hoped to avoid trouble by subsidies and by conciliatory treatment of the natives. This lame response confirmed Tenterden in the opinion that the project was ill-conceived and fraught with risks which could lead to governmental involvement. The authority of Zanzibar, he believed, was a fiction beyond the coastal strip. The only way that order could be maintained against the 'treacherous and unruly savages' of the interior was by 'strong measures backed by force'; such measures required an effective government, and they required money. William H. Wylde, the head of the Commer-cial and Consular department, attempted to reassure the Perman-ent Undersecretary as to the practicability of the project and the unlikelihood of risks for the government. The response in England, and particularly in Scotland, he noted had been overwhelming –

[1] Roeykens, *Léopold II et l'Afrique*, p. 342.

over £100,000 had been pledged. Further, Tenterden under-estimated the extent of the Sultan's power in the interior. Before Britain had interfered with the slave trade, his authority had been respected as far inland as Lake Tanganyika, and even now his influence was significant. It should be British policy, Wylde argued, to back the Sultan as the force of order as far into that interior as possible and to use all practicable means to extend his authority. In this way, Britain would contribute to the suppression of the slave trade and the expansion of legitimate commerce.[1]

Wylde did not convince Tenterden. Their exchange was an early indication of a basic difference of opinion among the per-manent staff of the Foreign Office as to the degree to which the Imperial government should use its influence in advancing desirable ends on the east coast of Africa. Wylde and T. Villiers Lister, head of the Slave Trade department, were generally supportive of a forward policy, while Tenterden and Sir Julian Pauncefote, the legal adviser, were disposed to extreme caution. Tenterden and Pauncefote received powerful support from Sir Henry Thring, parliamentary counsel to the Treasury and an eminent authority on international law, whose influence was far greater than his official role would suggest. Thring's analysis was devastating to the hopes of the promoters of British participation in Leopold's International Association. He pointed out that there was a vast gulf between the avowed objectives of the association and its means to carry them out. The slave trade could be abolished only by governmental action, not by a private body and certainly not by an association with little money at its disposal. Under these circumstances it would be unwise for the Prince of Wales to accept the presidency of a national committee which would be subject to control of the international executive committee, in-cluding the right to expend the national committee's funds. If the International Association proceeded with its program of establish-ing stations throughout Africa, it would inevitably find itself required to take military and political decisions, as had the British East India Company, and a British committee would be forced to follow a course laid down by an alien body which might be subversive of the British national interest.[2] Thring's memorandum was submitted to the Foreign Office after Alcock, accompanied by Frere and Rawlinson, had had their interview with Lord Derby.

[1] Roeykens, *Léopold II et l'Afrique*, p. 342.
[2] Memorandum by Thring, 13 December 1876, F.O. 84/1463.

The Foreign Secretary told them that he had no objection to the plan for a national committee, but stated he could give no positive judgment until he was given a more detailed plan.[1] That plan was never submitted. The movement for a British national committee collapsed.

There has been some controversy over the reasons for the sudden loss of interest in an idea which had commanded such widespread support.[2] The probable cause was that the participants were brought face to face with the implications of their scheme and recognized the unwisdom of pursuing it. Buxton expressed this belated realization when he wrote to Mackinnon on 16 December 1876, with regard to Thring's memorandum: 'It was alarming to find [the] tremendous duties we, according to his view, had taken upon our shoulders – War, conquest, trade and Government – We shall look to you Scotchmen to pull us through.'[3]

It is true that Mackinnon did not immediately accept the verdict that the national committee was dead. It was not formally buried until mid-January 1877. But these facts had little to do with Mackinnon's involvement in east Africa. Long before the abolition of the committee, and indeed before the Brussels Conference, Mackinnon had been contemplating a project for east African development. His meetings with Leopold had intensified his interest, and he had expanded his ambitions into a grand cooperative project in which he and the King of the Belgians would be prime movers. In this framework, a national committee could be useful to Mackinnon rather than his being an instrument of the national committee.

From Mackinnon's standpoint, the frustration of plans for a national committee was regrettable but not decisive. Of far more importance was the action of his confederate in Zanzibar. Sir John Kirk had followed through on the plans he and Mackinnon had discussed and had carried out his promise to induce the Sultan to express his support. Barghash's letter to Derby of 13 December 1876 was inspired by Kirk if not actually written by him. Barghash told the Foreign Secretary that he had seen in the newspapers and had had explained to him by Kirk the importance

[1] Memorandum by Derby, 11 December 1876, quoted in Roeykens, *Léopold II et l'Afrique*, p. 348.
[2] See Roeykens, *Léopold II et l'Afrique*, pp. 364–5, 367, and Anstey, *Britain and the Congo*, pp. 63–4.
[3] Buxton to Mackinnon, 16 December 1876, Mackinnon Papers, quoted in Anstey, *Britain and the Congo*, p. 62.

to Zanzibar of the Brussels Conference, and in particular the plans of certain Scottish gentlemen to open roads to Lakes Nyasa and Tanganyika and to Uganda. He was anxious, Barghash stated, to assist in the realization of these great objects.[1] Kirk accompanied Barghash's letter with a statement of his own. He admitted that he had called the Sultan's attention to the proceedings in Glasgow but maintained that the Sultan had responded of his own accord and wished to give his cordial support to the scheme.[2]

Kirk's assurance that the Sultan was genuinely interested was undoubtedly correct. There were good reasons for Barghash's being so. Beyond the financial benefit he would receive, there were important strategic considerations, in particular the threat from Egypt. During the mid-1870s the Khedive was intent on extending the influence of Egypt to the upper reaches of the Nile and, if possible, to the Great Lakes. There were two routes by which these ambitions might be realized, by the Nile itself or by a river and land route from the east coast. Late in 1875, on the advice of General Charles E. (Chinese) Gordon, the Khedive had dispatched an expedition under Captain H. F. McKillop to the port of Brava, on the Benadir coast, which was claimed by the Sultan of Zanzibar. McKillop's Egyptian force occupied the town with no opposition from the Sultan's troops. But Kirk had intervened with the Foreign Office, which compelled the Eyptians to withdraw.[3] The incident left Sultan Barghash badly shaken and anxious to prevent a repetition. Kirk assured him that if the British opened up the interior to commerce through Zanzibar, neither the Egyptians nor any other power could threaten his overlordship.[4]

The Foreign Office expressed gratification at Barghash's enlightenment in giving his support to the opening up of the interior of Africa.[5] Lord Derby passed on Barghash's letter to Mackinnon and Sir Thomas Fowell Buxton, and the two decided

---

[1] Barghash to Derby, 13 December 1876, quoted in Roeykens, *Léopold II et l'Afrique*, pp. 359–60. Reginald Coupland, *The Exploitation of East Africa, 1856–1890* (London, 1939), pp. 304–5, states that the initiative for the grand plan for east Africa came not from Mackinnon but from Barghash in a letter, undated, to Derby, which had not been traced. This viewpoint cannot be sustained.

[2] Kirk to Derby, 13 December 1876, F.O. 84/1454, P.R.O.

[3] For a detailed account of this incident, see Coupland, *The Exploitation of East Africa*, pp. 275–88. Additional insight is provided by E. R. Turton, 'Kirk and the Egyptian Invasion of East Africa in 1875: A Reassessment', *Journal of African History*, XI, 3 (1970), 355–70.

[4] de Kiewiet, 'History of the Imperial British East Africa Company', p. 21.

[5] F.O. notes on Kirk to Derby, 13 December 1876, F.O. 84/1454, P.R.O.

to proceed immediately with the construction of a road from Kilwa or Dar es Salaam to Lake Nyasa.[1]

Mackinnon was not merely concerned with building a road. His road was to be the means for the moral and economic transformation of eastern Africa and he intended to be centrally involved in that greater objective. His ardor for the grand scheme he had discussed with Kirk and Leopold had not faded, and he immediately set to work to make it a reality. In the process he became intimately involved with fellow-visionaries, including Horace Waller and Gordon. Waller's mature life had been dominated by his association with Livingstone. He had been with the great explorer on the Zambezi and he had caught Livingstone's passion for 'commerce and Christianity' as the salvation of Africa. By the 1870s he was established as an authority on eastern and central Africa, and as a spokesman for the humanitarian cause. Waller was the link between Mackinnon and Gordon. He had come to know Mackinnon through mutual associations in London, and he was also a friend of Gordon's. When Gordon in one of his frequent crises involving conscience and destiny turned to him for advice, Waller thought that fate had intervened. An enterprise backed by Mackinnon and represented on the spot by Gordon was almost certain to be a success.

The Gordon of legend is a religious mystic, a man of rigid principles who refused vast monetary rewards offered him by the Chinese Emperor, a man born to martyrdom, whose death was appropriate to his life. Gordon himself noted that a man who followed his conviction was anathema to an expedient society: 'There is no doubt but that whosoever *acts* after the true precepts of our Lord will be considered a madman. His precepts are out of the question and cannot be followed.'[2]

Gordon's passionate hatred of the slave trade is often cited as the primary motive for his acceptance in 1874 of the Khedive's offer of the governorship of Equatoria. His abhorrence of this infamous traffic is well documented, but his personal knowledge of it postdated his appointment. Gordon thrived on the exercise of power; and his passion for command was matched by his ability to exercise it. His performance in difficult positions won him a reputation which made statesmen willing to accept his irascibility

[1] de Kiewiet, 'History of the Imperial British East Africa Company', pp. 49–50.
[2] Gordon's 'Journal', 14 May 1875, in George B. Hill, *Colonel Gordon in Central Africa, 1874–1879* (London, 1881), pp. 82–3.

and insubordination. W. E. Gladstone, hardly a timid man, confided to Granville at the beginning of Gordon's last and fatal mission that 'I should not like to take the responsibility of ordering a man like Gordon not to do what he deems essential.'[1] That characteristic was Gordon's strength, as it was his weakness.

Gordon had been attracted to the governorship of Equatoria in large part because the Khedive had convinced him that the Egyptian government meant to employ him to expand the power of Egypt into Uganda and the Great Lakes area. This was a mission which appealed to Gordon's nature. Much of his energy during the first few months in his position was devoted to plans for the penetration of central Africa via the Nile, but personal observation convinced him that the most feasible route to the Great Lakes was not by the Nile route – 'a terrible affair'[2] – but from the east coast. In January 1875 he noted:

I have proposed to the Khedive to send 150 men in a steamer to Mombaz Bay, 250 miles north of Zanzibar, & there to establish a station & thence to push towards Mtesa. If I can do that, I shall make my base at Mombaz & give up Khartoum & the bother of the steamers, etc. . . . The Centre of Africa would be much more effectually opened out, as the only valuable parts of the country are the high lands near Mtesa, while all south of this [Lado] and Khartoum is wretched marsh. I hope the Khedive will do it.[3]

The Khedive, after some hesitation, adopted Gordon's advice and the consequence was the McKillop expedition. Though this project ended in a fiasco, Gordon was not shaken in his conviction that there were great possibilities in the development of Uganda and the Great Lakes through a route from the east coast.

The British reaction to McKillop's occupation convinced Gordon that Egypt could not carry out his scheme of developing an east coast route. Further, though he boasted of having established Egyptian sovereignty over Lake Albert and of having placed the Khedive in a position to gain control over Lake Victoria within a year, his great hopes had in fact been dashed. He had not 'annexed' Uganda or the Lakes; he had been unable to establish effective communications by the Nile River; and his efforts to end the slave trade had been thwarted because some of his own subordinates, including the governor of Khartoum, were in

---

[1] Note by Gladstone, 6 February 1884, on note by Granville, n.d. [February 1884], PRO 30/29/144, P.R.O.

[2] Gordon's 'Journal', 21 January 1875, in Hill, *Colonel Gordon in Central Africa*, p. 68.

[3] *Ibid.*, 29 January 1875, pp. 65–6.

collusion with the slave dealers. Gordon saw his energy being subverted to serve evil purposes. His extension of Egyptian authority had not been the means for the spread of legitimate trade but for the extension of the slave trade into new districts. The cause, Gordon convinced himself, was that he had insufficient authority. He was tempted by the suggestion of Nubar Pasha, one of the Khedive's closest advisers, that he set up a kingdom in opposition to the Khedive which would be under either the formal sovereignty of Mutesa, King of Buganda, or the Sultan of Zanzibar, and which would stretch from Victoria Nyanza to the sea. But he thrust aside this counsel of 'an ungrateful intriguer' and resolved to tell the Khedive that he could not continue to accept responsibility without power. He was not determined to resign; indeed, he listened to the Khedive's promises to give him full authority without suggesting such an inclination. He left Cairo for Europe with his future uncertain. But it was evident that he still dreamed of himself in a central role in the opening up of Africa. From Paris he wrote Tenterden in the Foreign Office of his frustrations in such terms that Tenterden and the staff had difficulty interpreting his meaning. In effect he seemed to be requesting that the government relieve him of the embarrassment of having to resign by finding him another assignment. But in conversations later in the Foreign Office he seemed to suggest that he might go back to the Sudan if he were given full control.[1]

It was while Gordon was anguishing over his future that he was brought into contact with Mackinnon. Soon after he arrived in London, Gordon met Waller, who informed Gordon of Mackinnon's hopes for the development of east Africa and heard of Gordon's frustrations. Gordon asked Waller's help in fending off the many invitations from members of the Geographical Society and other friends and then went on to pour out his frustrations over his experiences in the Sudan. Waller told him that he was putting himself in a false position by continuing in the service of the Khedive who was as much a slaver at heart as ever. Gordon acknowledged that Ismail was a hypocrite. But God had His own design, and Gordon had been spared to perform further services in his behalf. He could not escape the feeling that his destiny was in the interior of Africa. The country to the south of Lakes Albert and Victoria was 'enormously rich'; under effective civilized

[1] Gordon to Tenterden, 23 December 1876, and notes thereto, F.O. 84/1463, P.R.O.

government, its resources could be developed for the benefit of its inhabitants. Egypt could not provide such a government. His resignation would be the signal for a great hunt for slaves, and no pasha who would follow him could or would prevent the resumption of slave dealing throughout the area. In any case Egyptian rule could not be exercised effectively, since the Nile route was not practicable. Gordon referred to Nubar Pasha's suggestion that he go back to the Sudan, break through to the sea and repudiate the Khedive's authority. He had rejected this as a counsel of disloyalty but he saw no such complication in a project such as Mackinnon contemplated.[1]

Waller was ecstatic. Here was the perfect choice for the execution of his and Mackinnon's plans:

You may judge what all this was to me. It seemed as if some unseen hand was leading him [Gordon] into the presence of four or five men and ladies who sat round a breakfast table in Burlington H[otel] about a year ago.[2]

Waller reiterated that Gordon could not serve two masters – he must choose between his principles and the Khedive. In association with Mackinnon he would serve humanity. He would find that Mackinnon was no dreamy philanthropist but a practical man who had the means and influence to carry out a commercial operation modelled on the old East India Company. Gordon responded that Mackinnon's views and his were identical. As Waller wrote:

. . . the word 'philanthropy' to him conveyed the idea of all that is not practicable and is unmanageable. That large undertakings with Kings and so forth at their head bore with them the seeds of failure; that under no circumstances would he tie such a log around his leg as would inevitably accrue from following out the plans of other people.[3]

Waller's spirits rose even higher when Gordon outlined the requirements for success in the development of the Lakes area. First, he would require a port on one of the rivers near the Juba and would then work west and north. A capital investment of £5,000 would be sufficient for a start.[4] Gordon's requirements for

---

[1] Gordon to Waller, 4 January 1877, Waller Papers, Rhodes House, Oxford; Waller to Mackinnon, 12 January 1877, Mackinnon Papers.
[2] Waller to Mackinnon, 12 January 1877, Mackinnon Papers.
[3] *Ibid.*
[4] *Ibid.*

himself were in the Gordon tradition – full authority, minimum publicity, and small salary. He asked:

1. 'That quietness should be observed.'
2. A two-year contract.
3. Reasonable expenses and a salary of £150 a year.
4. Independence of action, 'as far as is compatible to my rank'.[1]

This indeed was destiny. Waller told Mackinnon 'There is your man and *the* man; money must do the rest'. Let Mackinnon bring together several of his wealthy friends, including Donald Currie, the shipping magnate, to pledge the necessary funds, and then convince Gordon to join him.[2]

Gordon, it seemed, required no convincing. On 9 January 1877 he told Lord Derby that he had decided to leave the Khedive's service[3] and two days later he notified Waller that he was free to accept an appointment for two years on the conditions that he had outlined earlier.[4] He apparently had committed himself to a new mission.

The role which Gordon conceived for himself was similar to that he had played in Equatoria – as the agent for the establishment and preservation of order and the rule of law. He admitted that he knew nothing of commerce and that his ideas were 'quixotic and impractical'. But he nevertheless could not resist giving advice in matters in which he confessed his incompetence. He proposed that a company acquire from the Sultan of Zanzibar a concession for ten years which would essentially grant all governmental rights and authority. The company would then establish a depot at some suitable port on the coast and from that point reach into the interior, proceeding cautiously.[5] This plan was essentially similar to Gordon's ill-fated scheme which had led to the dispatch of McKillop Pasha, but the auspices would be different. This time Kirk smiled on the project, and there was no reason to anticipate opposition from the Foreign Office.

Now that Gordon was available, Waller urged immediate action. He suggested to Mackinnon that perhaps the Sultan could be induced to sign a concession by correspondence, since Kirk had already prepared the way; if not, perhaps Waller's younger

[1] Gordon to Waller, 11 January 1877, Waller Papers.
[2] Waller to Mackinnon, 12 January 1877, Mackinnon Papers.
[3] Gordon to Waller, 9 January 1877, Waller Papers.
[4] Gordon to Waller, 11 January 1877, Mackinnon Papers.
[5] Gordon to Waller, 17 January 1877, Waller Papers, copy in Mackinnon Papers.

brother Gerald or his brother-in-law, Alexander Kirk, brother of John, might go to Zanzibar and make the arrangements. In any event, the prospect was brilliant. The British government must now give not only its blessing but its backing.

'We should have to make it perfectly clear to Lord Derby that the opportunity was so great and the convictions so well matured that an effort would be made to lay the foundation on nothing less than those of the East India Company. If you look closely you will see the spirit of a Clive in this man – let us try, by God's help, to make a Clive or greater if we can – less he is not and you will say so when you know him well.'[1]

There was one small remaining problem, Waller advised Mackinnon – it was probably useless to ask Gordon to participate in a cooperative scheme with Leopold II. If Mackinnon had gone so far as to commit himself to working with Leopold, Gordon's involvement was in doubt. Otherwise his acceptance was little more than a formality.[2]

With 'Chinese' Gordon, no decisions could be assumed to be a formality. He was beset with doubts, haunted by a sense of a destiny beyond his control or cognizance and by the conviction that Providence had preserved him for one more mission. What was that mission to be? He could not determine for himself. Fate intervened in the unlikely form of the Duke of Cambridge, Field Marshal Commanding-in-Chief of the British army.

The manner in which Gordon decided to inform the Khedive of his resignation suggests that he may have wanted to be dissuaded. He handed the draft of the telegram to the War Office to be put into cypher; predictably word of his intention was communicated to higher authority, and the Duke of Cambridge decreed that Gordon must go back; to do otherwise would be to break the promise he had made in Cairo to the Khedive that he would return. Gordon withdrew the telegram – perhaps with a sense of relief. He told Waller 'back I must go'.[3] for he could not be open to a charge of bad faith. He extracted the promise from the Foreign Office that if the Khedive did not provide sufficient support for the abolition of the slave trade he might withdraw from his position without further pressure.[4]

---

1 Waller to Mackinnon, 18 January 1877, Mackinnon Papers.
2 Waller to Mackinnon, 12 January 1877, Mackinnon Papers.
3 Gordon to Waller, 21 January 1877; Waller to Mackinnon, private, 22 January 1877, both in Mackinnon Papers.
4 Gordon to F.O., 30 January 1879, F.O. 84/1498, P.R.O.

There is a curious statement in Gordon's last letter to Waller in which he asked to be left in peace during the short time he had left in England and not to be pressed further about the east African scheme. He indicated that there was no reason why the project could not be carried out with another leader and gave Waller the address of Henry Dent,[1] Alfred's brother. This was almost precisely the time when Alfred Dent was engaged in the negotiations which led to his acquiring the leases which became the bases for creation of the British North Borneo Company.[2]

During Gordon's dalliance with Waller, Mackinnon apparently had no correspondence with Leopold. Father Roeykens concludes that the grand cooperative scheme had died, citing as evidence Mackinnon's interest in Gordon and Gordon's disinclination to work with Leopold.[3] Clearly Mackinnon had no plan at this time to develop a joint enterprise with the Belgian King, but it would be incorrect to assume that Mackinnon had given up the thought of cooperation. On the contrary, as his later actions made manifest, he continued to think of his venture as a British initiative which could be developed in concert with Leopold's schemes.

In the meantime, Mackinnon proceeded with his own plans in consultation with Kirk. Already the outlines were emerging of a great enterprise which would essentially extend throughout the Sultan's mainland territories. Mackinnon envisaged the commercial development of the coastal district and road connections with Lake Victoria and Lake Nyasa. He suggested to Kirk that Kilwa in present-day Tanzania might be the starting point for a road to the north end of Lake Nyasa. The southern area of the Sultan's dominions was not well known to Europeans; consequently Kirk made a reconnoitering expedition. His inspection convinced him that most of the harbors were unsuitable for immediate use because of the prevalence of tsetse fly. His advice was that Lindi, which had a good climate and an excellent harbor, might be a better base than Kilwa, but he indicated that no land route to Lake Nyasa was likely to compete with that of the Zambesi. If the obstacle of the Portuguese could be removed the water route would be far preferable. Until that time, a land route to Nyasa might be worthwhile as a means of encouraging legitimate trade and ending the slave system. If commercial considerations were paramount,

[1] Gordon to Waller, 28 January 1877, Waller Papers.
[2] Galbraith, 'North Borneo Company', pp. 107–8.
[3] Roeykens, *Léopold II et l'Afrique*, pp. 372–5.

however, the route from the more northerly coast of Zanzibar to the south end of Lake Victoria was far more promising than that to Lake Nyasa.[1]

Even on the southern coast, however, Kirk saw great commercial prospects. The cultivation of rubber had just begun, and the area had other valuable resources, including coal and iron. Kirk's reports, coming as they did from an acknowledged authority on Zanzibar, reassured Mackinnon that humanitarianism and commerce could both be served by a great east African company. Kirk also convinced Mackinnon that the company must be British and not international both because of the Sultan's preference and that of the Foreign Office.[2]

By the beginning of February 1877 Mackinnon had definitely decided to negotiate with the Sultan for a concession which would essentially transfer effective control of Zanzibar's mainland possessions. He proposed that an association headed by himself, Sir Thomas Fowell Buxton, Edward D. Young, who had served on Livingstone's Zambesi expedition, and other wealthy or influential men should acquire the right to administer the mainland in the Sultan's name. The association would have the right to make laws, maintain troops, negotiate treaties, levy taxes, indeed to exercise all the powers of government. It would also have the exclusive rights (1) to control river and lake navigation and the construction of roads, railways, and telegraphs; (2) to search for and exploit minerals and mineral oils; (3) to issue notes and coinage in the Sultan's name; and (4) to control or prevent the importation of arms and liquor. The concession on the mainland was to be for seventy years, except for the lease of customs at Zanzibar and mainland ports, where the company would hold a lease for sixty years, to begin at the expiration of an existing lease held by Indians. For these concessions, the Sultan would receive (1) a 'founder's share' in the Company entitling him to twenty per cent of the net profits after eight per cent dividends had been paid to the shareholders; (2) customs revenue equal to that which he received from the existing lease, plus half in any future increase at Zanzibar and one-quarter at other ports; and (3) a royalty not exceeding five per cent on the profits from mining.[3]

---

[1] Kirk to Mackinnon, 5 February 1877, Mackinnon Papers.
[2] *Ibid.*
[3] Coupland, *East Africa and Its Invaders*, pp. 307–8.

Mackinnon appointed Gerald Waller as his emissary to go to Zanzibar. Influenced by Kirk's advice, Mackinnon advised Waller to stress the role the Company would play in developing the territory between the coast and Lake Victoria to prevent the Egyptian government from extending its 'baneful influence' into that area.[1] Ironically, the Egyptian force from which any threat would be most likely to come was that commanded by Gordon. Gordon in the Sudan returned to his earlier ambition of extending the Khedive's dominion up the Nile through Busoga to Lake Victoria, repudiating Buganda's claim to dominion over Busoga. Gordon's ambition was thus in direct conflict with Mackinnon's.[2]

Waller arrived in Zanzibar on 4 April and immediately submitted the proposed concession to Kirk for inspection and comment. Kirk found that some provisions were contrary to the treaty rights of other governments. The Sultan was bound to a fixed import duty of five per cent to citizens of France, Britain, Germany, and the United States. Furthermore, the Company as the Sultan's agent probably could not exercise jurisdiction over these foreigners. Kirk wrote to Derby that the promoters of the scheme were obviously not well informed on the state of affairs in Zanzibar – a striking comment in view of the fact that he himself had been a principal confidential adviser to Mackinnon. But Kirk expressed to the Foreign Secretary his optimism that a great British company could bring a bright new era to Zanzibar; the slave trade would give way to commerce; the Sultan would be relieved of a vexing burden, and 'a prosperous and powerful Kingdom' would emerge which would bring order and justice and a better way of life to benighted Africa.[3]

This vision was excessively roseate, as Kirk himself was aware. Other contributions by the Consul General were also questionable. He told Mackinnon of his surprise that the Sultan had even been willing to consider the proposed concession, since it involved the alienation of the Sultan's authority to a private company and to foreigners and Christians.[4] Yet several months earlier Kirk had assured Mackinnon of the Sultan's interest in supporting a

---

[1] Mackinnon to G. Waller, 28 March 1877, in Roeykens, *Léopold II et l'Afrique*, pp. 389–90.
[2] Memorandum by Hill of conversation with Colonel Prout on Central African Affairs in Colonel Gordon's District, 22 August 1877, F.O. 84/1499, P.R.O.
[3] Kirk to Derby, 10 April 1877, in Roeykens, *Léopold II et l'Afrique*, pp. 397–8.
[4] Kirk to Mackinnon, 19 April 1877, Mackinnon Papers.

E

company to develop east Africa. Further, the Sultan's acquiescence in the principles involved had already been established.

Kirk's role in the negotiations was distinctive from that of any other party. He had advised Mackinnon, but he was not a spokesman for the proposed company. He was Barghash's most intimate adviser, but his objectives were not identical with the interests of the Sultan. He was the representative of the Foreign Office, but his views as to British policy in east Africa did not always accord with those of Whitehall. In the years which had passed since 1866 when he had arrived at Zanzibar as Agency surgeon, he had become a power in his own right. He was not only 'the man on the spot' with the influence which experience and first-hand knowledge commanded; he was the British presence in Zanzibar whose personal influence over the Sultan had been repeatedly demonstrated. Kirk's identification with Zanzibar was complete, so much so that he came to think of himself as the embodiment of the enlightened interests of the inhabitants. To achieve his objects he sometimes had to cajole the Sultan. Whenever British commitments were involved he had to convince his masters in Whitehall. The ends he sought were the elimination of the slave trade throughout east Africa and the development of a prosperous economy under British aegis which would benefit both Africans and European entrepreneurs. This was his passion; to this he devoted his life; and he identified himself personally with the cause. As is often the case with such involvement, his attachment was so great that he could not emotionally accept any other man in his role and he was not receptive to views which did not accord with his own. This egocentricity influenced his relationship with the proposed Mackinnon concession as with all other great policy questions which arose during his tenure in office.

Kirk saw in Mackinnon the possible means by which his dreams might be realized. In his anxiety to enlist Mackinnon's cooperation he had overstated the economic prospects of eastern Africa and had minimized the problems involved in the successful operation of a commercial company. But as the British representative in Zanzibar he had to insist upon certain changes, all adversely affecting the prospects of profit. Kirk laid these out frankly to Mackinnon as soon as he had reviewed the concession. He pointed out that the treaty obligations of Zanzibar severely limited the options of any company in raising revenue. The requirement of a standard five per cent *ad valorem* import duty could not be breached, nor could a company impose harbor and other port dues. The Sultan could not confer monopoly rights except in his own reserved monopoly of ivory and copal. The only means by which the company could achieve an advantage for itself would be through charges for the use of facilities it constructed. It could levy tolls at its own quays and jetties, but it could not prevent competitors from landing goods on the open beach, thus avoiding such charges. It could impose fees for the use of roads it constructed, but it could not stop anyone from using the various trails which had been beaten across country. Further, the company could not tax foreigners, including Indians.[1]

Reviewing this catalogue of prohibitions, a typical businessman must have concluded that the Mackinnon project was foredoomed to failure. All that was certain was negative; the sole bases for optimism were the highly speculative prospects for profits in the interior beyond the Sultan's dominions. Kirk admitted that if a company restricted its operations to the coast it would suffer heavy financial loss until years of effective government had made possible substantially increased trade, and for all its efforts the company would receive no special advantages. The only possibility for success was a rapid thrust to the Great Lakes to exploit the resources of the surrounding territories.[2]

When Lord Derby reviewed the proposed concession he noted, 'I cannot think the Sultan knows what he is doing. He is thinking of signing over nearly all his power, and for no corresponding advantage.'[3] The comment was misplaced. The Sultan was delegating to a company the onerous responsibility of government, in return for which he was guaranteed financial returns no less than he had previously received and a good prospect of increased revenue to himself from the expansion of trade. The remarkable phenomenon is not the Sultan's agreement but the continued interest of Mackinnon and his associates despite the gloomy prospects indicated in Kirk's analysis. Yet they persisted.

The negotiations in Zanzibar were conducted entirely through Kirk as an intermediary. Waller after presenting the draft concession to Kirk departed for Madagascar and Mozambique to examine the trade possibilities in those areas, leaving Kirk to

[1] Kirk to Mackinnon, 19 April 1877, Mackinnon Papers.
[2] *Ibid.* Kirk later reversed himself and recommended a policy of cautious expansion from the coast.
[3] Note by Derby on note from Wylde of 16 June 1877, F.O. 84/1485, quoted in Roeykens, *Léopold II et l'Afrique*, p. 399.

deal with the Sultan. When he returned at the end of April, Kirk informed him of the Sultan's general approval of the concessions, subject to modifications for the protection of treaty rights. When these changes had been made, the Sultan, said Kirk, was prepared to negotiate further, preferably with Mackinnon himself rather than an emissary.[1] Barghash also requested Kirk to be present as a translator and consultant, but Kirk declined because of possible conflict with his official status. The Sultan's alternate choice was Dr G. P. Badger, who had been a member of the Frere mission of 1873 and whom the Sultan had come to trust. Kirk's refusal and Badger's acceptance had significant consequences for the concession.

After Gerald Waller's return to Britain, he was employed in discussions with Edward Young and others on modifications to the concession. His estimate of the probability of success may be assessed by his request to Mackinnon that if the scheme proved abortive he would be considered for a position in one of Mackinnon's firms in India or elsewhere.[2] But he persevered, and by mid-August had prepared a redrafted concession which took cognizance of Kirk's strictures. Meanwhile Mackinnon had been actively promoting support from businessmen and from the permanent staff of the Foreign Office. Among the influential men he induced to back his scheme was Sir Charles Aitchison, Secretary to the Government of India's Foreign Department, who was home on leave before taking up his duties as Chief Commissioner in Burma. Mackinnon also during July saw Wylde, Lister, and other permanent officials of the Foreign Office and received general encouragement. But the cabinet at the time was preoccupied with the crisis in the eastern Mediterranean, and the staff advised Mackinnon that Derby could not be expected to give his attention to the concession until mid-August.[3] In any event, reference to other departments was in order, since the proposal involved considerations beyond the purview of the Foreign Office alone. Consequently the Foreign Office submitted the scheme for comment to the Colonial Office, Board of Trade, India Office, and Law Officers. Carnarvon at the Colonial Office replied on 28 July that the proposal was much too general to permit a formal judgment by the government. The outline, however, suggested

[1] Coupland, *East Africa and Its Invaders*, p. 310.
[2] G. Waller to Mackinnon, 30 June 1877, Mackinnon Papers.
[3] Mackinnon to Kirk, 26 July 1877, Mackinnon Papers.

that a well-thought-out proposal might well contribute to civilization and good government and the elimination of slavery. Such
a great object should be encouraged. The one caveat was that the
company should be subject to governmental control in all political
actions. Beyond that there should be a stipulation providing that the
concessionaires must be British subjects and preventing their
transferring their rights. The Board of Trade expressed disinterest
since Imperial trade with Zanzibar was largely in the hands of
Indians rather than British from the home islands. The Law
Officers saw no legal prohibition for the company to carry out its
scheme without governmental sanction. There might be difficulties
if the company committed acts in violation of such British statutes
as the Foreign Enlistment Act which forbade certain actions
without license of the government. There was also the possibility of
complication with foreign powers, but these were diplomatic
rather than legal questions.[1]

These responses were encouraging, but of critical importance
was the position of the India Office, and its reply was not immediately forthcoming because of the necessity for communication
with the Government of India. Acting on the advice of Foreign
Office officials Mackinnon did not wait for the India Office but
made a formal inquiry of Derby on 23 August, indicating that
without assurance of governmental support he was not prepared
to proceed. He suggested that if he withdrew, the Sultan would
likely grant similar concession to subjects of other unnamed states
who were assured of backing by their governments.[2] This mild
blackmail had no effect, and the threat was probably baseless, for
the only other concession hunters of which there is any record were
British and none was involved with any scheme of a magnitude
comparable to Mackinnon's.[3]

While he awaited a governmental reaction to his major scheme,
Mackinnon proceeded with his road-building project. Mackinnon
had preferred a road from Kilwa to the north end of Lake Nyasa,
since it would be much shorter than that from the other suggested
base at Dar es Salaam.[4] But the road builders had already begun
at Dar es Salaam when Mackinnon's letter arrived, and consequently their action was allowed to stand.

[1] 'Memorandum on Mr. Mackinnon's Scheme' by Wylde, 21 January 1878, F.O.
84/1527, P.R.O.
[2] Mackinnon to Derby, 23 August 1877, F.O. 84/1499, P.R.O.
[3] Coupland, *East Africa and its Invaders*, pp. 301–2.
[4] Mackinnon to Kirk, 26 July 1877, Mackinnon Papers.

Meanwhile the government's response to the grand scheme awaited the reply from the Government of India. Kirk nervously speculated on the possible consequences of delay. Derby's constitutional disinclination to act, compounded now by the reference to another department, he feared, gave an opportunity for Egypt to subvert the project. The Khedive had informers in the Foreign Office, Kirk was convinced, who provided him with copies of confidential correspondence, Kirk's among them. Knowledge of Mackinnon's plans would undoubtedly impel the Khedive to dispatch an expedition to claim lands as far away as the south end of Lake Victoria. The steamers were already ordered for service on the lake and the 'farce' of hoisting the Egyptian flag by the lake region would probably take place within six months.[1]

Kirk's nightmare of an Egyptian plot with British connivance did not seem to be borne out by the responses of government departments. The India Office under Lord Salisbury expressed a preliminary opinion on 13 September that there were no significant Indian interests involved and consequently that it was inappropriate to give any judgment at all. Two months later, after receiving the views of Viceroy, Lord Lytton, Salisbury reiterated that position. The Viceroy's comments were considerably more positive. Though Lytton held that the interests involved were primarily Imperial rather than Indian, he expressed confidence that the company's activity would benefit Indian interests. Like Kirk, the Government of India urged that the scheme be supported as a means of establishing British influence in Zanzibar before foreign rivals entered the field. The only reservation expressed by Lytton was with regard to the powers granted in the concession to make peace or war. Such powers, he said, should be granted only after the most careful consideration.[2]

The delay in the India Office reply and its non-committal nature might be seen as an indication of Salisbury's aversion to Mackinnon's scheme and an earnest of his own future position.[3] But there is an alternative explanation which is at least equally plausible. A delay during the summer months of matters of less than acute urgency was not at all uncommon, and there was nothing in the Foreign Office request to suggest that an immediate

[1] Kirk to Mackinnon, 18 September 1877, Mackinnon Papers.
[2] Memorandum by Wylde, 21 January 1878, F.O. 84/1527, P.R.O.
[3] de Kiewiet, 'History of the Imperial British East Africa Company', pp. 34–5.

decision was imperative. Salisbury's response as the representative of the India Office was entirely appropriate, just as was that of the Board of Trade, which also held the issues to be outside its immediate concern.

One other element in the correspondence is of interest – the suggestion that foreign powers might intrude if Britain did not bless Mackinnon's enterprise. Kirk in April 1877 had raised the specter of foreign intrusion as an argument for speedy governmental action to support the company, and Mackinnon and Lytton had taken the same line. At about the same time – in early 1878 – Mackinnon's friend Alfred Dent and Sir Julian Pauncefote of the Foreign Office were advocating governmental support for the British North Borneo Company on the basis among others that delay might result in North Borneo falling under the control of a protectionist power. In both cases the evidence presented of a foreign threat was not substantial. The only potential rivals for concessions whom Kirk named were British – Sir John Pender with a telegraph scheme and a Glasgow group headed by James Stevenson which sought to build a road to Lake Nyasa. But the warnings cannot be dismissed as mere scare tactics without foundation. In the late 1870s there were signs of greater activity by European states toward the underpowered areas of the world. Kirk reported that France had approached the Sultan in 1876 with a request for a base on the coast and in early 1877 with an offer to purchase Mafia Island. The overtures had been rejected.[1] Early in 1878, the French Chamber of Deputies voted 100,000 francs for an expedition across central Africa under the leadership of Abbé Michel-Alexandre Debaize, which began its transcontinental journey at Bagamoyo in the Zanzibar dominions.[2] The expedition was a tragic failure, but a new French initiative was evident, and this abortive venture was followed by other probes. In the winter of 1880–1, a French firm sought a concession from Barghash comparable in extent to Mackinnon's scheme. At the same time, French officials displayed a new aggressiveness in Madagascar. The commandant at Nosy Bey, an island off the north coast, which the French had acquired in 1841, informed a British naval officer in 1878 that the French government had instructed him to consider the whole of the western coast of Madagascar as being under French protection. This announcement marked the be-

---

[1] Kirk to Derby, 25 April 1877, F.O. 84/1485, P.R.O.
[2] Confidential Print, September 1878, F.O. 48/31, P.R.O.

ginning of several years of French harassment of the Malagasy, culminating in a treaty in 1885 by which the French in fact, though not yet in law, gained control over Madagascar.[1]

Kirk and others, of course, in 1877–8 could not foretell the great upsurge of European activity which occurred in east Africa in the 1880s but there were enough signs of foreign interest to warrant the concern they expressed to the Foreign Office. This sense of urgency was not shared by Derby. In December 1877 Mackinnon sought to stimulate action by presenting the Foreign Secretary with a revised copy of the proposed concession which he indicated he intended his agent to carry to Zanzibar by the next mail ship. The concession provided that the Sultan would transfer to the company all his powers on the mainland and all islands except Zanzibar and Pemba. The company would have the exclusive right to purchase land and had the power to levy taxes so far as consistent with existing treaties. The company would also have exclusive powers to regulate trade and river navigation, and to control construction of roads, railways, and telegraphs. The concessionaires themselves would be exempt from all taxes. The company would have the exclusive privilege to seek minerals, and to trade in ivory and copal, paying a royalty of not over five per cent to the Sultan. It would also have the right to coin money and establish banks. As before, the concession was for 70 years. The Sultan would receive the same returns as in the first concession and he could, if he desired, receive an interest-free loan of £50,000.[2]

The revised concession was much like the first version, except for the recognition of the limitations imposed by treaties. During the months since Kirk had first warned Mackinnon of the complications these treaty rights might involve, Mackinnon's advisers had concluded that the company could levy taxes, regulate trade and commerce, and perform other functions which Kirk had considered might possibly be considered a violation of treaties. The draft was reviewed for the Foreign Office by Wylde, who had been Mackinnon's principal confidant in the office and had assured him of his eagerness to advance the concession.[3] Wylde's recommendation reflected this enthusiasm. Mackinnon's project,

[1] The treaty, dated 17 December 1885, is in C. 4652, March 1886.
[2] Mackinnon to Derby, 17 December 1877, F.O. 84/1499, P.R.O.
[3] Wylde to Mackinnon, 27 August 1877; Waller to Mackinnon, 9 October 1877, both in MacKinnon Papers.

he asserted, offered the prospect of the transformation of east Africa. If it succeeded, the area would become a profitable market for British manufacturers. The existing anarchy would be replaced by a government which maintained order with justice. Slavery would cease, and the British government would be relieved of the expense of maintaining a naval squadron which had not been particularly effective in suppressing the slave traffic. These momentous developments would involve no expense to the British taxpayer. All that was required from the government was an expression of support. Wylde conceded that the operations of the proposed company might involve complications with other powers which had treaties with Zanzibar, but the risks were minimal. Mackinnon wanted only the same protection and assistance to which any British subject engaged in a legitimate business was entitled. Indeed, as the Law Officers had pointed out, the company could carry out its scheme without the necessity of governmental permission. Wylde proposed that the government commend Mackinnon for his enlightened objectives and assure him of its willingness to afford whatever support was appropriate to any British venture but to withhold formal sanction.[1] If Wylde's recommendation had been followed, Mackinnon would have received all the assurance he had sought. But Derby decided that the issue was of sufficient moment to require cabinet attention, and a further delay occurred. There were far more pressing problems facing the government. The Russo-Turkish war had turned disastrously against the Turks, and the danger of the collapse and disintegration of Turkey dominated the deliberations of the cabinet. Consequently, the cabinet did not consider the Mackinnon scheme until mid-February 1878, when it agreed with Wylde's recommendations, apparently with little debate.[2] The obstacle of Whitehall seemed to be removed; Mackinnon prepared to conclude a formal agreement with the Sultan, which in view of Barghash's earlier endorsement of the main principles he expected would involve no difficulties. He was soon disabused of these optimistic assumptions.

The agent of Mackinnon's discomfiture was a man on whom he relied as an ally – Dr G. P. Badger. When the Sultan in 1877 had requested the services of Badger as an interpreter when negotiations were resumed, both Kirk and Mackinnon had been pleased since

[1] Memorandum, 21 January 1878, F.O. 84/1527, P.R.O.
[2] Note, n.d. [February 1878], in *ibid.*

they considered Badger to be friendly and trustworthy. He proved to be neither. In September 1877, when he expected soon to depart for Zanzibar, Badger had written to Derby 'a few considerations' regarding the Mackinnon concession. At that time he professed complete support for the proposal, which he stated was eminently fair to the Sultan and was motivated by philanthropic rather than mercenary motives. If the company was successful it would effect a moral and economic revolution throughout east Africa. The project deserved the support of the government, he said.[1]

Badger obviously was not content to be a mere transmitter of other men's views. He considered himself to be a factor in his own right. His enlarged conception of his role contributed to a debacle. When Badger and Gerald Waller set out for Zanzibar in April 1878, Mackinnon had no reason to suspect that all was not well. During the first few days after their arrival on 29 April nothing occurred to disturb the optimism of the promoters. The Sultan, John Kirk reported, was 'quite hearty in the scheme. He does not draw back in the least'.[2] The only hazard Kirk foresaw was that the intemperate and arrogant Dr Badger might antagonize the Sultan sufficiently to cause a breakdown in the negotiations. Within a few days of his arrival Badger had fully vindicated Kirk's fears. He erupted into angry tirades and he wrote the Sultan 'insolent messages' and 'bullying letters'. Indeed, said Kirk, the negotiations would have terminated abruptly had it not been for the consul's intervention.[3]

Badger's conduct did not end the negotiations; they were stalemated by a bewildering change of position by the Sultan. He suddenly began to express objections to an agreement with which he had professed to be pleased. He now found that it was not in his interests to cede his monopoly rights to the ivory trade or the £20,000 annual revenue which the duties on ivory produced. He also raised the issue of the lease of the customs at Zanzibar, which had been held by an Indian, Tharia Topan. The lessee, Barghash stated, had threatened to withdraw immediately if Barghash granted Mackinnon the concession, three years before the scheduled expiration, unless the lease was immediately renegotiated at $50,000 less.[4]

[1] Badger to Derby, 22 September 1877, F.O. 84/1499, P.R.O.
[2] Kirk to Mackinnon, confidential, 4 May 1878, Mackinnon Papers.
[3] de Kiewiet, 'History of the Imperial British East Africa Company', p. 39.
[4] Barghash to Mackinnon, 22 May 1878, Mackinnon Papers.

The avowed reasons for the Sultan's change of front appear convincing. He was a monarch forced to walk a slippery path between his inclinations and the wishes of his subjects. His advisers had remonstrated with him against his inclination to transfer his rights, even his sovereign powers, to a European company. This action, they told him, would mean ruin for the inhabitants of Zanzibar. The Europeans would pre-empt the trade with the interior, and the Arabs would be deprived of their livelihood.[1] Kirk, with his usual cynicism, interpreted the Sultan's new concern to the success of his advisers in convincing him that he himself would suffer substantial financial loss by the concession.[2]

Kirk considered Barghash's professed objections to be specious, a mere cover for a decision to break off the negotiations. The counterproposals were 'utterly impossible'.[3] But there was nothing in the Sultan's counterproposals which was so inherently outrageous or non-negotiable as to lead to an abrupt end to discussion without a further effort to come to a conclusion. Clearly not only Barghash's but Mackinnon's interest had declined during the hiatus in the discussions. Kirk's testimony as to the hopelessness of the situation certainly would have cooled the ardor even of an enthusiast, but Mackinnon had quite evidently decided that the prospects for success were marginal, and the Sultan's counter-offer consequently was not given serious consideration. Writing to Mackinnon, Kirk had assigned the blame to the Sultan's advisers and to Badger. To Horace Waller, he stated that the responsibility was Mackinnon's. The scheme had been killed by 'the little Scotsman's halfheartedness'.[4] 'Mackinnon never was hot enough on it to have made it a success.'[5] This was ungenerous, and Kirk's penchant for overstated private indictments of those for whom he publicly professed admiration reflects discredit on him. But it is correct to assert that the scheme was dead without Mackinnon's personal intervention, and that he was not prepared to take such action.

As a result of the research of Marie de Kiewiet,[6] another factor in the abortion of the agreement has been suggested – the inter-

---

[1] *Ibid.*
[2] Kirk to Mackinnon, 31 May 1878, Mackinnon Papers.
[3] *Ibid.*
[4] Coupland, *East Africa and Its Invaders*, p. 317.
[5] Kirk to Waller, 14 November 1878, Waller Papers.
[6] Marie de Kiewiet was the first to bring to light the role of Salisbury. See her dissertation, pp. 42–5. See also Oliver and Mathew (eds.), *History of East Africa*, p. 361.

vention of Lord Salisbury. Before Badger and Waller departed for Zanzibar, Salisbury had replaced Derby at the Foreign Office because of the gravity of the Eastern Question and the need for a strong man to work with Disraeli.

Salisbury in 1878 had little interest in Africa[1] – indeed it may be argued that he continued to have little interest subsequently. His preoccupation was British security in Europe. His approach was in the aristocratic tradition of the Old School. He was a student – eventually he would be a master – of the amoral art of diplomacy, one requirement of which was success in dissimulation. He used the staff of the Foreign Office as sources of information and advice, but on issues of high policy the decisions were his own and the bases for his actions he did not confide to his subordinates. This aversion to consultation or even to information characterized his career as Foreign Secretary, and it was galling to his subordinates. One who did not suffer in silence, the brash young George Curzon, when he served as Parliamentary Undersecretary in 1896, burst out to Salisbury:

I have to be mouthpiece of the office here, and it would, I think, be an easier task if I knew always what was going on. I hope I am not making an improper request. It is certainly not actuated by curiosity, and if you tell me that it is undesirable that I should know and see more I shall be content. But I do feel the difficulty of having to speak here as if I knew all, whereas I only know part, and I am sure you will exonerate me from mentioning it.[2]

The appeal had no effect. Salisbury made his great decisions alone, at Hatfield, and Hatfield was a considerable distance from Whitehall as measured by Salisbury's mentality.

Thus in 1878, the staff of the Foreign Office were not involved in Salisbury's discussions with Badger, and there is no record in the official files of Badger's visit to Salisbury except Badger's subsequent reference to it in a private communication which inadvertently was included in the official correspondence.[3] Undoubtedly the initiative was Badger's. He left the interview with Salisbury with considerably less enthusiasm for Mackinnon's scheme than he had expressed previously. The precise nature of

[1] Kirk complained that the Foreign Office under Salisbury cared nothing about the affairs of Zanzibar and east Africa. See, for example, Kirk to Mackinnon, 17 October 1878, Mackinnon Papers, and Kirk to Waller, 17 November 1878, Waller Papers.
[2] Leonard Mosley, *Curzon* (London, 1960), p. 63.
[3] Badger to Salisbury, 3 July 1878, F.O. 84/1528, P.R.O.

Salisbury's reservations cannot be determined from the available correspondence. Probably, like Derby, he considered the proposed agreement disadvantageous to Barghash, and the Sultan's expression of gratitude for Salisbury's 'useful advice'[1] indicates that the Foreign Secretary had suggested modifications in the concession which contributed to Barghash's changed position. The reasons for Salisbury's intervention almost certainly did not relate to his sense of fair play. Salisbury was not a man who showed concern for the welfare of native potentates for humanitarian reasons. Barghash had significance to him only in relation to Imperial interests. Salisbury's coolness was probably based primarily on the risk of complications with other treaty powers from any special privileges granted Mackinnon. Wylde had pointed to that possibility and minimized the danger; Salisbury evidently considered that changes in the concession were necessary to reduce the possibility of conflict.

When Salisbury replied to the Sultan's letter of appreciation the first draft referred to the negotiations as having been unsuccessful; the final version, to their not yet having resulted in agreement. In both cases, he expressed regret.[2] The regret may well not have been feigned. Salisbury was not opposed to Mackinnon's enterprise as such; he was concerned with the avoidance of governmental involvement. Whatever his motivation the course of the negotiations was significantly altered by Salisbury's intervention, but their collapse cannot be attributed to him alone. The critical momentum was lost by the delay in governmental reviews. Also Mackinnon did not during this time display the energy which might be expected from a man imbued with great zeal for the grand project. Instead, he suspended action in the renegotiation of the concession until he had received an official response to his inquiry about the governmental attitude. Even after he had received a satisfactory statement from Derby, he delayed a further several weeks before dispatching Waller and Badger to Zanzibar. He did not go himself, despite his awareness of the Sultan's desire to negotiate with him personally rather than with subordinates. Kirk's attribution of the failure to Mackinnon's halfheartedness, while overly severe, thus was not entirely unjustified. Mackinnon's involvement with his east African scheme at this time was in the character of the dilettante rather than of the true believer. When the Sultan

[1] Barghash to Salisbury, 19 May 1878, F.O. 84/1527, P.R.O.
[2] Salisbury to Barghash, 27 August 1878, F.O. 84/1526, P.R.O.

proposed modifications to the agreement, he immediately terminated the project and returned to the glamorous environment of Leopold's imperialism, where he luxuriated as friend, associate, and adviser of the King of the Belgians.

The burial of the Mackinnon project left open the future of east Africa's relation to Europe. The operation of a British company from the coast into the interior might well have discouraged the assertion of German claims. The vague, undefined British influence exercised on the Sultan through Kirk was not an effective deterrent. The Mackinnon scheme, however, was not well-developed and carefully conceived; it would almost certainly have soon ended in failure, and the British government would have been confronted earlier, as it was later, with the issue of whether it would accept the receivership of a defunct business. Though the 'might have beens' are always fascinating to contemplate, the historian must deal with the 'weres', and in 1878 and for several years thereafter the east African interior remained outside the control of any European state.

At the end of 1878, all that was left of the dream of a new East India Company in Africa was a road out of Dar es Salaam already returning to a state of nature, its track overgrown with tropical vegetation and its bridges infested with termites.[1] The only lasting effect of Mackinnon's involvement in east Africa seemed to be the alienation of the Sultan. The workmen who had been sent out to supervise the road building, Kirk reported, had been drunken rowdies who had antagonized the local population and the Sultan's officials. 'It will inevitably end,' he said, 'in all employees here being Germans. They work for half what the same quality of English will and are sober. We cannot compete with them as a nation. Our market price is too high, and we are as a class not worth the additional money. The Germans are good linguists, we seldom are.'[2] Kirk's assessment of the German character he later revised; his prediction of their involvement was realized in a way which he did not anticipate.

---

[1] O'Neill to Kirk, enclosure in Kirk to F.O., 18 February 1879, PRO 30/29/367, P.R.O. The road which Mackinnon and Buxton had projected was to sustain wheeled traffic between Dar es Salaam and Lake Nyasa. The work was abandoned in 1881 when the road had reached 73 miles from Dar es Salaam. Oliver and Mathew, *History of East Africa*, p. 248.

[2] Kirk to Waller, 14 November 1878, Waller Papers.

3

The scramble reaches Zanzibar, 1879-1886

In international relations there are no friendships, only interests. Sultan Barghash had ample opportunity to reflect on this reality in the years after the end of his negotiations with Mackinnon for the original great concession. Salisbury's 'friendly' advice, for which Barghash had expressed such warm appreciation, had disastrous consequences for Zanzibar. It frustrated an arrangement by which Zanzibar might have retained control of its mainland dependencies under the protection of Britain and left it exposed to the intrusion of Germany and to partition. In Salisbury's hierarchy of values, the welfare of Zanzibar was of no significance; cooperation with Germany was of paramount importance. Consequently the erstwhile friend became an accessory, indeed a collaborator, in the coercion of the Sultan to succumb to German demands.

By the end of the 1870s, Zanzibar was no longer an independent state. British influence was already paramount. The issue was whether Britain would transform a loose relationship into substantive control or Zanzibar would be exposed to pressures from other European powers. John Kirk directed his efforts to extending Zanzibari authority into the interior through agreements with local rulers or, where necessary, by the employment of Mathews' little army. But the feuds of the major chiefs frustrated this policy. The Arabs of Unyanyembe, in the district around Tabora, were usually at odds with the powerful Nyamwezi chief Mirambo. Further, the loyalty of the leading Unyanyembe Arab, the renowned Tipu Tip, was transferable to the highest bidder and cooperation with Mirambo became impolitic after his soldiers killed two Englishmen.[1] At the onset of European interest in the exploitation of east Africa, consequently, there was no established Zanzibari

[1] See Alison Smith, 'The Southern Section of the Interior, 1840–1884', in Oliver and Mathew, *History of East Africa*, pp. 291ff.; Kenneth Ingham, *A History of East Africa* (New York, 1965), pp. 62–8.

authority behind the coastal belt which could withstand the claims of any state which decided to challenge it.

In the months after the collapse of his grand plan, Mackinnon's interests danced over a number of alternative projects. He devoted considerable time and energy to a scheme for the construction of a railway from Delagoa Bay to the Transvaal but opposition in the Portuguese Cortes obstructed the ratification of the necessary treaty.[1] He also dabbled in Florida real estate in collaboration with Henry S. Sanford, the free-wheeling American ex-minister in Brussels, who was now also deeply involved in promoting Leopold's ambitions.[2] But he retained his fascination with tropical Africa, and this continuing attraction was kept active by his association with the King of the Belgians. During the years since the Brussels conference of 1876, Leopold's ambitions had taken on form and substance. He had decided that he would be the architect of a great empire in central Africa. Stanley's explorations of the Congo convinced him that one route of his penetration to the interior must be that great river, but by 1880 he had not yet decided to make it the only means of access. The land route to central Africa from the mainland of Zanzibar might prove more efficient. If so, Leopold wished to be able to employ this route, and his friend Mackinnon offered the means to do so. As Leopold conceived it at the end of 1879, the plan was to connect the east and west coasts of Africa by land and river routes dotted with stations which would be used for provisioning and defense. From this main axis, secondary lines would reach out to the north and south.[3] He was not prepared to limit himself as to how far they might extend in these directions. In this scheme, he relied upon the cooperation of Mackinnon for the development of the eastern portion of the system. Mackinnon and Leopold thus reinforced each other in the conviction that the road which Mackinnon had started from Dar es Salaam must be extended to Lake Nyasa. In the spring of 1879, Mackinnon and Leopold's representative agreed that the Belgian committee of the International Association would have the right to participate in the syndicate which Mackinnon intended to form to build the road and that Leopold's expeditions would be able to use the road and to acquire land for

[1] For this project, see Morier to Mackinnon, most confidential, 7 June 1879; same to same, 4 July 1879, both in Mackinnon Papers.
[2] Sanford to Mackinnon, 20 November 1879, Mackinnon Papers.
[3] Strauch to Mackinnon, 17 Febraury 1880, Mackinnon Papers.

their way-stations.[1] Conversely, Mackinnon and his friends would invest in Leopold's venture for the development of the Congo, the Comité d'Etudes du Haut Congo. Mackinnon pledged a sub-scription of 20,000 francs (£800);[2] another subscriber was James F. Hutton, prominent in the Manchester Chamber of Commerce, who was engaged in the trade of west Africa. Among Mackinnon's associates who also expressed interest in participating were the Duke of Sutherland, with whom Mackinnon had been associated in other financial ventures, Lieutenant General Sir Arnold Kemball, who acted as an adviser to Sutherland in his multifarious in-vestments, and Donald Currie, the head of the Union Steamship Company. The interests of these men were to be closely associated with Mackinnon's in east Africa as well.

While Mackinnon prepared to seek a lesser concession from Barghash, others were also manifesting an interest in east Africa, among them the missionary societies. Missionary activity was at first concentrated on the coast, with the exception of recon-noitering expeditions, but by the mid-1870s stations were being established in the interior. In the Nyasa country, the Scottish Presbyterians and the Free Kirk established stations which became the basis for a close and enduring relationship between the peoples of that area and Scotland. The London Missionary Society had a mission at Lake Tanganyika. The Universities (Church of England) Mission which originally concentrated on Zanzibar and the coast also reached into the interior. By the 1880s, in addition to its work on the island itself, the Mission maintained three principal stations on the coast, four in the Usambara mountains area, one at Masasi, one in the Yao country, and one at Lake Nyasa. These east African stations were sustained by public subscriptions of about £18,000 per year and a govern-ment grant of £5 per head on all freed slaves entrusted to the Mission's care.[3] The United Free Methodists maintained three or four missionaries in the 1880s at stations near Mombasa and one in the Galla country. The society which was to be the most

---

[1] Lambert to Mackinnon, 21 March 1879; Mackinnon to Lambert, 22 March 1879, Mackinnon Papers.

[2] Lambert to Mackinnon, 24 March 1879; same to same, 26 March 1879, both in Mackinnon Papers. The Comité was succeeded by the Association Inter-nationale du Congo (A.I.C.) in November 1879.

[3] 'British Missions in Eastern Tropical Africa', by Holmwood [1886?], in F.O. 97/602, P.R.O. The mission maintained plantations for freed slaves on the island of Zanzibar

F

important in relation to British influence in Buganda was the Church Missionary Society. This society, supported by the Church of England, had an annual income in the 1880s of approximately £220,000 a year with which to support stations throughout the world. At its east African headquarters at Mombasa, it maintained church schools and plantations for freed slaves. Its tenure at Mombasa dated from 1844 when Johann Krapf had arrived at that settlement, and in the next forty years it established over a dozen stations, first on the coast and then into the interior in the Kilimanjaro area, Usagara, and Lake Tanganyika. By the end of the decade of the 1870s, the Church Missionary Society was contemplating the establishment of a Buganda mission at about the same time as the White Fathers founded by Cardinal Lavigerie were beginning missionary activity in the same area.[1]

The interest of the Church Missionary Society in Buganda developed at the same time as men with more mundane ambitions were directing their attention to the area. In the view of the pillars of the Society there was no necessary disharmony between the spiritual and commercial impulses. The lay secretary, General George Hutchinson, believed that the success of evangelization was dependent on the development of trade. But at the end of the 1870s there was no coordination between the plans of the missionaries and those of commercial adventurers. Among the latter, the most powerfully backed was a group headed by Captain C. E. Foot, R.N., whose objects were strikingly similar to Mackinnon's defunct scheme. The parallelism was enhanced by the involvement of Dr Badger, whose support of Foot's plan was as warm as it had been of Mackinnon's before Badger's interview with Salisbury. Badger's earlier solicitude for the Sultan had now given way to a profession of the inevitability of progress. The Sultan, he indicated, had two choices: he could accept a scheme which opened up his territories to trade while allowing him to retain his dignity and his revenue or he could resist and be swept away. The developing demands of Europe and America required that east Africa be brought into the modern world as a market and as a source of raw materials. 'Anglo-Saxon energy and enterprise' could not be thwarted by the foibles of a petty native potentate. If Barghash were recalcitrant, Badger said, the Europeans and Americans would have to negotiate agreements with those powerful

[1] For a discussion of missionary activity see Roland Oliver, *The Missionary Factor in East Africa* (London, 1952).

chiefs on the mainland who were 'more generous and large minded' than the Sultan.[1] What gave Foot's scheme significance was the backing of the Manchester Chamber of Commerce, whose views were remarkably like Badger's. At the end of the 1870s the economic condition of the textile industry of Manchester was bleak. This stagnation of trade stimulated the search for new markets and central Africa seemed to offer promise for profit. The Chamber of Commerce had been particularly impressed by a report from Frederic Holmwood, Kirk's vice-consul, who was in England on leave at the beginning of 1879. Holmwood, from accounts of explorers and his own travels, had become convinced that east Africa was potentially an important field for commerce and settlement, and communicated his optimism to English audiences. The Manchester Chamber of Commerce was sufficiently impressed to request the Foreign Office to assign him to temporary duty in Whitehall in order that his services would be available to the directors.[2] The result of his meeting with the Chamber at the end of February was an expression of support for a national company to develop east Africa, an idea being advanced by Captain Foot and Edward Jenkins, M.P. Among those who endorsed the idea was Mackinnon's close associate, James Hutton.

The idea for such a company was derivative of Mackinnon's grand scheme but more immediately it developed from the discussions on a charter for the British North Borneo Company. Alfred Dent's concessions from the Sultans of Brunei and Sulu seemed to be a model for similar concessions by the Sultan of Zanzibar or, if he were recalcitrant, by chiefs on the mainland.[3]

Endorsement by the Manchester Chamber of Commerce was useful, but Chambers of Commerce do not form companies or raise money. What was required were capitalists who were willing to risk their funds. These entrepreneurs were not in evidence. As Holmwood ruefully admitted, Manchester was anxious to embark on the African trade but not to the extent of providing capital for such a venture. Rather, it hoped to profit from the efforts of others.[4] The Foot project collapsed. For the time being Mackinnon and Leopold had no competition.

---

[1] G. Waller to Mackinnon, 10 January 1879, Mackinnon Papers.
[2] F.O. to Armitage, President, Manchester Chamber of Commerce, 28 February 1879, F.O. 84/1556, P.R.O.
[3] G. Waller to Mackinnon, 10 January 1879, Mackinnon Papers.
[4] Holmwood to Wylde, 1 March 1879, F.O. 84/1556, P.R.O.

In December 1878 a Belgian expedition had set out from the coast with the object of establishing a post on Lake Tanganyika. Its progress inland was beset with misfortunes and tragedies. Two of the original four leaders died and a third resigned in despair and went home to Europe. A relief party had a similar fate. Beyond the toll imposed by disease, the expedition was plagued with problems of finding and retaining porters. Three-quarters of the porters deserted. Further, chiefs along the way demanded lavish gifts, *hongo*, as the price for allowing the expedition to proceed through their territory. A miserable remnant finally arrived at the Lake in August 1879,[1] but this pioneering column scarcely was a demonstration of the efficiency of the land route to the interior. Leopold, however, was not readily deterred. One lesson he had learned from the tribulations of his first caravan was that a substitute must be found for human porterage. Manpower even when it was available was expensive, inefficient, and unreliable. He and Mackinnon turned to a means of transport which they hoped would have none of these deficiencies – elephants. Mackinnon had Horace and Gerald Waller talk to African experts in England and they all agreed that the use of elephants, preferably African, could be an admirable solution to the porterage problem. From Zanzibar, Kirk added his endorsement. He was convinced, he said, that the experiment would work, but he recommended African elephants as being much more hardy than those from India. Until a railway was built, the elephant might well be the engine of commerce.[2] Gerald Waller inspected an African elephant for sale at £150 f.o.b. Victoria Docks,[3] and preparations were made to try out the idea. Leopold, on Mackinnon's recommendation, employed as chief elephant tender Captain Carter, a British officer who had travelled in east Africa and also had had some experience with elephants.[4] The second Belgian expedition, accompanied by Carter, arrived in Zanzibar at the end of May 1879.[5] Four elephants joined the party shortly thereafter, but they were Indian, not African. Kirk grumbled that the experiment with Indian elephants was utterly useless as a means of capturing the African variety,[6]

[1] Coupland, *East Africa and Its Invaders*, pp. 331–2.
[2] Kirk to Mackinnon, 3 May 1879, Mackinnon Papers.
[3] Waller to Mackinnon, 20 March 1879, Mackinnon Papers.
[4] Sanford to Mackinnon, 4 April 1879, Mackinnon Papers.
[5] Kirk to Salisbury, 30 May 1879, PRO 30/29/367, P.R.O.
[6] Kirk to Mackinnon, 26 July 1879, private, Mackinnon Papers.

but at first it appeared his pessimism was unwarranted. The first two animals died within a few weeks, but the performance of the others delighted the promoters – Sanford noted that 'thus far the only success has been the elephants!'[1] One elephant survived throughout most of the expedition and the usefulness of elephant transport was demonstrated, but the experiment was not repeated.

While the second expedition was in progress, Gordon reappeared as a factor in the plans of Mackinnon and Leopold. His second experience in the Sudan had been as depressing to him as his first. He was expending his energies to no purpose, he concluded; the Egyptian government was hopelessly corrupt, and the subordinates through whom he tried to work were 'brigands of the worst description'.[2] He handed in his resignation in the summer of 1879, and his possible availability immediately roused great interest – Gordon and the elephants could be the combination to open up the Great Lakes to European commerce. Leopold approached Gordon through Mackinnon, who arranged for a meeting of the two in Brussels in March 1880. Before they met, Gordon had responded with enthusiasm to Leopold's exhortations to join with him in a crusade against slavery. There was one problem, however – he could not detach himself emotionally from the Sudan. Even though he had resigned from the service of Egypt, his heart was still set on the liberation of the Sudan from slavery and misrule. This was no problem to the expansive Leopold. He gave assurance that while the Sudan had not hitherto been within the immediate sphere of the International Association, he was prepared to extend its activities in that direction if Gordon would join his service.[3]

Leopold at this time was disenchanted with Stanley. Since the expenses of Stanley's expeditions came largely from the royal purse, Leopold was acutely aware of the expenditures involved, and they were sizeable indeed, far greater than he had bargained for. At the time he engaged Stanley, the King had set an upper limit for African expenditure of 500,000 francs (£20,000) a year. But in 1879 the royal treasury had been depleted by approximately 700,000 francs, of which 302,000 were directly attributable to Stanley's operations.[4] The prospect was appealing of substituting

[1] Sanford to Mackinnon, 15 October 1879, Mackinnon Papers.
[2] Diary, 11 April 1879, in Hill, *Gordon*, p. 349.
[3] Strauch to Mackinnon, 17 February 1880, Mackinnon Papers.
[4] Sanford to Mackinnon, 14 February 1880, confidential, Mackinnon Papers.

for the extravagant Stanley a leader of proven ability whose dedication to frugality was legendary.

There was one serious problem which Leopold's persuasiveness could not dispel – the vagueness of status of the International Association. It had no flag and no international recognition. Without such recognition Gordon was convinced that it could not be effective in its avowed purpose of civilizing Africa. He suggested that expeditions from east Africa might be conducted under the flag of Zanzibar.[1] Leopold stated that he would not consider becoming an agent for the extension of the jurisdiction of Zanzibar. Gordon and the King then touched upon the possibility of establishing a settlement between the southern limits of Egypt and the northern point of Zanzibari jurisdiction on the coast, assuming that there was a gap which could be occupied. This conversation, however, Gordon did not take seriously, since he assumed that the Foreign Office would oppose any settlement by Leopold in the intervening territory, even if such a gap existed, and that foreign powers would raise legal objections to any acts of the Association which infringed on the rights of their citizens. The King, he wrote, thought otherwise but did not give any reason for his opinion.[2] Leopold asked Gordon to inquire unofficially of the Foreign Office as to their attitude toward an International Association based on the east coast, and the response was as Gordon had expected. The scheme was legally impossible, in the opinion of the Foreign Office staff. Without sovereignty the Association could assert no authority; 'the establishment of a community of cosmopolitan description on no man's land and under no flag of any state' was unthinkable.[3]

Gordon's first surge of interest was already giving way to skepticism before he left Brussels, and his doubts were reinforced when he talked to Horace Waller in London. The flag problem loomed even greater; he could not serve without a flag nor could he accept employment under that of Belgium, which he thought Leopold might decide to use. But beyond that he could not desert the cause of anti-slavery in the Sudan to replace Stanley in the Congo as Leopold suggested.[4]

[1] Waller to Mackinnon, 2 March 1880, Mackinnon Papers.
[2] Gordon to Waller, 2 March 1880, Waller Papers.
[3] Gordon to Tenterden, 10 March 1880, F.O. 84/1585, P.R.O. The comments are Sir Julian Pauncefote's but they represent the opinions of the permanent staff of the Foreign Office.
[4] Waller to Mackinnon, 2 March 1880, Mackinnon Papers.

Leopold was not yet ready to give up. On receiving Gordon's declination of service under the terms they had discussed, he returned to an idea he had previously rejected out of hand. He contemplated engaging Gordon and negotiating a concession from the Sultan of Zanzibar for a telegraph, lighthouses, and roads. He would then 'lend' Gordon to the Sultan as the mainland governor general in order to be able to use the flag of Zanzibar.[1] Gordon, however, was losing interest. He professed disbelief that the Sultan would appoint him to a command in which he would not only be independent of Zanzibar but serving another master.[2]

Gordon in the spring of 1880 was under great emotional stress. Waller described him as 'extremely excitable.'[3] He was indeed in a state of turmoil as to the direction of his life, convinced that he was anathema to officials in high places in the British government yet determined to be involved again in some great cause. A discussion in April with Leopold and Colonel Maximilian Strauch, the Secretary General of the Association, left Gordon even more beset by doubts. He concluded that he could not work with both the King and the Sultan, for Leopold's objects would in fact involve the extinction of the Sultan's rule on the mainland. He would not enter any project relating to the Zanzibar coast unless it was in the service of Leopold, but he was convinced that Leopold's ideas were impractical.[4]

Gordon's depression continued through the spring. At the end of March he had rejected appointment as commander of the colonial forces in Cape Colony, offering as one of his reasons the 'great delight of the present government in England at my exile, which I grudge them', and the separation from the Near East, in which he had spent most of his life.[5] Shortly after the election of a Gladstone government, he unaccountably accepted the position of private secretary to the new Viceroy, the Earl of Ripon, and sailed for India. This incongruous assignment, predictably, did not last long. Gordon when he took it admitted that 'the post is very unlikely to suit me or me it', but that he was taking it on 'probation'.

[1] Sanford to Mackinnon, 16 March 1880, Mackinnon Papers.
[2] Gordon to Waller, 20 March 1880, Waller Papers.
[3] Waller to Mackinnon, 2 March 1880, Mackinnon Papers.
[4] Gordon to Waller, 6 April 1880; same to same, 7 April 1880, both in Waller Papers.
[5] Notes on telegram, Bonat to Gordon, 23 March 1880, Waller Papers. Two years later he accepted this appointment and went to Basutoland where the 'Gun War' was in progress. His tenure in the position was short.

He had an expectancy of some ten years of life; how he spent his last years, he said, mattered little.[1] This mood quickly passed. He resigned as soon as he arrived in India, and was again expressing enthusiasm at the prospect of returning to Africa to join one of Leopold's east African expeditions. On 4 June 1880 he wired Waller from Bombay to ask Mackinnon and Leopold whether it was advisable to visit Zanzibar on his homeward voyage, but three days later sent another cable, 'Do nothing. Am going to China.'[2] After a short stay in China, Gordon again set out for home and telegraphed Kirk without notice or background. 'Would my visit Zanzibar be desirable?' Kirk was not certain what this somewhat cryptic message meant. Before Gordon's abrupt decision to go to India, Horace Waller had written Kirk inquiring about the possibility of Gordon's joining the Sultan's service.[3] The telegram, however, did not indicate whether this was again in Gordon's mind or whether he meditated other plans, perhaps service under Leopold. With this uncertainty, Kirk's answer to Gordon was appropriately cautious: 'Personally most glad to see you. Can say no more.'[4] Gordon's actions at his time were certainly erratic, indeed almost bizarre.

The discussions between Gordon and Leopold might be called fantastic were it not for Leopold's subsequent record of accomplishing the incredible. It is significant to note that the links between these two exotics were Mackinnon and Waller. Gordon became associated with Mackinnon through Waller, and with Leopold through Mackinnon, and Leopold's ambitions in east Africa were associated with Mackinnon's. What is not entirely clear is the extent to which Leopold and Mackinnon were acting in concert and to what extent in parallel. Leopold considered Mackinnon to be a useful ally, but he acted in cooperation with him only when it was convenient to do so. Leopold, through his intermediary, Sanford, invited Mackinnon and Hutton, as the only British subscribers to the Congo project, to withdraw from participation, thus eliminating any association with Mackinnon in that area, and his plan for access from east Africa north of Zanzibar's jurisdiction also apparently did not involve Mackinnon. The arrangement between the two seems in effect to have been that Leopold would

[1] Gordon to Waller, 6 May 1880, Waller Papers.
[2] Telegrams, Gordon to Waller, 4 June 1880, 7 June 1880, Waller Papers.
[3] Waller to Mackinnon, 2 March 1880, Mackinnon Papers.
[4] Coupland, *East Africa and Its Invaders*, p. 298.

usually work through Mackinnon in any matters within the jurisdiction of Zanzibar and independently elsewhere.

While Leopold was negotiating with Gordon, Mackinnon was attempting to come to an agreement with Barghash with regard to facilities for the road from Dar es Salaam to Lake Nyasa. To make the road financially feasible, Mackinnon required a lease of harbor facilities at Dar es Salaam, and the right to collect customs, wharf dues, and taxes at the port, the grant of land four or five miles on either side of the road, and the right to impose tolls.[1] These rights, in particular the concession of the port, the Sultan was unwilling to grant, offering as his reason the undesirability of leasing only one port rather than the whole coastline. Despite Kirk's importunities on behalf of Mackinnon, Barghash remained recalcitrant, so much so that Kirk suspected he was influenced by sinister forces. Kirk knew that Stanley in March 1879 had warned the Sultan against accepting British proposals such as Mackinnon's which, he predicted, would result in the loss of his power and possibly his throne. The American and French consuls had also talked to the Sultan in much the same terms.[2] Frederic Holmwood suggested that the Sultan was so irritated over the inadequacies of his ship, the *Glasgow*, built by British contractors, that he refused to entertain any proposals from British businessmen. If Mackinnon would find a purchaser for the *Glasgow* and build him a new and better ship for a good price, Holmwood was confident that the Sultan would come to terms regarding Dar es Salaam.[3] These judgments of Barghash's actions in terms of credulity or petulance underestimated him. The Sultan was aware of the cross-currents with which he had to contend if he were to survive. The British would support him so long as he served their interests; they were not prepared to back him against another European power, and the French government through its consul had made it clear to him that concessions such as Mackinnon was seeking were in violation of Zanzibar's commercial treaty with France restricting import duties to a maximum of five per cent.[4] If he were to grant Mackinnon a concession he would at the least have to

[1] Kirk to Salisbury, 30 May 1879, PRO 30/29/367, P.R.O.

[2] Kirk to Mackinnon, 3 May 1879, Mackinnon Papers; Coupland, *East Africa and Its Invaders*, pp. 333–4.

[3] Holmwood to Mackinnon, 1 June 1879, Mackinnon Papers.

[4] Kirk eventually concluded that he had exaggerated the personal influence of Stanley and emphasized the French pressure on the Sultan. Kirk to Mackinnon, 16 October 1879, Mackinnon Papers.

contend with French protests, and in all likelihood with demands for similar concessions to French interests. These were compelling reasons for hesitation. Mackinnon decided that further negotiation was useless, and for the next few years his interest in east Africa was almost entirely confined to his shipping line. Early in 1881, Kirk visited Dar es Salaam and took the opportunity to inspect Mackinnon's road. He assured Mackinnon that by cutting a road through the coastal jungles he had performed a great service for Africa and for humanity,[1] but the commendation was for past services, not for a continuing contribution.

Leopold made one last effort to revive the dream of a trans-continental trading empire. Early in 1880, he inquired about the possibility of a Zanzibar port's being assigned to the International Association as a base for exploration and commerce. Later in the year a formal request was made by Alfred Rabaud, Consul for Zanzibar in Marseilles. Rabaud proposed that the Sultan assign to the Association a station on the coast near Malindi or Mambrui, avowedly to be used for the training of African elephants. That it would be no mere elephant school was indicated by the proposal that the base be granted rights of self-government, if not sovereignty, under a lease of perhaps ninety years. Rabaud explained that the Belgian consul general in Zanzibar knew nothing of the proposal since it involved Leopold in a private capacity rather than as the constitutional head of the Belgian state.[2] The Sultan took no action, and the elephant school was forgotten. Leopold continued to have an interest in Zanzibar and east Africa but primarily as a source of manpower for his Congo requirements rather than as a route of communication. The Sultan at first cooperated with Leopold but finally indicated that he was not willing to allow young men to be lost to Zanzibar to fulfill the needs of the International Association. Leopold thereupon turned to Mackinnon for help, and through his intercession with the Colonial Office, manpower was supplied from Lagos and other British colonies on the west coast of Africa.[3]

[1] Kirk to Mackinnon, 5 February 1881, Mackinnon Papers. Mackinnon expended approximately £1,500 on the road to March 1879 and relatively little thereafter.

[2] Kirk to Granville, 27 July 1880, F.O. 84/1575, P.R.O.

[3] There is considerable correspondence in the Mackinnon Papers and in the F.O. 84 series with regard to labor recruitment for Leopold and others. Kirk estimated that about 600 laborers had been recruited for the Congo from Zanzibar's territory. One factor in the Sultan's termination of the practice was

Observing the African scene and the energy emanating from Leopold's African Association, Kirk was disquieted by the inactivity of his countrymen. 'It is, I think, a disgrace,' he wrote Salisbury in March 1880, 'that no British company should have before this time stepped in to share the chance of success and reap the advantages that must attend those who are first in the field.' The focus of his disquiet, however, was not east but central Africa, in particular the Congo. If the river proved to be navigable, the power which controlled it would possess the resources of central Africa. The most likely heirs, Kirk thought, were the Americans or the French, since Belgium was obviously too weak to control it and Leopold's efforts seemed 'too artificial to be permanent'. But Kirk was not seriously worried about his side of Africa: 'On the East coast our countrymen have a better footing and one we are not likely to lose.'[1] Kirk's prophetic powers failed him both with regard to Leopold and to east Africa. During the same year in which he expressed confidence in the ability of British, in particular Indian, traders to discourage foreign competitors there was already evidence of greatly increased European interest in the mainland. A German expedition in 1880 examined the land between Karema on Lake Tanganyika, and Mpwapwa in the Usagara district with the reported intention of establishing a colony. This was not the first evidence of German activity. As early as 1864 Baron Carl von der Decken had written during his exploration of the Juba River that it would be advantageous for Prussia to establish a colony in that area, particularly after the Suez Canal was completed. In 1875 Vice-Admiral Livonius had advocated a German protectorate over Zanzibar, and after Leopold's Brussels Conference of 1876 various German societies had been founded to promote interest in Africa. These manifestations were not taken seriously by Whitehall or by Kirk because of Bismarck's well-known aversion to colonies. In 1880 also there were at least two French projects in east Africa, one involving the occupation of Usagara and the other the establishment of a center for trading in ivory at Tabora.[2] None of these threats to British influence materialized, but they were auguries of what was to come.

the possibility that the French would claim similar rights, and their labor requirements for their Indian Ocean colonies were substantial. Kirk to Lister, 23 November 1882, F.O. 84/1623, P.R.O.
[1] Kirk to Salisbury, 8 March 1880, F.O. 84/1574, P.R.O.
[2] Ingham, *A History of East Africa*, pp. 132–3.

Private societies in Britain also directed their attention to east Africa. The Royal Geographical Society in 1878 had granted £1,500 for an expedition under Keith Johnston for a survey of the best route for the completion of Mackinnon's road from Dar es Salaam to Lake Nyasa, and in 1882 provided £3,000 for an exploration of possible routes from the coast to Lake Victoria to Joseph Thomson, who had assumed the leadership of the 1878–9 expedition after Johnston's death. But the official attitude in the early 1880s continued to be one of reliance upon free trade and informal influence. The Anglo-French treaty of 1862 providing for mutual respect for the independence of Zanzibar had been effective in eliminating the threat from France; British officials at the beginning of the 1880s were not yet aware that a policy based upon this treaty was no longer sufficient. The myth of Zanzibar sovereignty from the coast to the Lakes could survive only until it was challenged. That challenge came in 1884, with the arrival of Carl Peters, and the bankruptcy of Whitehall's east African policy was exposed. Officials had occasion to ponder a succession of missed opportunities, the last of which came just before Peters arrived back in Berlin with his treaties. Ironically, Sir John Kirk[1] contributed to the German success.

The opportunity was presented by an expedition commissioned by the Royal Society and the British Association avowedly to study the flora and fauna in the district around Mount Kilimanjaro. The leader, Henry H. (Harry) Johnston, had credentials as a naturalist, but his fame was to be as an empire builder. His first venture as an imperialist was in east Africa. Within a short time of his arrival at Kilimanjaro he had purchased land from Mandara (Rindi), chief of the Moshi subtribe of the Chagga, and from chiefs in the Taveta area, the latter agreement entailing not only land but governmental rights. In July he wrote the Foreign Office asking for permission to hoist the British flag to forestall the French, the Germans, or the International Association. When Johnston's proposal arrived, the staff of the Foreign Office were still in a state of shock at the transformation of the 'anti-colonial' Bismarck into an aggressive imperialist. The British government, relying on the advice of its ambassador in Berlin, Lord Ampthill, had developed an assessment of the characteristics of German policy which did not prepare it for the entry of Germany into the colonial sphere. Ampthill had recognized that the imperial spirit was fully as

[1] Kirk was made a K.C.M.G. in 1881.

strong in Germany as it was in France and needed 'but a spark of encouragement from the Imperial Govt. to become a national conflagration'.[1] But to the moment when Bismarck declared a German protectorate over Angra Pequena, Ampthill continued to express confidence that Bismarck's opposition to colonies would continue.[2] The Foreign Office instructed its officials in west Africa to give every assistance to the mission of Bismarck's emissary, Gustav Nachtigal, which was masked as a scientific expedition, and Lord Granville, the Foreign Secretary, was deeply wounded at Bismarck's duplicity when Nachtigal in July declared German protectorates over Togoland and the Cameroons.[3] If only Bismarck had been forthright about his intentions, Granville lamented, the British government would have been accommodating. Britain had no desire to obstruct German colonial ambitions, said Granville, bewildered at the virulence of Bismarck's attack on Britain for its long delay in answering his inquiries about British claims in south-west Africa.[4] This new abrasiveness, he and other members of the cabinet agreed, must be for electioneering purposes.[5]

The 'mine which Bismarck had sprung'[6] necessitated a reconsideration of British colonial policy both in Africa and the South Pacific. Gladstone might proclaim, as he did at Midlothian on 1 September 1884, that he looked 'with satisfaction, sympathy and joy upon the extension of Germany in those desert places of the earth',[7] but his joy was not universally shared by his colleagues or by permanent officials. This was manifest in the Foreign Office's response to Johnston's request for support. Lord Edmond Fitzmaurice, the Parliamentary Undersecretary, considered Johnston's proposal to be worthy of attention, particularly 'as coming from a man who is not a fanatic or an enthusiast but above all a scientific man'. The attraction was enhanced by Johnston's assurance that a road could be constructed from the

---

[1] Ampthill to Granville, 29 March 1883, F.O. 64/1144, P.R.O.

[2] Ampthill to Granville, 30 May 1884, F.O. 244/383, P.R.O.

[3] Granville to Malet, 20 January 1885, F.O. 244/399, P.R.O.

[4] Regarding Bismarck's dispatch of 5 May 1884, which inaugurated his new policy, see Sybil Crowe, *The Berlin West Africa Conference* (London, 1942), pp. 51–3, 211–18, and Wolfgang Windelband, *Bismarck und die europäischen Grossmächte, 1879–1885* (Essen, 1942), pp. 486–7.

[5] Gladstone to Granville, 9 September 1884, PRO 30/29/29A; note by Derby, n.d., on F.O. to C.O., 30 October 1884, C.O. 537/124B, both in P.R.O.

[6] The phrase is Sir Percy Anderson's in a letter to Lister, private, 20 December 1884, PRO 30/29/195, P.R.O.

[7] *The Times*, 2 September 1884.

coast, the bush cleared and houses built for only £5,000, which would be forthcoming from private sources.[1] Granville agreed with his lieutenant. Consequently Kirk in September 1884 was surprised to receive a cable from the Foreign Office asking for his immediate reply by telegraph as to whether Britain should accept Mandara's request for the protection of the British flag and Johnston's proposal for the establishment of a British colony.[2] Kirk, without any information on which to reply to a proposal which ran directly contrary to his policy of supporting Zanzibari authority, suggested that a decision be delayed until Johnston returned to the coast. The Foreign Office with its new sense of urgency, pressed him for an earlier answer to forestall the danger of action by some other power.[3] But Kirk continued to insist that precipitate action was unwise. Mandara was an 'utter savage' whose allegiance to the British was meaningless and whose power in the Kilimanjaro–Taveta region was uncertain. There were a dozen chiefs on the mountain who were jealous of each other, but united in enmity to Mandara 'who is rather a tyrant'. No colony could survive without access to the coast:

... it would be as impossible to hold the country around the Himalayas without possessing Bombay or Calcutta as to attempt to rule the Chaga without possessing Mombasa or Tanga. Nor do I think that a colony in the true sense of the term where the white race can permanently exist and perpetuate itself can be founded anywhere in Central Africa.[4]

Furthermore, Kirk argued, Johnston exaggerated the resources of the country. It probably had little more to offer than ivory and rubber, and it could not be developed effectively until a railway was built. Most important, the declaration of a British protectorate over Mandara would be an invitation to the dismemberment of Zanzibar, since it would imply that the country of the Chagga and other peoples of the interior was independent of the Sultan.[5]

Kirk admitted that there was a danger that if Britain did not act, other countries might. Indeed he was certain that the new aggressiveness of France and particularly of Germany meant an early extinction of even the pretence of an independent Zanzibar.

[1] Fitzmaurice to Granville, 20 September 1884, F.O. 84/1687, P.R.O.
[2] Telegram, F.O. to Kirk, 23 September 1884, F.O. 84/1676, P.R.O.
[3] Telegram, F.O. to Kirk, 24 September 1884, F.O. 84/1676, P.R.O.
[4] Kirk to Granville, 23 November 1884, F.O. 84/1679, P.R.O.
[5] Telegram, Kirk to Granville, 27 September 1884, confidential, F.O. 84/1678; Kirk to Granville, 23 November 1884, F.O. 84/1679, both in P.R.O.

But the declaration of a protectorate over the Chagga he insisted would hasten that eventuality by undermining the authority of Zanzibar. It would be far better to send out missionaries who could hold the area as against other Europeans and perhaps to encourage sportsmen to shoot game there, rather than resorting to the extremity of raising the British flag.[1] He could not resist reminding the Foreign Office that if it had followed his earlier advice and backed the Sultan's authority more strongly the need for immediate action might have been averted. Wistfully he also recalled the occasion when the British flag had been hauled down in Mombasa after the cession to Captain Owen in 1820, and the opportunity had been lost for control of the coast which could have been effected with little difficulty.[2]

Kirk's self-justification and nostalgia were not helpful, nor was Kirk's advice palatable to those members of Gladstone's cabinet and of the Foreign Office staff who were determined that the humiliating experience the government had recently undergone in west Africa should not be repeated in the east. On the advice of Sir Edward Hertslet, the Foreign Office instructed Kirk to try to secure a declaration from the Sultan that he would not cede his sovereign rights to any other power.[3] This Kirk accomplished immediately;[4] Barghash needed no convincing that his Sultanate was in peril and that his best chance for survival was in accepting British advice. The more difficult question was that of Kilimanjaro. The cabinet was divided among those who believed immediate action was imperative to keep the area around the mountain British and those who saw no justification for taking any action at all. The advocates of a forward policy predominated; they included both elder statesmen – Derby and Kimberley – and the brash newcomers – Chamberlain and Dilke. But what should be the precise nature of the response? Here again opinion was divided between those who advocated the assertion of British authority directly and those who counselled using the Sultan as the cover for British paramountcy. Probably decisive in influencing the cabinet to the latter view was the advice of Clement Hill of the Foreign Office, who in turn was much influenced by Kirk. Hill pointed out that the assertion of direct control could be expensive and

[1] Kirk to Granville, 23 November 1884, F.O. 84/1679, P.R.O.
[2] Kirk to Anderson, 24 November 1884, F.O. 84/1679, P.R.O.
[3] Telegram, F.O. to Kirk, 27 November 1884, F.O. 84/1676, P.R.O.
[4] Coupland, *East Africa and Its Invaders*, p. 388.

might involve complications with the French, whereas if the Sultan's authority were extended to the interior, Britain would achieve all the substantial benefits of a protectorate without the liabilities. The commercial system of Zanzibar was all that a free trader could desire.[1]

The policy proposed by Hill was accepted by the majority of the cabinet. On 5 December Granville sent instructions to Kirk that the Sultan should be induced to send a military force of his own to assert the authority of Zanzibar. Kirk was to accompany the expedition to negotiate treaties on behalf of Britain with chiefs who refused to recognize the Sultan's overlordship and were too powerful to be pacified easily.[2] But the decision had been made without Gladstone's participation and when he saw the dispatch his reaction was predictable. Obviously there must be some strong justification which would motivate rational statesmen to adopt such a course, he said, but the dispatch did not indicate what it was. The cabinet seemed to be reacting in panic to a German hobgoblin which seemed to appear whenever British or colonial expansionists wanted annexations.[3] A memorandum from Hill describing in detail the rationale for the decision[4] merely reinforced Gladstone's opposition. There was no adequate reason for Britain's being 'dans cette galère'. Britain's interests were in the maintenance of free trade; these interests had not been sacrificed by German annexations on the west coast. It was senseless annexationism to advocate that Britain find compensation for German west coast annexations by taking land on the east.[5] He was, he said, 'puzzled and perplexed at finding a group of the soberest men amongst us to have concocted a scheme such as that touching the mountain country behind Zanzibar with an unrememberable name.'[6] Gladstone's intervention blocked any action. The opportunity to assert British authority in east Africa without challenge had been lost. Kirk wrote Mackinnon that 'the

---

[1] Memorandum by Hill, 29 November 1884, and notes thereto, PRO 30/29/144,
[2] P.R.O.
    Granville to Kirk, 5 December 1884, F.O. 84/1676, P.R.O.
[3] Gladstone to Granville, 9 December 1884, in Agatha Ramm, *Correspondence of Gladstone and Granville*, II, 293.
[4] Memorandum by Hill, 9 December 1884, F.O. 84/1693, Confidential Print, 10 December 1884, F.O. 84/1676, both in P.R.O.
[5] Gladstone to Granville, 12 December 1884, PRO 30/29/144, P.R.O.
[6] S. Gwynn and G. M. Tuckwell, *Life of Sir Charles Dilke* (2 vols., London, 1917), II, 83–4.

government is sickening. It is the old story of delay, nothing done'.[1]
But he himself had been a contributor to delay at that critical time
in September and October 1884, when the cabinet had been most
anxious to protect British influence in east Africa.[2] It is far from
certain that if Britain had capitalized on the opportunity provided
by Johnston's expedition Germany would have been deterred from
acquiring other regions of the east African interior. But it is clear
that Gladstone's opposition left east Africa exposed to German
intervention.

While the British cabinet debated, the Germans were active. On
10 November 1884 Carl Peters and two companions from the
German Colonization Society had landed on the coast without
Kirk's knowledge. In a series of forced marches they struck into
the interior and emerged a month later with twelve treaties.
Within three months of his arrival in east Africa he had founded
the German East Africa Company, and at the beginning of March
1885 the Colonization Society, as the parent body of the Company,
received a charter from the Emperor granting it full power to
govern Usagara and adjacent territories covered by Peters' treaties.[3]
The ease with which Peters received the cooperation of his
government casts doubt on the genuineness of Bismarck's expression of opposition to Peters' journey. The Chancellor had
assured the British ambassador at the end of November that
Germany had no desire to negotiate a protectorate over Zanzibar.[4]
But that assurance left unanswered the question of what the limits
of Zanzibar were. The charter to Peters' Society made it clear that
Germany did not recognize Zanzibari authority behind the
coastal belt. At the same time as Peters was penetrating the
interior, Gustav and Clemens Denhardt on the coast were in
communication with the chiefs of Witu and Lamu, over whom the
Sultan of Zanzibar claimed jurisdiction. T. V. Lister, still rankling
over the frustration of the forward policy he had advocated, asked
whether it might not be wise at least to advise the Sultan to issue a
proclamation defining the limits of his territories. A telegram to
Kirk to that effect was drafted, advising him that the proclamation

---

[1] Kirk to Mackinnon, 16 December 1884, Mackinnon Papers.
[2] I agree with Roland Oliver, *Sir Harry Johnston and the Scramble for Africa*
(London, 1959), p. 76, that part of the responsibility for failure to act must be
assigned to Kirk.
[3] John Flint, 'The Wider Background to Partition and Colonial Occupation',
in Oliver and Mathew, *History of East Africa*, p. 369.
[4] Malet to Granville, 18 November 1884, F.O. 244/383, P.R.O.

G

should avoid extravagant claims but including at his discretion the Kilimanjaro district. The proclamation should state, the draft indicated, that the Sultan was issuing it as the head of an African state not represented at the Berlin Conference then in session in order to avoid European intervention into Zanzibar territory. The telegram was not sent.[1] In fact, the time had already passed when it could have had any effect. In June 1885 Germany announced a protectorate over Witu.[2] The authority of Zanzibar had now been repudiated by Germany both in the interior and on at least part of the coast. The commander of the frigate *Gneisenau* which reconnoitered the coast declared that he had found the government of Zanzibar 'the most artificial which he had met', and that in the north, the so-called Benadir coast, the Sultan's officers admitted that they had no power beyond the walls of the cities which were their headquarters.[3] This was not mere rationalization to justify aggression, for Kirk himself admitted that the Sultan had little authority in the interior and that there were wide stretches of coast within his dominions where there was no governmental authority.[4] By the rules laid down at the recently concluded Berlin Conference, the British had a weak position for the protection of Zanzibar against German probes, and in any event the Gladstone government concluded that good relations with Germany were far more important than propping up the authority of the Sultan. The Sultan was consequently defenseless.

During the autumn and early winter of 1884-5, Britain reassessed its position in Europe. The occupation of Egypt and the consequent estrangement from France had made Britain vulnerable to Bismarck's pressure if he chose to exercise it in areas not considered vital to the security of Britain and the settlement colonies. In the first half of 1885, Britain's international position was particularly weak. France continued hostile, war threatened with Russia over Afghanistan, and the fall of Khartoum with the death of Gordon was a blow to British prestige as well as evoking public indignation against the Gladstone government. Under these conditions, the Liberals were anxious to avoid antagonizing Germany. Concessions in east Africa seemed a small price to pay

---

[1] Note by Lister, 27 January 1885, on Kirk to Granville, 31 December 1884, F.O. 84/1676.
[2] Coupland, *East Africa and Its Invaders*, pp. 416–17.
[3] Kirk to Granville, 17 February 1885, F.O. 84/1724, P.R.O.
[4] Kirk to Granville, 13 March 1885, F.O. 84/1724, P.R.O.

for Bismarck's cooperation. Some members of the cabinet, including Gladstone himself, professed to consider it no price at all. Granville in May 1885 instructed Sir Edward Malet, the British ambassador, to assure Bismarck that Britain had no objection to German schemes of colonization on the east African mainland, that on the contrary they welcomed them, and no British enterprise would be permitted to encroach on German claims.[1] When Bismarck complained that the Sultan had sent a military force to the Usagara and threatened war with Zanzibar, without ascertaining the facts – the report was in error – the Foreign Office ordered Kirk to induce Barghash to withdraw.[2] As Malet pointed out, cooperation meant the reversal of British policy toward Zanzibar, but Britain had little choice:

If we cannot or will not work with Germany we shall be in a very awkward position because the German protection will be rendered effective despite us and our influence with the Sultan must collapse, to say nothing of the chance of Zanzibar being bombarded.[3]

There were limits to British pliability. Not even the Gladstone government was prepared to abandon all of east Africa to the Germans. Nor was Bismarck inclined to push Britain to that point. The problem of 1885–6 was the delineation of British and German spheres in a manner which could be interpreted at least as an act of statesmanship if not a diplomatic victory. The continued existence or extinction of the Sultanate was an issue only in terms of this *modus vivendi* of the great powers. Zanzibar was now an issue of European rather than of British imperial policy.

Kirk was made aware of the new realities when he attempted to forestall a German move on Kilimanjaro and the Chagga country by encouraging the Sultan to send a force under General Mathews to the area to show the flag.[4] He reported jubilantly to the Foreign Office that the chiefs of the area had declared their loyalty to Zanzibar.[5] But instead of congratulations he received a caution to avoid any measures which might involve political complications with Germany.[6] Again, however, there were limits to British deference to Bismarck's wishes. The Foreign Office ignored his

[1] Granville to Malet, 25 May 1885, F.O. 403/93, P.R.O.
[2] F.O. to Kirk, 27 May 1885, F.O. 84/1722, P.R.O.
[3] Malet to Granville, 4 June 1885, secret and confidential, F.O. 403/93, P.R.O.
[4] Kirk to Granville, 28 April 1885, F.O. 84/1725, P.R.O.
[5] Telegram, Kirk to F.O., 3 June 1885; letter, Kirk to F.O., 3 June 1885, both in F.O. 84/1726, P.R.O.
[6] Oliver, *Johnston*, p. 86.

suggestion that Mathews be removed as head of the Sultan's troops,[1] and while it counselled Kirk to be cautious in expressing views or giving advice to the Sultan, it did not immediately replace him. When Kirk left Zanzibar in July 1886, he did so with a newly awarded G.C.M.G. and he continued to be consulted thereafter as an adviser to the Foreign Office.

Salisbury, who returned to power in June 1885, was not prepared to sacrifice the prestige of Britain to German 'swagger',[2] but he placed no higher value on the economic importance of east Africa than had his predecessors. From a different set of assumptions, Salisbury reacted similarly to Gladstone in response to protests of business and humanitarian groups at the encroachments of Germany. British interests already established were entitled to the same protection accorded other British subjects but he would not keep 'every other nation out on the bare chance that some day or other our traders will pluck up heart to go in'.[3] He made his observation not only as a statement of general principle but with reference to a proposal which revived some of the elements of the Mackinnon scheme which he had contributed to frustrating in 1878. On this occasion, Mackinnon again was a participant but the initiative came from Manchester and Mackinnon's friend Hutton. The renewed initiative was stimulated by Johnston's arrival in England filled with plans for the future of the east African highlands and by the return on leave of Holmwood, who shared Johnston's enthusiasm and his determination that the country should be Britain's.

Mackinnon continued to be the principal figure to whom would-be entrepreneurs in east Africa turned for advice, encouragement, and money. Albert Grey, the future fourth earl, was among those whom Mackinnon had advised on African financial opportunities and when Grey heard Johnston's account of the promise of Kilimanjaro and the danger it would be lost, it was natural that he should escort him over to a nearby hotel where Mackinnon was staying in order that Johnston should tell his story to the man who would be the most likely means of saving the area for Britain. Johnston later wrote that Mackinnon had refused to have anything to do with this or any other east African project.[4] This may well have been his response to this unknown young man, but Johnston's

---

[1] Malet to Granville, 24 May 1885, F.O. 244/398, P.R.O.
[2] Salisbury to Malet, 24 August 1885, in Gwendolen Cecil, *Life of Robert, Marquess of Salisbury* (4 vols., London, 1921–32), III, 229–33.
[3] Cecil, *Salisbury*, III, 85.
[4] H. H. Johnston, *The Story of My Life* (Indianapolis, 1923), p. 149.

memoirs are notoriously inaccurate, and his account of the interview gives a distorted description of Mackinnon's thinking at the time. In 1885, as in the 1870s, Mackinnon was susceptible to involvement in a scheme for the development of east Africa, but not to the extent of throwing his energy and money away on a hopeless endeavor. As he watched the British government give way before the aggressive Germans he had concluded that the future of Zanzibar was as a German protectorate, since Britain would sacrifice east Africa rather than antagonize Bismarck.[1] His earlier experience with Salisbury did not contribute to faith in British politicians and his subsequent overtures to the government had met with rebuff. In 1884, Mackinnon and Sir Donald Currie were the principal figures in the creation of the Companhia Africana, an Anglo-Portuguese syndicate. This company was assigned governmental and commercial rights in Portuguese East Africa under charter from the Portuguese government but its projected area of operations extended far beyond acknowledged Portuguese jurisdiction, into the Congo basin. Mackinnon suggested that the company could be a means of protecting British interests against French and German expansion if the British government would also grant a charter similar to that assigned the North Borneo Company or contemplated for Goldie's National African Company. With such support he would guarantee to double the capital.[2] It was an eccentric idea, worthy of a Leopold, and the Foreign Office predictably declined,[3] but Mackinnon was confirmed in his opinion that the British government was comatose, completely unable to respond to the opportunities of the times. Africa would belong to those like Leopold who had the energy to take it. Mackinnon and his friend Hutton were actively involved in 1885 in the formation of a syndicate to build a railway in the Congo basin.[4]

Despite his jaundiced opinion of the British government, however, Mackinnon had not entirely lost his attraction to east Africa, and when Hutton and a group of Manchester businessmen and politicians expressed an interest in another company he gave them his moral support. Again, the inspiration came from Holm-

[1] Mackinnon to Lister, 3 October 1885, F.O. 2/75, P.R.O.
[2] Memorandum by Mackinnon, 3 January 1885, confidential, F.O. 84/1731, P.R.O.
[3] F.O. to Mackinnon, 2 February 1885, F.O. 84/1733, P.R.O.
[4] There is correspondence between Mackinnon and Hutton on this project in the Mackinnon Papers. The syndicate failed to get the concession from Leopold.

wood, who by 1885 had elaborated upon his earlier ideas to include a light railway which would reach Kilimanjaro from the coast, carrying Manchester textiles in exchange for ivory, rubber, cattle, and other products which he continued to insist were available in abundance.[1] Holmwood's focus on Kilimanjaro and the details of his proposal were similar enough to Johnston's to suggest that there had been communication between the two.[2]

Railways were being widely touted in the 1880s as the road to riches. The intoxication was international. The French were undertaking a railway from the Senegal toward the Niger; Portugal, nearly bankrupt, was planning another in Angola from Loanda to Ambaca, and both the French and the International Association were planning railways in the Congo. Railways would be the means for the civilization of Africa and for its economic development. That seemed undeniable. But there were also such considerations as capital costs and operating expenses and the question whether the traffic would justify the investment. Unless governments were prepared to subsidize construction and to guarantee profits in order to promote their political objectives, investment in African railways seemed certain to fail. Such guarantees were not in the British imperial tradition. Governmental assistance, it was true, had been offered to Indian railways, but India was *sui generis*, not to be used as a precedent in other areas.

Holmwood's belief in the railway was not shaken by such sober considerations, and of course the capital to be employed was not his. His appeal was to the great capitalists of Manchester who had made their wealth in textiles and were now alarmed at the shrinking of the world's markets. East Africa would buy their products, but the markets could be reached only by a railway. Holmwood proposed that in its initial phase the railway should be built from Mombasa into the interior for a distance of 140 miles, at a total cost which he estimated at £700,000. The diversion of ivory alone from the old trade routes he predicted would produce an annual income of £20,000, and the export of hides and other products would add £30,000. With expenses deducted, he thought a return of five per cent could be expected; indeed, the likelihood was that it would be higher:

[1] *Manchester Guardian*, 13 February 1885.
[2] Oliver, *Johnston*, p. 85.

Looking at the fact that in the country under consideration, the accumulation of wealth or even the use of any form of coinage must long continue unknown, and that every pound of ivory and other produce exported will therefore be represented by an equivalent in the shape of imports, it might not be imprudent to estimate the probable return of such an undertaking still higher.[1]

Other officials were not convinced of the 'prudence' of Holmwood's proposals, though they acknowledged the persuasiveness with which he had made his case – Anderson noted that 'his prospectus ought to empty any pocket'.[2] But the staff of the Foreign Office would not believe that investors in Manchester or elsewhere would be attracted to such a scheme without guarantees that they would not lose their money – 'Manchester will not advance a sixpence unless the money is safe.'[3] Germany now sat astride the main trade routes to the interior, and was thus able to cut off trade with the southern districts of the interior. The railway would not pay, at least for a considerable number of years; governmental support was essential. The Foreign Office saw no prospect of a British subsidy. The thought was briefly entertained that perhaps the Sultan might be induced to provide it and quickly discarded as being too outrageous for serious consideration.[4]

Beyond the financial problems there were other complications. In Lister's opinion, the weakest part of the scheme was that it ignored the necessity for the subjugation of the Masai, through whose areas of wandering the railroad would pass.[5] The fearsome reputation of the Masai continued to be a deterrent, though in fact their power to obstruct European intrusion had been greatly weakened by an epidemic of smallpox in 1883–4 and by an outbreak of rinderpest which destroyed large numbers of their cattle.[6]

Far more important than possible African opposition was the reality of the German presence in east Africa. No decision on Holmwood's project could be made without consideration of the German reaction. To whom did Kilimanjaro belong? The Germans

---

[1] Holmwood to F.O., 19 February 1885, F.O. 84/1730, P.R.O.
[2] Minute, 'Zanzibar', by Anderson, 14 April 1885, F.O. 84/1737, P.R.O.
[3] *Ibid.*
[4] *Ibid.*
[5] Note by Lister, 25 April 1885, F.O. 84/1737, P.R.O.
[6] In 1893 Sir Percy Anderson noted: 'It is known now that early travellers exaggerated their numbers, power, and ferocity. They have to be taken into account but present no serious difficulty.' Memo, Anderson, 10 January 1893, F.O. 83/1237, P.R.O.

did not recognize the sovereignty of Zanzibar, and Dr Karl Jühlke had acquired treaties with chiefs in the area which gave Germany a counterclaim to those based on Mathews' expedition. The danger of provoking German anger was an additional cause for governmental caution in reacting to any proposals based on Holmwood's ideas.

When the leaders of the Manchester Chamber of Commerce first discussed the possibility of opening up east Africa, they were not, of course, fully cognizant of the political considerations which weighed so heavily with the Foreign Office. The financial problems, however, were clear, and it was a measure of the Chamber's concern over the condition of trade that they gave Holmwood's views such respectful attention. They had watched with alarm as huge areas of Africa had been brought under the control of protectionist states. Hutton, now President of the Chamber, had repeatedly exhorted the government to be more active in representing the interests of British merchants.[1] Now Germany threatened to swallow east Africa, and the flabbiness of the British response made necessary not only private pressure but private initiative. The group which was brought together to advance this purpose was prestigious, including industrialists, financiers, and influential politicians. Among them was Lord Aberdare, who was a stalwart of the Liberal party, a close friend of Granville's and a former member of the cabinet, now chairman of the National African Company, soon to be chartered as the Royal Niger Company. Also included were P. M. de Rothschild, members of Parliament from the Manchester area and William Mackinnon. The other members of the group turned to Mackinnon as the man who had nearly preserved east Africa for British commerce in 1878. The government of that day had lost the opportunity by indifference and delay, they believed, and must accept responsibility for the loss to Germany of potentially valuable territories and the best trade routes to the interior. What was left could be saved if the government would respond quickly and affirmatively. The plan for which they sought support was essentially the same as Mackinnon's scheme of the 1870s with modifications made necessary by the German presence. In April 1885 the group formally presented Granville with their plan. It involved the Sultan's assigning to Mackinnon and his new associates, to be

---

[1] See, for example, Holmwood to Granville, 9 February 1885, F.O. 244/399, P.R.O.

called the British East African Association, all of his powers on the mainland and all islands except Zanzibar and Pemba. In compensation, the Association would give the Sultan a guaranteed annual revenue and one founder's share in the company which entitled him to a percentage of the net profits after eight per cent had been paid on the shareholders' paid-up capital. Aside from the reduced territory involved, the principal difference from the earlier concession was provision for the construction of a railway, which the promoters contemplated would run from Tanga or an adjacent port to the foot of Kilimanjaro, with a subsequent extension to Victoria Nyanza.[1] Mackinnon would have preferred Dar es Salaam, to take advantage of the work which had been done on his road, but Dar es Salaam was the natural outlet for the German protectorate in the Usagara, and the group concluded it would not be politic to risk German outrage.[2]

For several weeks before the formal proposal was sent to Whitehall Mackinnon, Holmwood and Hutton had discussed their ideas in general terms with Anderson and other members of the staff of the Foreign Office. They received a respectful hearing. They and their backers were men of substance, not to be lightly dismissed. Nor was there any wish to do so. Not even Anderson, considered by some of his colleagues to be excessively pro-German, recommended inaction in the face of German expansion. But on the other hand, there was general recognition that the possible German reaction must be carefully assessed; even Lister, usually a member of the 'forward' party, advocated caution and the avoidance of any guarantees which would commit the government to protect the proposed enterprise.[3]

In arriving at a consensus as to the appropriate response, the Foreign Office had to weigh several factors: the seriousness of the promoters; their expectations of assistance, political and financial, from government; the effect of such support on Anglo-German relations; and the position of the Sultan in the altered circumstances in east Africa. From the outset it was clear that the interest of the promoters was dependent upon assurances of governmental support in any negotiations with the Sultan and in protection of

---

[1] Memorandum to Granville, 22 April 1885, F.O. 84/1737, F.O. 403/93, P.R.O. The signatories were Aberdare, Mackinnon, Hutton, Rothschild, John Slagg, Jacob Bright, Henry Lee, Henry Broadhurst, and W. H. Houldsworth.
[2] Aberdare to Granville, 24 April 1885, F.O. 84/1737, P.R.O.
[3] Note by Lister, 25 April 1885 on minute, 'Zanzibar', by Anderson, 14 April 1885, F.O. 84/1737, P.R.O.

the company's rights against challenge from Germany or any other European state. In turn, the governmental response was conditioned by the risks such backing entailed. Germany had made it clear that it had no respect for Zanzibar's pretensions on the mainland except perhaps for some areas on the coast. What then would be the German reaction to a company operating under the Zanzibari flag which proposed to assert governmental authority as far inland as Kilimanjaro and eventually the Great Lakes? The Foreign Office decided that before rumors of the project reached Berlin it would be desirable to inform the German government sufficiently to allay suspicion. Granville at the end of May instructed Malet to tell Bismarck of the plan for a railway from the coast to the Lakes but to reassure him that Britain would not countenance any proposals which conflicted with the interests of territory under German protection or affected that part of the Sultan's dominions lying between the German protectorate and the Indian Ocean.[1] This approach was in accordance with previous British suggestions for a delimitation of spheres of influence, which Bismarck had rejected. But with the prospect of a powerful British company in the field, there seemed reason to hope that he would be willing to negotiate such an agreement. Meanwhile Granville saw no objection to Kirk's ascertaining informally whether the Sultan would be receptive to granting a concession and whether he claimed the Kilimanjaro district.[2]

In the months since the first shock at the German irruption into west and east Africa, the sense of urgency which had briefly gripped the government had subsided. Anderson noted in June 1885, 'the present situation doesn't seem to me desperate either as regarding the Sultan's interests or our own.' The only danger was that the Sultan might act impetuously: it was in the British interests to promote caution rather than to stimulate action. Anderson professed to believe that the German intrusion was in fact not a serious threat to British commerce. The British Indian community on the coast could more than hold its own against German competition. Mackinnon and his associates, also, if they were serious, could outdo the Germans without any special privileges, since they had more experience and access to greater capital. Indeed the most likely prospect was that the German

[1] Granville to Malet, 25 May 1885, F.O. 403/93, P.R.O.
[2] Telegram, Lister to Kirk, 27 April 1885, F.O. 403/93; F.O. to Kirk, 22 May 1885, F.O. 84/1722, both in P.R.O.

commercial speculation in east Africa would fail, with or without competition from Manchester, and that the field would be left again to the British Indians.[1] Anderson in common with his colleagues, assumed at this time that Germany would not long continue to support unprofitable commercial activity for the sake of prestige and that whether or not it retained sovereignty, the economy would fall under the control of the most efficient, who were likely to be the British, in particular the Indians. These assumptions did not contribute to aggressive counteraction against Germany. The prevailing attitude at the Foreign Office through 1885 was that if Hutton, Mackinnon, and their associates were serious they could be successful without any British guarantees beyond those provided any other British subjects, and that if the Sultan were willing to grant a concession to the East African Association, well and good, but he must be careful not to antagonize Berlin. Further, Sir John Kirk must not by his words or actions give any basis for German or French allegations that he was exercising undue influence on behalf of British interests.[2] The advent of Salisbury did not change this policy. *160695*

Without pressure from Kirk, the Sultan reacted negatively to the proposed concession, but no effort was made to induce him to change his mind.

The entry of Germany compelled the Foreign Office to reassess the traditional policy toward the Sultan. Under the altered circumstances, perhaps his usefulness was at an end. But after consideration of the alternatives, the conclusion was that it was still in the British interest to prop up his authority. The Sultanate was admittedly an anachronism, but its abolition would involve Britain in responsibilities it was not prepared to assume. The principle continued to be accepted that the only important British interest was commercial, the right of equal access and equal treatment. So long as Germany did not discriminate against British traders, Salisbury professed to be unconcerned. Britain would react only if Germany adopted such extreme measures as establishing ports free only to themselves and imposing heavy tariffs on the citizens of other states.[3] In practice, Salisbury was not prepared to be quite so accommodating. The best guarantee

---

[1] Memorandum on the Zanzibar Question, by Anderson, 9 June 1885, in Confidential Print, F.O., 11 June 1885, F.O. 84/1739, P.R.O

[2] Minute, 'Zanzibar', 14 April 1885, F.O. 84/1737, P.R.O.

[3] Salisbury to Malet, private; 24 August 1885, F.O. 243/2, P.R.O.

of equal access was the preservation of the independence of what was left of Zanzibar against the encroachments of foreign powers.

Bismarck, on his part, particularly after the fall of the Gladstone government, expressed a desire to come to an understanding with Britain on east Africa much as had been done with New Guinea. In June 1885 the two governments agreed to establish a joint commission in which France would also be represented to determine the boundaries of Zanzibar.[1] At the same time, and as a corollary, the British and the Germans would seek to define their respective spheres of influence.

Bismarck made it clear that he expected Britain to support Germany in its claims on the Sultan. Barghash had angered the Chancellor by protesting directly to the Emperor against the protectorates in Usagara and Witu, and to bring him to reason Germany sent a squadron which arrived in August 1885. Kirk had to accept the humiliation of being required by his government to cooperate with the Germans in imposing upon the Sultan terms which he considered unjust. Not only was Zanzibar required to recognize the protectorates but to concede to Germany access to Usagara from the coast, including the right to a port – the Germans selected Dar es Salaam. Barghash was allowed only the shred of dignity of asserting that he had capitulated under protest, and the Germans agreed that legally he retained sovereignty over the coast which they had in fact torn from his control.[2] Kirk was obliged by his instructions to cooperate in inducing the Sultan to acquiesce in the rape of Zanzibar. Indeed, Kirk worked more cordially with the Germans than Salisbury had intended,[3] and the prime minister was annoyed at receiving Bismarck's thanks for services beyond what he had intended to provide.[4]

Zanzibar was about to be dismembered – that was evident. Britain intended to salvage as much as possible for itself, short of antagonizing Germany. On the mainland, it would be helpful to the British case, if it were evident that a powerful British company was preparing to open the country to trade.[5] The government, however, was not prepared to give any support, and Mackinnon

[1] Malet to Granville, 3 June 1885, F.O. 84/1714, P.R.O.
[2] Coupland, *East Africa and Its Invaders*, pp. 429–32.
[3] Salisbury to Malet, private, 18 August 1885, Salisbury Papers, A/44, Christ Church, Oxford.
[4] Plessen to Salisbury, private, 15 August 1885, Salisbury Papers G, Christ Church, Oxford.
[5] Lister to Mackinnon, 4 September 1885, F.O. 2/75, P.R.O.

was not willing to act without at least a concession from the Sultan.[1] There was, consequently, a stalemate, with each party accusing the other of apathy and inaction. Anderson had maintained from the first that Mackinnon, Hutton, and the other members of the Association would not risk any money without security. Mackinnon, in particular, he alleged, was halfhearted. Were it not for Mackinnon's holding back, Hutton might be more energetic. With all of the zeal which great visions can evoke when unencumbered by personal responsibility Anderson deplored Mackinnon's hesitation. The peoples of the Great Lakes, he maintained, provided a greater market for trade than those of the Congo, and the lands around Kilimanjaro were apparently admirably suited for European settlements. It would be a pity if through lack of energy on the part of British traders all of this would be lost to the Germans.[2] Mackinnon with equal vehemence deplored the passivity of his government which was in such striking contrast to the activity of Bismarck in support of German enterprise. Both the Association and the government agreed that Holmwood's railway project was now temporarily out of the question, and the impending delimitation commission put further discussion on a concession from the Sultan in suspense. But there was an opportunity to strengthen the British position and lay the basis for the future operation of the Association by revitalizing Johnston's Kilimanjaro and Taveta concessions.

The initiative apparently came from a meeting between Anderson and Johnston at the end of October. Lieutenant Colonel H. H. Kitchener, the British representative on the delimitation commission, was about to set out for Zanzibar. The case for the inclusion of Taveta and Kilimanjaro in the British rather than the German zone would be strengthened if Johnston's claims could be transformed into actual occupation. Johnston did not have the capital; perhaps the Association might accept the responsibility. Johnston accordingly wrote Hutton offering to transfer his concession,[3] and within a few days Hutton had accepted.[4] Hutton immediately informed Mackinnon, whose cooperation he considered essential, and the two agreed that a company should be organized and agents appointed to take

[1] Mackinnon to Lister, 3 October 1885, F.O. 2/75, P.R.O.
[2] Memorandum, Anderson, 2 July 1885, F.O. 84/1740, P.R.O.
[3] Note by Anderson, 4 November 1885, F.O. 84/1744, P.R.O.
[4] Hutton to Johnston, 2 November 1885, F.O. 84/1744, P.R.O.

possession, with Smith, Mackenzie, and Company at Zanzibar assuming responsibility for all of the arrangements. The intention was to keep these actions a secret until preparations had been completed, but the story of the transfer appeared in the *Manchester Guardian* at the beginning of November, probably from Johnston's inability to keep silent.[1]

Just as Hutton and Mackinnon were proceeding in response to what they thought was governmental initiative, the policy changed again and action was again suspended. Britain and Germany agreed in December that their respective claims should be examined by the commission and that in the meantime they should dissuade their citizens from altering the situation. The German Colonial Society ignored this concessions truce and their parties continued to be active on the coast and in the interior until a protest from the British and French governments caused Bismarck to order them to desist.[2]

The proceedings of the delimitation commission had little to do with an objective examination of the territorial rights of Zanzibar. Each member acted in accordance with what he considered to be the interests of his government. Kitchener, with the military man's appraisal of strategic possibilities,[3] found the claims of Zanzibar to the coast and much of the interior to be impressive. The German representative, on the other hand, was eager to reduce Zanzibar to as small an area as possible, and where the facts collided with German pretensions he chose to ignore them. When he was invited to inspect the Kilimanjaro area, he replied that he had no wish to do so, since the Sultan's influence would probably ensure that all the evidence would be in the British interest. The French member usually sided with Kitchener, since the French interest in east Africa was more akin to the British position than to the German. Each of the commission members kept in close touch with his government, and his positions were essentially dictated by the instructions he received from home.[4] At no stage of the discussions was the Sultan of Zanzibar or his representative consulted concerning the decisions being made about the future of his state. He was only an 'Oriental

---

[1] Hutton to Mackinnon, 5 November 1885, Mackinnon Papers.
[2] Minute by Pauncefote, 8 February 1886; F.O. to Waddington, 10 February 1886, both in F.O. 84/1797, P.R.O.
[3] See his 'Notes on British Lines of Communication with the Indian Ocean', 22 December 1885, F.O. 84/1797. P.R.O.
[4] Coupland, *East Africa and Its Invaders*, pp. 448–68.

Prince to whom are not accorded the usual rights prescribed by international law'.[1]

The negotiations on Zanzibar were thus in fact conducted from the European capitals through the 'men on the spot'. This was an unsatisfactory arrangement from every standpoint. The agent might imperfectly represent his government and have to be reminded of his proper role. The German representative, Dr Schmidt, was unable to contend effectively against his British and French colleagues, and Bismarck consequently insisted that only unanimous decisions of the commission should be recorded, all other issues being left for consideration by the home government, and Paris and London gave way. In effect, Schmidt was thus given the right to decide the commission's report. The commission's unanimous recommendations recognized the Sultan's jurisdiction over the coast from the Mninjani River at the head of Tunghi Bay to Kilwa, to the towns of Kismayu, Brava, Merca, and Mogadishu on the 'Benadir coast', and to the island of Lamu. The issues of the interior were left undecided.[2]

The commission disbanded in June 1886, just before Salisbury was returned to power after a brief Liberal interlude. The final negotiations for the partition of east Africa were thus conducted under his auspices[3] through Anderson. The settlement arrived at was more generous to the Sultan than the 'unanimous agreement' of the commissioners but considerably more restrictive than the Anglo-French majority had supported. It conceded to Zanzibar the coast to a depth of ten miles from Tunghi Bay to Kipini and to the towns of Kismayu, Brava, Merca, and Mogadishu with a ten-mile radius around each, and to Warsheikh with a radius of five miles. Zanzibar was recognized as sovereign over the islands of Lamu and Mafia as well as over Zanzibar itself and Pemba. Witu was recognized as German. The interior was partitioned on a line from the Umba River to Lake Victoria with the British sphere to the north and the German to the south. Both countries agreed to assume the collection of customs duties in their respective coastal areas, paying the Sultan a percentage of the revenue on a sliding scale. Germany promised to accept the Anglo-French declaration

---

[1] The statement is Kirk's in a letter to the Foreign Office, 4 June 1886, F.O. 84/1776, P.R.O. He was not being sarcastic.

[2] Coupland, *East Africa and Its Invaders*, p. 466.

[3] Lord Iddesleigh was Foreign Minister until 14 January 1887, but the control of Anglo-German policy was still in Salisbury's hands.

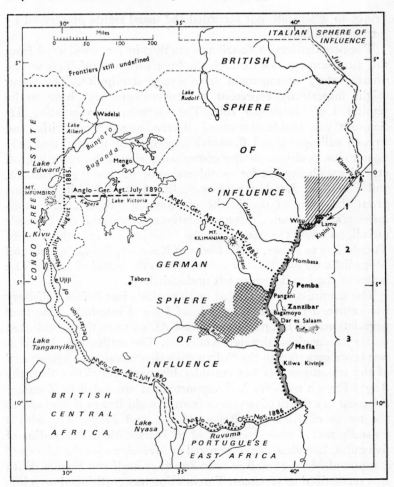

Agreements of 1885/1886.   – – – – Agreements of 1890/1891.

Approximate area claimed by Germany as Witu Protectorate October 1889. German claim renounced, July 1890.

Approximate area claimed by Germany under protectorate of February 1885.

Sultan of Zanzibar's coastal dominions as acknowledged by Anglo-German-French Delimitation Commission, 1886.

1   Zanzibar northern Ports leased to I.B.E.A. Co. 1889.

2   Northern coastline of Zanzibar leased to I.B.E.A. Co. 1887.

3   Southern coastline of Zanzibar leased to German E.A. Co. April 1888. Sold to Germany December 1890.

Map 3   The partition of east Africa, 1884–91

of 1862 guaranteeing the independence of Zanzibar.[1] This
stipulation may be regarded as epitomizing the cynicism of the
scramble. But it was not inserted primarily to provide a humanitarian gloss to the unsavory proceedings. The continued fiction of
an independent Zanzibar and the newly invented 'sphere of influence' made it possible for Britain to continue its traditional
policy of protecting its interests through influence and without
responsibility. The recognition of a British special interest in the
northern sector by Germany and eventually by France provided a
safeguard against the encroachment of another power. The
Sultan's adherence to the Berlin Act at British behest was a further
protection, since it gave international recognition to his fiscal
authority on the coast, thus retaining for Britain the right of most
favored nation treatment.

Salisbury had paid his tribute to German friendship at the
expense of Zanzibar. 'The Sultan of Zanzibar', he admitted, 'is
being hardly treated',[2] but as he and his ambassador in Berlin
recognized, Bismarck was capable of being embarrassing and 'his
friendship is worth preserving even at some sacrifice'.[3] Count
Herbert Bismarck acknowledged Salisbury's cooperation when he
wrote to Count Hatzfeldt:

Salisbury has truly shown great loyalty, and I was anxious that he should
receive the praise of all his countrymen and opponents, who, and amongst
them even his enemies, are accessible to the widespread influence of the
Missionaries. I share your Excellency's conviction that Salisbury has gone
as far as ever he could, and that we can claim no more from him. His high
position and his retention of office is worth more to us than the whole of
Africa. My father is exactly of that opinion.[4]

The Sultan of Zanzibar paid a high price for Bismarck's good
will toward Salisbury. The task of imposing the terms of the
Anglo-German agreement on the hapless Sultan did not fall to
Kirk. He had been called home in July 1886 to a leave from which
he would not return. A man on the spot with the strength and
prestige of Kirk was not needed in the conditions of 1886; indeed,

---

[1] Flint, 'The Wider Background', in Oliver and Mathew, *History of East Africa*, p. 374.
[2] Salisbury to Malet, 23 February 1887, F.O. 343/2, P.R.O.
[3] Malet to Salisbury, 22 January 1887, private, Salisbury Papers, A/61, Christ Church, Oxford.
[4] H. Bismarck to Hatzfeldt, 19 December 1888, Edgar Dugdale, *German Diplomatic Documents* (4 vols., London, 1928–31), I, 243.

H

his continued presence was undesirable. Vice-Consul Holmwood, who had worked so energetically to forestall Germany, was required to force the Sultan to accept the terms of an agreement to promote Anglo-German amity at the expense of Zanzibar. When Barghash pleaded for a postponement of six months, the Foreign Office replied that it had done all that it could on his behalf and that further delay might be dangerous to his interest.[1] Barghash succumbed. Holmwood reported that the Sultan was now completely in his hands and depended on him for advice. But, he added, 'At the same time I never forget the nature of the Arab and shall always be on my guard against change and even treachery should it possibly be his interest at any time to break away from my influence.'[2] The irony of the statement did not occur to Holmwood.[3]

During the months in which the fate of Zanzibar and the mainland was in the hands of the politicians, Hutton's and Mackinnon's plans for commercial development were largely in abeyance. Their only significant action was the dispatch of an expedition under J. W. Buchanan of Smith, Mackenzie, and Company to represent their interests at Taveta and the Chagga country. Buchanan's party remained at Taveta for several months.[4] In the partition, Taveta remained in the British zone.

East Africa did not engage much of Mackinnon's attention in 1886. For most of the year he and Hutton and Stanley were deeply involved with their Congo railway syndicate, but negotiations with Leopold failed.[5] A brief dalliance with Carl Peters had the same result. Peters had found that German capitalists were not eager to invest their money in an enterprise so highly speculative as his German East Africa Company. Early in 1886 he approached Mackinnon with the remarkable proposal that the British East African Association transfer the 'Johnston concessions' to a group headed by himself and join in an amalgamated company in which the Association would have one-third interest. As partner with

---

[1] F.O. to Holmwood, 6 December 1886, F.O. 84/1771, P.R.O.

[2] Holmwood to Anderson, 23 November 1886, F.O. 84/1776, P.R.O.

[3] Barghash did not long survive. In March 1886 he died and was succeeded by a younger brother approved by Britain. Holmwood's tenure in Zanzibar was short. Bismarck considered him inimical to Germany and Salisbury transferred him.

[4] The German government protested Buchanan's expedition on the erroneous assumption that it was accompanied by a military escort provided by the Sultan. Holmwood to F.O., 15 September 1886, F.O. 97/603, P.R.O.

[5] Hutton to Mackinnon, confidential, 16 September 1886, Mackinnon Papers.

Peters, Mackinnon would help to raise capital in London and elsewhere for the enlarged German East Africa Company. The Mackinnon road out of Dar es Salaam would also be transferred to the new company. Mackinnon declined Peters' offer of amalgamation but did offer to sell the road after ascertaining from the Foreign Office that its retention would be of no value to British interests.[1]

The rejection of Peters' overtures was an expression not of nationalism but of business judgment. The prospects of Peters' company were no more impressive to British capitalists than they were to German. Peters had offered no convincing evidence that Mackinnon, Hutton, and their fellow-promoters would enjoy better prospects in working with him than in remaining independent. Peters proposal, however, gave Mackinnon his first opportunity to engage in the kind of personal diplomacy which he was to find so exciting in future years. Perhaps the two companies could come to an understanding and partition the interior commercially as the governments were doing politically. Peters and Mackinnon met in London in August 1886. Peters again pressed Mackinnon to invest in the German company – as evidence of its bright future, he said, the Chancellor himself had invested 100,000 marks (£5,000). The German government would be a guarantor of its success. Mackinnon wistfully replied that he wished some eminent persons in the British government had the courage to follow Bismarck's example.[2] But he was cautious. He told Peters that British subjects would be unlikely to invest unless Britain had sovereignty over part of east Africa. Once the limits of British and German influence were established they could talk seriously about cooperation. Given the uncertainties at the time as to the future of east Africa, neither in fact could consider a definite agreement. Peters had two objectives – to attract British capital to his company and to assert its claims. He maintained that the company had rights over a substantial part of the interior between the Tana and Rovuma rivers based on treaties and prior discovery, and that unless

---

[1] Mackinnon to Lister, 19 April 1886, F.O. 84/1783, P.R.O.
[2] Peters later denied he had said this, but circumstantial evidence seems to back Mackinnon's version. Each reported the other's statement to his own government, which in turn repeated it, and Mackinnon and Peters each protested that the other had been guilty of inaccuracy and breach of confidentiality. The correspondence is contained in F.O. 84/1794, P.R.O. It was, as Iddesleigh noted, 'a curious story'. Note by Iddesleigh on Mackinnon to Anderson, F.O. 84/1794, P.R.O.

the Sultan of Zanzibar could prove his rights to the territory, the German company would be in possession and Mackinnon and his friends would have to buy the German rights. Mackinnon conceded that if the commission found for Germany, Peters would indeed be justified in claiming compensation for the transfer of its rights. He repeated, however, that it was necessary for the British crown or a company holding a charter from it to have sovereignty over part of east Africa, including at least half of Kilimanjaro, before British subjects would invest in or cooperate with a German company. This, as Peters pointed out, was a weak argument – British capital was invested in many areas under foreign sovereignty – but it was the best which Mackinnon could advance in support of a line of demarcation favorable to Britain. Mackinnon, indeed, does not seem to have considered the discussion to have been a serious business conversation. It was a means of communicating through Peters to the German government and its negotiators. Shortly after his first interview with Peters Mackinnon's interest in further negotiation was cooled by Kirk, who arrived in England in mid-August and who rapidly became his principal adviser on east African affairs. The German East Africa Company, Kirk told Mackinnon, was 'an unscrupulous pack of adventurers'; Peters was a rogue; and his treaties were all frauds.[1] In October, Kirk gave Mackinnon confidential information on the partition agreement which had been reached, to put Mackinnon on guard against Peters in case he should offer concessions which had already been made by the German negotiators.[2] Kirk had no scruples of principle against dealing with Peters – he prided himself on being a realist, and principles were irrelevant to power politics in east Africa.[3] His objection to Peters was that he had nothing of value to offer.

The assignment of Kilimanjaro to Germany discouraged Mackinnon;[4] he had hoped to make the area an important center for development in a revived east Africa concession; and he relapsed for a time into passivity. But Mackinnon did not long remain inactive. His imagination was stirred by reports of the courageous stand for civilization in the equatorial province of the Sudan by one Emin Bey, a disciple of Gordon, who by the

[1] Kirk to Mackinnon, 17 August 1886, Mackinnon Papers.
[2] Kirk to Mackinnon, n.d. [23 October 1886], Mackinnon Papers.
[3] Kirk to Mackinnon, 11 October 1886, Mackinnon Papers.
[4] *Ibid.*

force of his personality had kept the area in perfect order since the death of the general.[1] The idea of the Emin Pasha 'relief expedition' was born.

[1] Kirk refers to the great work of Emin in his letter to Mackinnon of 23 October 1886, Mackinnon Papers.

4

The Emin Pasha Relief Expedition

Historians are allegedly prone to cynicism, since they are required to probe into motives, and avowals of nobility and idealism are frequently a mask for hard, calculating self-interest. The antecedents of the Emin Pasha Relief Expedition certainly involve abundant evidence of more or less conscious hypocrisy. The list of supporters is sufficient to produce skepticism as to its humanitarian character – it included in addition to Mackinnon, Sir Evelyn Baring, the African department of the Foreign Office, and Henry Morton Stanley, as well as Leopold II; and a parallel German enterprise included among its avowed humanitarians Carl Peters. Each of these would-be rescuers had his own reasons of self-interest for advocating action, but all publicly professed their devotion to the cause of the defense of Christianity and civilization. The fact that they found this to be necessary, however, is indicative of the receptivity of the public to this humanitarian appeal, and perhaps some of them at least were not entirely immune to it themselves. Certainly in the case of Mackinnon there is no question of the sincerity of his belief that he was serving a higher purpose by his actions on behalf of Emin; if he also advanced other, material, objectives, of course, so much the better.

Emin Bey or Emin Pasha, born Edouard Schnitzer, became famous in the immediate aftermath of Gordon's death as 'the noblest . . . of Gordon's lieutenants'[1] who embodied the same attributes as his martyred leader. As Gordon had died heroically at Khartoum rather than sacrifice the people with whom he had cast his lot, so Emin had remained in Equatoria to defend its people against the fanatics who had struck down Gordon. Gordon had died because of the cravenness of the Gladstone government; it would be monstrous if his successor also was killed for his courage and his devotion to Christian principles. Emin himself contributed

---

[1] *The Times,* 15 December 1886, cited in de Kiewiet, 'History of the Imperial British East Africa Company', p. 78.

substantially to the mythology which enveloped him. Even before Gordon's death he had inspired the leaders of the Anti-Slavery Society by his vision of a united province of Bahr al-Ghazal and Equatoria, separated from the rest of the Sudan, enjoying enlightened European rule which would, of course, eliminate slavery.[1] H. M. Stanley, already renowned for an expedition to rescue a great humanitarian, responded to the opportunity to act as the agent of British conscience by the relief of Emin. He transferred the energy which he had devoted to the 'Gordon Association for the Nile' to the project of vindicating Gordon through Emin and hopefully uniting the peoples of the southern Sudan into a confederation for protection against the slavers.[2]

Perhaps the most impressive manifestations of popular concern for the fate of Emin were in Scotland. The deep moral commitment which was evident in the African missions of Scottish religious groups extended to the Sudan where Emin had allegedly built a citadel of law and justice. Robert W. Felkin, an Edinburgh physician who had become a devoted admirer since his meeting with Emin on the Upper Nile in 1879, was actively involved in promoting the myth of the peaceful, prosperous principality threatened by the forces of barbarism.[3] Emin's reports also reinforced the impression that Equatoria was rich in resources, in particular ivory. Emin declared that the province made an annual profit of £8,000 after all the costs of government had been deducted, and he had accumulated, he said, a store of ivory valued at approximately £60,000.[4] Humanity and profit thus would be served by supporting him – and patriotism as well. Emin had expressed the hope that Britain would annex his country. No one seemed to see any incongruity in a Silesian's devotion to the Union Jack; it was assumed that he recognized Britain's peculiar commitment to 'a humanitarian and civilizing mission'.[5]

Reinforcing the sentiment for action in the Sudan was a movement among the missionary societies for intervention in Buganda. A new king, Mwanga, had succeeded Mutesa in 1884, and the first years of his reign had been marked by anti-Christian and anti-

[1] Emin to C. H. Allen, 26 March 1883, PRO 30/29/148, P.R.O.
[2] G. N. Sanderson, *England, Europe and the Upper Nile 1882–1899* (Edinburgh, 1965), p. 28.
[3] Robert W. Felkin, 'The Position of Dr Emin Bey', *The Scottish Geographical Magazine*, II, no. 12 (December 1886), 705–19.
[4] de Kiewiet, 'History of the Imperial British East Africa Company', p. 79.
[5] Emin to Felkin, n.d., Mackinnon Papers.

European activity. Arabs who inhabited his kingdom had convinced him that the Christian missionaries were the advance agents for European domination. Mwanga had responded by summary action against Christian converts. Early in 1885 he had executed three followers of the Church Missionary Society; and in October 1885 he had been responsible for the murder of Bishop James Hannington. Thereafter the missionaries were in constant fear for their lives and the persecution of converts culminated in the martyring of more than thirty in May 1886. The missionaries were allowed to escape, but their property was plundered.[1] These atrocities evoked indignation in England and added to demands for action which became coupled with the relief of Emin by a military force which would chastize Mwanga on its way to Equatoria.

Consul Holmwood, from a different perspective, advocated an expedition to Equatoria and Buganda under the flag of Egypt. Nothing, he wrote, would give such an impetus to the opening up of Africa as a show of force which would humble 'such scoundrels' as Mandara and the Kenya chiefs. The force would have to be large enough to overawe the King of Buganda – he thought 500 or 600 disciplined troops from Egypt or Zanzibar would be sufficient.[2]

These calls for action left the government at home unmoved. With a cold eye for national interest, the cabinet saw no justification for the risks and expense which such an expedition would entail. The prime minister was now Salisbury, but the same caution was evident which had infuriated Victoria and her fellow Britons toward Gladstone. The Liberal government had been condemned for its delay in sending an expedition; Salisbury was determined to send no expedition at all. The War Office did not share Holmwood's optimistic views as to the magnitude of the necessary force and the problems it would encounter. The Intelligence branch knew little about the interior between the Indian Ocean and the Lakes since it had never considered the area sufficiently

[1] Roland Oliver, *The Missionary Factor in East Africa* (London, 1952), pp. 103–8. Most Christians escaped Mwanga's persecution, and the terror did not last long. Shortly afterward he allied himself with young Christians to help him achieve independence from the old chiefs who had put him on the throne. John A. Rowe, 'The Purge of Christians at Mwanga's Court', *Journal of African History*, v, 1 (1964), 55–72.

[2] Extract, Holmwood to Anderson, 28 September 1886, F.O.B. 84/1775, P.R.O.

important to warrant close examination.[1] But what little it did know convinced it that the human and natural obstacles were formidable. At least 1,000 men, including carriers, would be required to proceed through the Masai country to Buganda. Food and water would be scarce,[2] and in Buganda they would encounter a fighting force reputed to be between 40,000 and 50,000. It would be 'the height of folly,' said Wolseley, then the adjutant general, to send an armed expedition.[3] Salisbury agreed. Neither the Upper Nile nor Buganda was of such importance as to justify the government's sending an expedition by whatever route. As Lord Iddesleigh noted, the government was not prepared to accept the risk of having to rescue the rescuers.[4] Whitehall, however, was prepared to bless a mission under private auspices, provided the risks were borne by the sponsors and those they sent out.

Various groups in 1886 were considering action to rescue Emin, and the government considered popular feeling too strong for it to take a passive or negative position. When Mackinnon came forward as the principal backer of an expedition headed by Stanley, the Foreign Office consequently was supportive. Percy Anderson noted that 'if we stopped Mackinnon the Scottish Geographical Society and African Lakes Company would be ready to start'.[5]

Mackinnon's motives for offering his money and his energy were certainly in part humanitarian. He was obviously affected by the moral issue which seemed to be involved in the rescue of Emin Pasha and believed he was acting in accordance with Christian principles. But from the beginning of his involvement he saw the prospect of using the expedition for the relief of Emin to achieve more substantial ends. Emin's plea may have been the 'spark'[6] which ignited Mackinnon to action, but it is doubtful that he would have responded to a mission only of mercy. A memorandum in Mackinnon's papers is entitled 'Syndicate for establishing

---

[1] Brackenbury to Wolseley, 29 September 1886, enclosure in Thompson to F.O., 29 September 1886, private, F.O. 84/1790, P.R.O.

[2] Thompson to F.O., 30 September 1886, F.O. 84/1790, P.R.O.

[3] Thompson to F.O., 2 October 1886, and note by Wolseley, same date, F.O. 84/1775, P.R.O.

[4] Memorandum by Iddesleigh, 25 November 1886, F.O. 84/1794, P.R.O.

[5] Note, n.d., on Secretary, African Lakes Co, to Stanley, 30 December 1886, F.O. 84/1796, P.R.O. The Lakes Company had contemplated sending an expedition by the Zambesi and the Great Lakes.

[6] Anstey, *Britain and the Congo*, p. 214.

British Commerce & influence in East Africa & for relieving Emin Bey'.[1] The conjunction is appropriate, as is the priority of emphasis. The plan as outlined was to use the expedition for the relief of Emin as the occasion for opening communications with Victoria Nyanza and the Sudan and to establish a chartered company for the exploitation of the territories between the coast and the Lakes. The government would give its assistance by its support of concessions from the Sultan of Zanzibar as well as the conferral of powers comparable to the Royal Niger Company. Stanley would not only be the rescuer of Emin but the agent of the projected company in negotiating treaties with the chiefs in the territories within its proposed sphere of operation.[2] Mackinnon's objects included the possible opening up of Buganda, not by force but by negotiation – but no plans were developed to that end. Indeed, Stanley seems to have been vested with considerable discretion to act in accordance with circumstances as he found them, including picking up whatever advantages he could for Mackinnon and associates by agreements with chiefs when he arrived in the Lakes area. The latter understanding was not communicated to the government. The Foreign Office saw no objection to Mackinnon's announced plans; on the contrary this private initiative was welcome, and a *modus vivendi* was reached with Mackinnon in November 1886. Mackinnon offered to raise £10,000 for the objects of the expedition, including the establishment of trading posts, if the government would match it. Since a levy on the Treasury was proscribed, officials sought for an alternative and discovered it in the government of Egypt. The territory occupied by Emin was claimed by Egypt – obviously it was Egypt's responsibility to contribute to his rescue. Without difficulty an agreement was reached between Mackinnon and the Foreign Secretary, Lord Iddesleigh, for a financial contribution of £10,000 from Mackinnon's syndicate and from Egypt.[3] The Egyptians, of course, were not consulted. It was agreed further that no responsibility for the expedition would fall on either the British or Egyptian government. Salisbury commented that his arrangement seemed eminently fair to all concerned.[4] Indeed, from the standpoint of the British government, it must have seemed ideal, for at no

---

[1] Memorandum, private and confidential, 27 November 1886, Mackinnon Papers.
[2] *Ibid.*
[3] Mackinnon to Iddesleigh, 27 November 1886, F.O. 84/1861, P.R.O.
[4] Note by Salisbury, n.d., on *ibid.*

cost and no liability it was attracting British commercial men into
the area of east Africa which it had hoped they would be willing
to exploit. With this encouragement, Mackinnon quickly proceeded to raise the money, much of which he contributed from his
personal fortune. The names of the major contributors indicate
the combination of humanitarian and commercial motives as well
as the predominance of Mackinnon's involvement.[1]

	£
W. Mackinnon	2,000
P. Mackinnon	1,000
P. Denny	1,000
Baroness Burdett-Coutts	100
Baron Burdett-Coutts	400
J. S. Jameson	1,000
Countess De Noailles	1,105
Gray, Dawes & Co.	1,000
W. Mackinnon (for	
H. J. Younger)	500
D. MacNeil	700
A. L. Bruce	500
James F. Hutton	250
Royal Geographical Society	1,000

The subsequent story of Stanley's expedition is well known –
his decision to adopt the Congo route, the long silence during his
arduous progress up the Congo, the reports of Stanley's death,
and his reappearance after well over a year with a force so depleted by death and illness that it was hardly able to sustain itself,
much less to offer Emin relief.[2] What yet remains unclear is the
precise relationship between the expedition and Mackinnon's
own plans. Leopold's interest was evident, as was the necessity of
Stanley's deference to his primary employer. The Foreign
Office, despite the reservations of Sir John Kirk,[3] offered no
opposition to the Congo route. Iddesleigh found convincing
Stanley's argument that this route was more feasible and that an
attempt to pass through Buganda would endanger the lives of
British and French missionaries and of the personnel of the

---

[1] Statement of Accounts, Emin Pasha Relief Fund, 1 January 1887 to 31
December 1887, F.O. 84/1990, P.R.O. The eventual cost of the expedition was
approximately £28,000. Financial Statement, 28 February 1890, Mackinnon
Papers.
[2] H. M. Stanley, *The Rescue of Emin Pasha* (London, 1890).
[3] Kirk to Mackinnon, 14 January 1887, Mackinnon Papers.

expedition.[1] At least some of those concerned for the fate of the Europeans in Buganda agreed with Stanley's decision. They had feared that if Stanley had elected to take the route from the east coast through Buganda he would have been denied permission to pass through and could have then proceeded only by the use of force. Under such circumstances, even if he had been successful, he would have endangered the lives and work of the missionaries.[2] Mackinnon's acquiescence is more difficult to understand, for the change in route seemed to vitiate his plan for the opening up of the interior from the east coast. A partial explanation is certainly that only by satisfying Leopold could he employ Stanley, and Stanley was important to Mackinnon's plans. Before Stanley left for Africa, Mackinnon came to an understanding with him that after he had effected the rescue of Emin he would join Mackinnon's company as chief administrator and from his headquarters in Mombasa direct the extension of the communication system from the coast toward the Lakes. After Stanley's reappearance, when the Imperial British East Africa Company was already formed, Mackinnon reaffirmed his offer.[3]

Mackinnon's deference to Leopold was not pleasing to those who were urgent in their advocacy of early action to secure east Africa for Britain. Among them was Euan Smith, the Consul General at Zanzibar. Euan Smith was particularly anxious that communications be established from the coast to Buganda, for despite the partition agreement he did not trust German intentions and the land in the interior, including Buganda, remained open to capture by an aggressive German such as Peters. He had advocated – and he understood Mackinnon to have similar views – an 'amicable arrangement' with the Masai to ensure the safe passage of caravans to the Lakes and the negotiation of a treaty of friendship with Buganda which, as a powerful and prosperous kingdom, he considered the key to a profitable trading empire in east Africa.[4]

---

[1] F.O. to Admiralty, pressing and confidential, 8 January 1887, F.O. 84/1856, P.R.O.
[2] Felkin to de Winton, 13 April 1888, citing correspondence in *The Times*, Mackinnon Papers.
[3] Mackinnon to Stanley, 5 April 1889, Mackinnon Papers. For a somewhat different interpretation, see de Kiewiet, 'History of the Imperial British East Africa Company', pp. 86–90.
[4] Euan Smith to Salisbury, 18 December 1888, Salisbury Papers, A/79, Christ Church, Oxford.

Beyond Buganda in Equatoria the nature of Mackinnon's intentions other than the rescue of Emin is not clear. Stanley's dual responsibility to Mackinnon and Leopold adds to the lack of clarity. When Stanley met Emin for the first time on Lake Albert in May 1888 he delivered a letter from the Khedive informing Emin that if he and his soldiers refused to accompany Stanley to the coast their refusal would automatically involve their discharge from the Egyptian army. He then communicated to Emin proposals from Leopold and from Mackinnon. Leopold offered the governor-ship of Equatoria as a province in an enlarged Free State. The Pasha would be appointed a general in the Belgian army with authority to fix his own emoluments and would receive in addition an annual payment of £12,000 for the administration of the province. Emin would compensate the King by the annual export of ivory and other produce valued at £12,000 to the Congo for the account of the Free State. Emin after several days of discussion with Stanley decided not to accept Leopold's offer because of the unlikelihood that the Free State would long survive. Its condition was unhealthy even under Leopold, and at his death it would undoubtedly collapse. Only after the rejection of Leopold's offer did Stanley present Mackinnon's proposal to settle Emin and his followers on the eastern shore of Victoria Nyanza where they would work for Mackinnon's company. Mackinnon's offer left pay and other conditions of service for future agreement but Emin decided to accept it and prepared to withdraw with his men toward Victoria.[1]

Stanley does not appear to have represented the cause of Leopold with unreserved enthusiasm in his discussions with Emin; indeed, the role he adopted of neutral communicant reinforced Emin's disinclination to join Leopold's service, for the dire predictions regarding the future of the Congo Free State went unrebutted. If he had intended to influence Emin toward Mackinnon he would not have acted differently, and perhaps this was his purpose. At this time Stanley was at odds with Leopold and was contemplating joining Mackinnon's service. When he later arrived in Zanzibar with Emin, he gave Euan Smith the impression that he was completely English in his sympathies and that he nourished a secret grudge against Leopold.[2]

[1] Euan Smith to Salisbury, secret, 14 March 1890, F.O. 84/2060, P.R.O.
[2] Euan Smith to Salisbury, private, 30 December 1889, Salisbury Papers A/79, Christ Church, Oxford.

He conformed to the letter of Mackinnon's agreement with Leopold, but no more.

Stanley's animus toward Leopold was not shared by Mackinnon. The sequence in the approach to Emin indicates that Mackinnon had conceded Leopold priority of opportunity in Equatoria and that he himself would concentrate his activity to the south. But Mackinnon did not exclude the Upper Nile entirely from his future plans if Leopold was unsuccessful in establishing a footing. In October 1888, before the outcome of the expedition was known in Britain, Mackinnon negotiated an indenture with Felkin as Emin's agent, by which the East Africa Company acquired Emin's rights in Equatoria.[1] Probably his intention was to transfer these rights to Leopold if the King proceeded with his plans at the time of the dispatch of Stanley's expedition. Euan Smith wrote Salisbury in December 1888 that Mackinnon's object on the Nile was to establish a station at Wadelai,[2] and Langer is probably correct in his surmise that Leopold's and Mackinnon's communication systems would link up at that point.[3]

Mackinnon looked upon Leopold as a friend and ally; Germany was a threat. Though the Anglo-German spheres of influence agreement had already been signed before Stanley departed for Africa, there were no guarantees that Germany would concede that the Upper Nile, which was not included, was a British preserve. Sir John Kirk, remembering the recent surprise German irruption into east Africa, saw the possibility that private German citizens would enter the race for the relief of Emin, and if they won call upon their government for recognition of whatever claims they had established.[4] This fear made him the more concerned about Stanley's selection of the Congo route. Reports of a project for a German Emin Pasha Relief Expedition filtered back to Britain. Mackinnon pressed the government to elicit from Germany a promise that this rival expedition would not be supported, and, if possible, a formal recognition that Buganda and the Upper Nile were in the British sphere, but received the unsatisfying response that the German government had indicated that it had no connection with the enterprise and had no intention of support-

---

[1] Indenture, 7 October 1888, Mackinnon Papers.
[2] Euan Smith to Salisbury, 18 December 1888, Salisbury Papers, A/79, Christ Church, Oxford.
[3] William L. Langer, *The Diplomacy of Imperialism, 1890–1902* (2 vols., New York, 1935), I, 114.
[4] Kirk to Mackinnon [15 December 1886], Mackinnon Papers.

ing it. The Foreign Office in fact saw no cause for alarm; its intelligence indicated that the expedition was not likely to take place, and if it did, there was no cause for concern as long as it remained a purely private undertaking.[1] This cool indifference was infuriating to those zealots such as Kirk and Harry Johnston who had advised Mackinnon to launch the British expedition and who had been exasperated by the decision to take the long route rather than to push on from the east coast. Johnston wrote Mackinnon in November 1888 that the Germans would likely get to Emin first, and Britain would lose the Sudan as it had lost Kilimanjaro. If this happened, he declared, the fault would be Mackinnon's: 'If you let the Germans get to Emin Pasha first, I shall never forgive you.'[2]

Johnston often resorted to hyperbole to make his point, but his fear was genuine and was shared by Kirk. In fact, the estimate of the Foreign Office was more realistic. In 1888, Bismarck was not inclined to use domestic pressures as a justification for actions which would embarrass Salisbury as three years earlier he had embarrassed Gladstone. He had received assurances from the Salisbury government that it would not use Stanley's expedition as an excuse for the extension of British influence,[3] and his preoccupation was with Europe. Carl Peters had been useful earlier, but Bismarck now considered him a dangerous mountebank who must be kept in check, and Peters' association with the German Emin relief discussions made Bismarck even cooler. 'Peters corrupts', he noted; and his 'impractical fantasies' could cost Germany dearly.[4] Peters' wild talk of Africa as Germany's India and of a challenge to Britain in the Upper Nile was a menace to German interests. Bismarck told the explorer Wolff in December 1888:

This is going too far, the English sphere of interest reaches as far as the sources of the Nile, and I run too high a risk. Your map of Africa is very

---

[1] Mackinnon to F.O., 26 September 1888, and notes thereon, F.O. 84/1929, P.R.O. Salisbury in 1888 had not substantially changed his attitude from his earlier position that the issue was not governmental. In 1886, he had written of possible German involvement, 'It is really their business if Emin is a German.' Note on Holmwood to Iddesleigh, 23 September 1886, F.O. 84/1775, P.R.O., cited in Robinson and Gallagher, *Africa and the Victorians*, p. 199.

[2] Johnston to Mackinnon, 26 November 1888, Mackinnon Papers.

[3] Henry M. Bair, 'Carl Peters and German Colonialism' (Stanford Doctoral Dissertation, 1968), p. 176.

[4] *Ibid.* p. 181.

nice indeed, but my map of Africa lies in Europe. Here lies Russia and here lies France, and we are in the middle, that is my map of Africa.[1]

Given Bismarck's posture at the end of 1888, the German plans for a relief expedition involved no threat to the British position on the Upper Nile, and Peters' appointment to command it added personal distaste to the Chancellor's aversion to involvement. The diplomatic scene might change, of course, in which case Peters might suddenly be restored to favor, and this was Peters' hope. He wrote later, 'The German Emin Pasha Expedition was no pleasure trip, but a large-scale, colonial-political undertaking.'[2] Bismarck continued to cooperate with Salisbury, however, and Peters received no governmental support. He arrived in Zanzibar at a time when the British and German governments were acting jointly in a blockade of the east Africa coast, ostensibly to block the slave trade but in fact to put down the Abushiri uprising against German rule. At such a time, Peters' presence was particularly obnoxious to Britain and the presence of his armed force might contribute to further disturbances against Germany. Consequently the German government instructed its consulate in Zanzibar not to allow Peters to land. Peters and his men skirted the blockade and made a landing in June 1889, and their subsequent activities in the interior complicated Anglo-German relations, but the expedition was no longer for the relief of Emin Pasha. As Peters' party proceeded inland, they heard in February 1890 that Emin and Stanley had left Equatoria and were en route to the east African coast.

Emin, in fact, had ceased to be of much value to either Britons or Germans since the first eruption of popular feeling. His force defending freedom and justice had turned out to be a miserable rabble barely surviving at Wadelai, and the successor to Gordon had been transformed through Stanley's accounts into a mild, ineffective, would-be naturalist, utterly incompetent to assume great responsibilities, 'a poor prisoner in the hands of his own mutinous soldiers'.[3] What little authority he had exercised had disintegrated when he had informed his troops of his intention to withdraw from Equatoria, and a substantial body of them had mutinied. This was the condition of affairs when Stanley returned

---

[1] Lowe, *The Reluctant Imperialists*, I, 131.
[2] Bair, 'Carl Peters and German Colonialism', p. 189.
[3] Stanley's report, enclosure in Euan Smith to Salisbury, 28 December 1889, F.O. 84/1982, P.R.O.

I

from the Congo with what was left of the rear column of the relief expedition. The Emin who accompanied Stanley to the coast was a discredited leader with no troops, entirely dependent on Stanley for protection. The idea of his employment by Mackinnon was quietly dropped.[1]

Emin's conversations with Stanley and with Euan Smith stimulated their fears of German intentions. He told them that he had been offered employment by the Germans, who were secretly preparing an expedition for Victoria Nyanza but with Buganda as its ultimate destination, and that they expected to be welcomed by the French missionaries who hated their British counterparts and their converts. This intelligence was particularly impressive because it conformed to other reports which Euan Smith had received,[2] and it proved to be an accurate statement of Peters' intentions, for in February 1890 Carl Peters arrived in Buganda and concluded a treaty of friendship with Mwanga. Emin, however, was not a factor in the threat represented by Peters. The two met in May 1890 and Emin entered the service of Germany, to die in 1892, on a mission into the interior, but his significance had ended before he left Equatoria.[3]

Peters, however, was a continuing source of worry until the signature of the Anglo-German treaty in July 1890. With Equatoria a vacuum and the future of Buganda uncertain, there was an opening for Germany if it chose to exploit it, and Salisbury, despite his early expressions of confidence in Germany's assurances, was by early 1890 beginning to manifest alarm. His concern was intensified when Wilhelm II, an avowed sympathizer with Peters' ambition for German empire, removed Bismarck in March 1890.[4]

This shift from apathy to apprehension was related to a fundamental change in policy toward Egypt. Until 1889 Salisbury had maintained that the British occupation was strictly temporary and that withdrawal would take place when there was reasonable assurance of the stability of the Egyptian government. He had unsuccessfully sought agreement from the European powers to accept a British formula for withdrawal based upon the right of re-entry if stability should break down. He had at first not been

[1] Euan Smith to Salisbury, secret, 14 March 1890, F.O. 84/2060, P.R.O.
[2] *Ibid.*
[3] Bair, 'Carl Peters and German Colonialism', p. 202.
[4] Robert O. Collins, 'Origins of the Nile Struggle', in Prosser Gifford and William Roger Louis, *Britain and Germany in Africa* (New Haven, 1967), p. 133.

willing to fix a date without such an agreement because, as he told his negotiator, Sir Henry Drummond Wolff, in 1885, 'the relief from our hated presence is the one bribe we have to offer' to induce other powers to accept the British terms.[1] But in 1887 Salisbury had promised that Britain would withdraw from Egypt in three years if it was guaranteed the right of re-entry 'upon the appearance of danger from without'.[2] The rejection of this proposal led to a reconsideration of the British position in Egypt which had important implications for Imperial policy toward the Upper Nile and Buganda.

By mid-1889 Salisbury had essentially accepted the argument of Sir Evelyn Baring that the prospect of a stable Egyptian government in the immediate future was illusory and that Imperial interests dictated that the British occupation be indefinitely prolonged.[3] To Baring, this decision had a corollary that no other European power must be allowed to establish a base on the Upper Nile, from which it could dominate Egypt.[4] The answer was not an expedition against the Dervishes. The Egyptians were in no position to mount such a campaign, and a British expedition was out of the question since Parliament would refuse to sanction the expenditure. The alternative was reliance on diplomacy. It was relatively easy to warn off the Italians from their ambitions to possess Kassala in the eastern Sudan, but intrusion by a great power would be a much more formidable threat. The German government, both under Bismarck and his successors, was probably sincere in its professed disinterest, but Salisbury had learned not to put his trust in princes. Since direct intervention remained out of the question the Foreign Office turned to the East Africa Company as an agent of the Imperial interest. The languid attitude which had been manifested by Iddesleigh's endorsement of the Congo route for Stanley's expedition was no more. Now the Foreign Office was importunate in prodding Mackinnon to energetic measures to establish the British presence in Buganda and the Upper Nile. The consequences for Mackinnon and his Company were disastrous.

[1] Salisbury to Wolff, private, 18 August 1885, A/44, Salisbury Papers, Christ Church, Oxford.
[2] A. P. Thornton, 'Rivalries in the Mediterranean, the Middle East and Egypt', in F. H. Hinsley (ed.), *The New Cambridge Modern History*, XI (Cambridge, 1962), 588.
[3] Robinson and Gallagher, *Africa and the Victorians*, p. 283.
[4] Lowe. *The Reluctant Imperialists*, p. 138.

5

The charter

In the last months before his death in March 1888 Sultan Barghash, sick and dispirited, bewailed the faithlessness of his British protectors. He had put himself in the hands of a power which had made a mockery of its noble pretensions. He could understand the Germans – they were at least forthright in their rapacity. But for the British to act as accessories to this brutal aggression upon him was treachery beyond his comprehension. His trusted adviser John Kirk was gone; Kirk's successor Holmwood, on whom he had come to depend, was removed because his continued presence was not pleasing to Germany.[1] Barghash felt betrayed, but he had no recourse against his betrayers. There was no alternative to continued reliance on the unreliable, for Britain was more likely to preserve what was left of his estates than was Germany.

Barghash could not comprehend the abrupt change in British policy because his world was utterly different from that of Whitehall. There was also a gulf between the government and those Britons whose lives were bound up with Africa. The explorer Joseph Thomson, always a man of direct expression, stated that 'East Africa in recent years presents an example which still stinks in the nostrils of all who love our country and our country's honour'.[2] Archdeacon John P. Farler, who had devoted himself to mission work in east Africa for fourteen years, was equally indignant. He wrote early in 1889:

British subjects in East Africa are now witnessing the destruction of all their interests; commercial men and traders are watching the ruin of their commerce; while missionaries are looking upon their civilizing work rendered abortive, with the lives which have been laid down and the

[1] Holmwood was replaced by Charles Euan Smith in June 1887, F.O. to Holmwood, 14 June 1887, F.O. 84/1850. Essentially his removal was at the behest of Bismarck, who maintained that he was acting in violation of the Anglo-German understanding to which Salisbury was committed.

[2] Joseph Thomson, 'Downing Street versus Chartered Companies in Africa', *Fortnightly Review* XLVI, n.s. (August 1889), 178.

money they have spent in opening up and civilizing the country made of no avail. While I can sympathize with Germany in her desire to found a colonial empire, I must enter a protest against her planting herself on the ruins of British interests or on ground already occupied by England.[1]

In this condemnation there was not only moral outrage but an assumption that Britain should act on the basis of its east African interests. Neither criterion was central to government policy. East Africa was of minor significance; the need for the good will of Germany overrode British local interests.

Sir Edward Malet in congratulating Salisbury on the continuation of Anglo-German amity noted that 'my experience of the very disagreeable things which Bismarck was able to do to us when those good relations didn't exist makes me satisfied that his friendship is worth preserving even at some sacrifice'.[2] As Malet and Salisbury saw it, that sacrifice was of British pre-eminence in east Africa. Their arrangement with Germany was not a cynical betrayal of the Sultan; such a description implies a recognition of wrongdoing; and there is no evidence that Salisbury ever thought of the Sultan's rights as worthy of support for their own sake. East Africa had significance as an area of the slave trade, as a market, actual and potential, and as a strategic base. When humanitarian organizations demanded the abolition of the slave traffic, the government responded by pressing the Sultan to decree its elimination on pain of losing his throne, but there was no thought that his rule would be replaced by direct British responsibility with its attendant expense. The fiction of Zanzibar sovereignty was useful and the spectacle of an Oriental potentate cooperating with the British navy against the abominable trade was elevating. In fact, as the government was aware, these measures were ineffective without control of the interior[3] and the Sultan was unable and Britain unwilling to undertake that responsibility. So far as the economic prospects of east Africa were concerned, the official British attitude, liberal or conservative, was that private enterprise must make its own way and government should confine itself to the role of preventing discrimination against British

---

[1] J. P. Farler, 'England and Germany in East Africa', *Fortnightly Review* XLV, n.s. (February 1889), 157.

[2] Malet to Salisbury, 22 January 1887, private, A/61, Salisbury Papers.

[3] Kirk in a memorandum to the Foreign Office, 27 January 1887, stated that warships had never been able to intercept more than five per cent of the slaves carried from east coast ports and that the weakening of the Sultan's authority on the mainland had increased the magnitude of the trade. F.O. 84/1851, P.R.O.

traders. The Anglo-German agreement of 1886, in the view of the
Foreign Office, provided adequate safeguards.

The east coast of Africa had significance in relation to the route
to India, a fact symbolized by the control of the Zanzibar agency
until 1883 by the Indian government. But the importance of the
Indian Ocean route had declined after the opening of the Suez
Canal, and in the 1880s the Admiralty considered France to be the
only serious threat to Indian Ocean communications. Some
strategists were alarmed at the changing balance of power in the
eastern seas. Kitchener during his assignment as delimitation
commissioner had expressed concern that a German fleet based
on the east coast could be a threat to British security in the
Indian Ocean and had urged that, at the least, the Royal Navy
should acquire a base at Mombasa to counter the acquisition of
Dar es Salaam by Germany and of Diego Suarez in Madagascar
by France.[1] The Admiralty, however, indicated that so long as
Britain controlled the island of Zanzibar, there was no strategic
necessity to acquire Mombasa, despite opinions by the staff of
the Foreign Office and by Kirk that Mombasa could be excellent
insurance against the possibility that Zanzibar might fall into other
hands.[2] A considerable influence in the Admiralty's indifference
was the recognition that the expense for the new base would have
to be assumed from Admiralty funds.

The other strategic area was Buganda, which was assumed to
have importance in relation to the headwaters of the Nile as well as
being the object of attention of the Church Missionary Society,
Aborigines Protection Society, and British and Foreign Anti-
Slavery Society as a possible field for their respective endeavors.
But in the 1880s there appeared to be no justification for direct
governmental action to open the way to Buganda.

After the agreement with Germany on spheres of influence there
was an acknowledged British zone on the coast, an acknowledged
German zone, and an interior which remained outside the acknowledged limits of the claims of either power.[3] The British government had no intention of committing itself to expenditures in the

---

[1] 'Notes on British Lines of Communication with the Indian Ocean', by Lt.
Col. H. H. Kitchener, 22 December 1885, F.O. 84/1797, P.R.O.

[2] Admiralty to F.O., confidential, 6 November 1885, F.O. 84/1744; same to
same, confidential, 26 February 1885, F.O. 84/1781; notes, n.d., on Kitchener's
memorandum of 22 December 1885, PRO 30/57/8; telegram, Kirk to F.O.,
19 February 1886, F.O. 84/1772, all in P.R.O.

[3] See agreed answer to question by Munro Ferguson, F.O. 84/2082, P.R.O.

British sphere and certainly not in the interior but it recognized the dangers of inactivity. If private enterprise should wish to undertake such responsibilities, the governmental attitude would, of course, be benign, provided no commitments were involved. In this environment, Mackinnon providentially reappeared. On 22 February 1887, Barghash cabled Mackinnon that he was ready to agree to a concession under the same terms as previously proposed if an association were formed under Mackinnon's leadership and if the British government approved.[1] The communication fitted British requirements so neatly that it might have been written by an agent of the government and indeed it was. Holmwood explained that the Sultan in his extremity had asked for advice and that he had told Barghash his best chance to salvage what was left of his position was to give his 'unreserved acceptance' of a concession to Mackinnon. Holmwood then drafted the telegram to Mackinnon's agents which the Sultan signed.[2]

Holmwood's advice to the Sultan was not spontaneous. The impetus, however, did not come from the government, but from the revival of Mackinnon's interest in east Africa as a result of his involvement with the Emin Pasha Relief Expedition. If the plan to make Emin Pasha an instrument for the spread of Christianity and commerce under British auspices were to succeed, a base on the coast was necessary. Just as the Germans required Dar es Salaam, so must the British have Mombasa. But the Salisbury government had made it clear that it would accept no responsibility either with regard to Emin or for the lease of Mombasa. If anything was to be done, private initiative must do it. Mackinnon in his discussions with Stanley and with Kirk about the relief expedition, concluded that he should seek from the Sultan the right to use Mombasa and to collect customs duties there, and Stanley was authorized to represent Mackinnon with the Sultan when he stopped in Zanzibar to make arrangements for the expedition. In these plans they acted with the full knowledge and support of Sir Percy Anderson,[3] who had established himself as the most influential member of the Foreign Office staff on African questions and who was eager for Mackinnon to take an initiative which the government was not willing to assume.

---

[1] Telegram, Barghash to Mackinnon, 22 February 1887, F.O. 84/1852, P.R.O.
[2] Holmwood to F.O., 14 March 1887, F.O. 84/1852, P.R.O. Mackinnon to Barghash, 14 March 1887, F.O., 84/1860, P.R.O.
[3] Kirk to Mackinnon, private, 26 January 1887, Mackinnon Papers.

Stanley arrived in Zanzibar in February 1887 and as soon as the state ceremonials were completed, proceeded to act on behalf of Mackinnon's concession, stressing the advantage to the Sultan's self-interest of such an agreement, and received from the Sultan the promise that he would sign a concession as soon as possible.[1] Stanley characteristically did not interpret his mission to the Sultan narrowly. He listened sympathetically as the Sultan recited the outrages to which he had been subjected. The Portuguese were acting like a great power in claiming a boundary with Zanzibar north of that which the Germans and British had recognized as being under the Sultan's sovereignty. Furthermore, they had seized his steamer. Stanley promised to use his influence to gain redress for these grievances and telegraphed Mackinnon to intervene with the British government. Through the efforts of Mackinnon and Kirk, the Portuguese were prevailed upon to return the steamer.[2] Britain also agreed to use its good offices in cooperation with Germany to induce Portugal to accept settlement of the boundary dispute by arbitration or a joint commission.[3]

Stanley and Holmwood were both activists – Holmwood's inability to adjust to placid coexistence with Germany was soon to cause his removal – and they agreed that the best course to protect what was left of the British position was the renewal of the Mackinnon scheme of 1878, adjusted to the altered conditions resulting from Anglo-German partition. They appear to have had no difficulty in convincing the Sultan, grateful for Stanley's and Mackinnon's intervention, that his interests would be served by acceptance of the terms he had rejected several years earlier.[4] Precisely what the Sultan meant by his proposal to renew the concession of 1878 was unclear. Mackinnon supposed that he intended to include the lease of the Zanzibar, Pemba, and Mafia customs as well as of Mombasa and the other ports reserved to him on the mainland. Such an arrangement would clearly have been unacceptable to Germany, but Mackinnon was desirous of making as extensive an agreement as possible.[5]

The problem, as in 1878, was the attitude of the British government. Mackinnon, who attributed his earlier failure to lack of

---

[1] Henry M. Stanley, *In Darkest Africa*, 2 vols. (London, 1891), I, 62.
[2] Mackinnon to Barghash, 14 March 1887, Mackinnon Papers.
[3] Portugal declined to accept any form of arbitration, and the dispute continued.
[4] Telegram, Smith, Mackenzie and Co. to Mackinnon, 25 February 1887, F.O. 84/1860, P.R.O.
[5] Mackinnon to Barghash, 14 March 1887, F.O. 84/1860, P.R.O.

support from Whitehall, would not proceed without a prior statement by the government of its support. He did receive informal assurances from the staff of the Foreign Office that they were favorably disposed to a concession provided that its terms did not involve complications with Germany, but this expression of good will was not enough. Mackinnon desired more; how much more caused uneasy speculation at the Foreign Office. An interview between Mackinnon and Salisbury did not remove this concern. Salisbury assured Mackinnon that his proposed company could negotiate treaties with chiefs in the interior of the British sphere beyond the coastal belt assigned to Zanzibar in order to establish the company's authority, but Mackinnon gained the impression that the prime minister had gone beyond that to assure him of 'more than the ordinary support'.[1] It was a common experience of those who dealt with Lord Salisbury to come away from discussions with the impression that he had promised them more than he would later admit. Whether in this instance Mackinnon assumed more than words warranted, it is clear that he expected more than Salisbury was willing to deliver. Anderson feared that Mackinnon with Holmwood's support was aiming at a *de facto* British protectorate over Zanzibar which would inevitably produce a rupture with the Germans.[2] There was a basic conflict between the objectives of Mackinnon and Salisbury, and each accused the other of dereliction because he did not act supportively. Salisbury's principal interest was peace with Germany; any British activity in east Africa must be compatible with Anglo-German harmony. Mackinnon prodded by Kirk[3] aimed at a great east African trading empire which would forestall the nefarious ambitions of Carl Peters and others who would steal from Britain what was rightfully hers. Salisbury expected Mackinnon loyally to perform functions which the government did not wish to assume; Mackinnon believed that in the patriotic cause he had undertaken he was entitled to governmental support. There could be no amity between men with such divergent views; the conflicts which plagued the government's relations with the British East Africa Company were foreshadowed in 1887, as indeed they had been in 1878.

[1] The quotation is from Anderson in a note 19 March 1887, F.O. 84/1860, P.R.O.
[2] Note 'Zanzibar', 19 March 1887, F.O. 84/1860, P.R.O.
[3] Kirk to Mackinnon, 23 March 1887, Mackinnon Papers.

The Foreign Office's instructions to Holmwood made it clear that the government would not support any agreement which could be construed as a challenge to Germany. Any concession, they indicated, must be limited to farming the customs and no part of the Sultan's territory within the German sphere could be included. No other powers than those required for fiscal purposes must be conferred and there should be no implication that the concessionaires would receive any governmental support beyond that usually accorded British subjects.[1]

This was hardly the kind of support for which Mackinnon had hoped. But John Kirk, on whom he relied in matters governmental, advised him to push ahead and to employ General Mathews to travel through the interior acquiring chiefs' signatures on treaties. With these treaties in British possession, Kirk assured him, the Foreign Office would become more cooperative; without them, the interior was still open to invasion by any nation other than Germany.[2]

The urgency of immediate action seemed underscored by the report that Peters would sail at the end of April from Aden to Zanzibar with twenty Germans. The report was correct, and prior experience with Peters caused alarm among Mackinnon and his associates that this free-wheeling imperialist contemplated another coup. The official purpose of Peters' visit was not threatening. In January the British and German governments had each agreed to settle with the Sultan the one outstanding issue left from the delimitations agreement – the amount of rent for the ports in their respective spheres, and Peters as chief representative of the German East Africa Company was designated as the negotiator. He was specifically enjoined not to annex any new territories without first securing the consent of both Germany and Britain, and he agreed,[3] but Peters had not made his reputation by quiet acceptance of governmental dicta. In any case, Mackinnon and other private citizens did not know of Peters' instructions and assumed the worst.[4] To attempt to shut out Peters, Mackinnon and his associates resolved that they should not wait for the

---

[1] F.O. to Holmwood, 23 March 1887, F.O. 84/1850, P.R.O.
[2] Kirk to Mackinnon, 23 March 1887, Mackinnon Papers.
[3] Minutes 'Zanzibar', by Anderson, 17 January 1887, F.O. 84/1850, P.R.O.; Bair, 'Carl Peters and German Colonialism', p. 132.
[4] On this occasion Peters in fact did abide by his instructions, though his overbearing conduct toward the Zanzibaris caused difficulties with the Sultan, *Ibid.* p. 158.

settlement of the terms of a general concession but should press for an immediate transfer of Mombasa and the ports and territory to the north.[1] At the beginning of May, the Sultan agreed to a draft concession applying to the British sphere. Mackinnon sought to gain the Sultan's consent to separate agreements, one including both the mainland in the British sphere and the islands of Zanzibar and Pemba and the other involving the mainland alone, leaving it to the Association to agree to either or to reject both, but the Sultan declined to sign any document to which the other party was not also bound. He declared that after his recent experiences he would never incur such a risk again.[2] Mackinnon decided that, in view of Peters' presence in Zanzibar and the uncertainty of the future, an immediate settlement was necessary. The Sultan agreed to the transfer to Mackinnon's Association of the administration and customs rights at his ports north of the German sphere for fifty years for an annual payment based on current custom revenue plus fifty per cent. He also agreed to cooperate with the Association in inducing chiefs in the interior behind the coastal belt to transfer their sovereign rights to the Association. The agreement was signed on 24 May 1887.[3] The Sultan selected the day as one of good omens because it coincided with both Queen Victoria's birthday in her golden jubilee year and the new moon of Ramadan.[4] He must have felt that he needed all the powers of heavenly conjunctions which he could summon in view of his recent unhappy experiences with his fellow men, in particular Lord Salisbury, whom he believed had betrayed him to the Germans and might betray him again. His estimate of the future was reinforced by advice from Holmwood, Kirk, and Badger,[5] all of whom advised him that unless he immediately came to terms he might have no assets to sell.

In giving Barghash such warnings, these advisers were not creating a hobgoblin to frighten the Sultan – they were frightened themselves. During his leave in England, John Kirk's attachment to Zanzibar had not faded. His years as the British presence had developed a deep personal commitment to the policies he had

---

[1] Memorandum by Mackinnon, 7 May 1887, private and confidential, F.O. 84/1863, P.R.O.
[2] Holmwood to F.O., 9 May 1887, F.O. 84/1852, P.R.O.
[3] G. Mackenzie to Lee, 25 May 1887, F.O. 84/1863, P.R.O.
[4] Holmwood to F.O., 4 June 1887, F.O. 84/1852, P.R.O.
[5] Kirk to Mackinnon, 16 April [1887], Mackinnon Papers; telegram, Badger to Barghash, 13 April 1887, F.O. 84/1863, P.R.O.

espoused. Salisbury by his words and actions repudiated those policies. Kirk looked at the auguries and found them ominous. Indeed, Salisbury's decision to remove Holmwood from Zanzibar he correctly attributed to German pressure, and an interview with Salisbury early in May convinced him that even Zanzibar itself was expendable for the good will of Germany. Wistfully he wrote that he could only return to Zanzibar to carry out a 'strong policy', but he knew that Salisbury neither intended to pursue such a policy nor to ask him to go back.[1] Kirk had become an anachronism in the new era.

To Kirk, the imminent departure of Holmwood and the landing of Peters were no coincidence. He suspected some secret understanding by which Zanzibar would pass from British to German influence. This plot, he believed, involved Salisbury alone; not even his most trusted adviser, Sir Percy Anderson, was privy to it. His advice was to act quickly both to secure the concession from the Sultan and to acquire treaties with chiefs in the lands between the coast and the vicinity of Kilimanjaro and with these in hand to confront Salisbury and ask him to state plainly the government's position.[2] Mackinnon followed Kirk's advice to the extent that he ordered Edmund Mackenzie to proceed vigorously both with regard to the concession and to the negotiation of treaties. But he concluded that he could not wait to approach Salisbury until these measures had been carried out. He required assurances immediately. Consequently in May 1887, as soon as an agreement for the concession seemed assured, Mackinnon presented a petition to the Foreign Office asking for a statement of the kind of support the government was prepared to provide his Association. He set down two conditions which he maintained were essential to success – that the government give the East African Association the same support that it had provided the British North Borneo Company and the Royal Niger Company and an assurance that mail service at least once every four weeks from Aden to Zanzibar would continue to be subsidized for his shipping line.[3]

Before he received Mackinnon's demand, Salisbury had already developed a personal dislike for the little Scotsman, which this latest memorandum reinforced. Mackinnon, he complained,

---

[1] Kirk to Mackinnon, private, 5 May 1887, Mackinnon Papers.
[2] *Ibid.*
[3] Memorandum on Zanzibar by Mackinnon, 7 May 1887, F.O. 84/1863, P.R.O. The contract was due to expire in September 1888.

pumped up schemes which were defective in form and substance and when they collapsed, blamed the government. He was a dilettante in imperial ventures.[1]

Mackinnon in Salisbury's eyes was not only lacking in zeal but in reliability. Perhaps he was not dishonest, but he had a penchant for translation of comments by Salisbury and the staff at the Foreign Office into commitments which they had not intended. After his first interview with Mackinnon, Salisbury had concluded that he would prefer to deal with him by correspondence 'because then we shall both know exactly what has been said on either side'.[2] Furthermore, Salisbury maintained, Mackinnon was asking for governmental backing without demonstrating his own commitment by the presentation of a well-organized plan of action, the government essentially was being asked to endorse hopes and dreams. He noted:

We know that Mackinnon was not in earnest in a negotiation of this kind he undertook ten years ago. The extraordinary slovenliness of his present proceedings make me doubt his being in earnest now. The undertaking which he asks us to support is quite nebulous. We do not know exactly the rights the unformed company are to have: or the amount of trade from the ports in the specified coast, which is to yield the customs duties on which the solvency of the company will depend.

I do not think that we can afford to be equally indistinct in our reply. If, in response to a request for Borneo treatment, and an assured mail contract we reply by promising the fullest assistance compatible with imperial interests and international engagements we shall be held and justly held to have encouraged him to expect the two specific things for which he asks.

As to Borneo treatment, I could not express an opinion without having the Borneo papers before me. But both in the case of Borneo and the Niger, we negotiated with a formed and not an unformed company.[3]

Beyond his disinclination to act in response to vague plans, Salisbury was concerned with a basic issue to policy. Mackinnon seemed to be demanding special treatment for a venture which was essentially commercial. The Foreign Minister was not convinced that there were national interests involved of sufficient moment to warrant guarantees of governmental support. Mackinnon was entitled to the same treatment as any other British trader; any governmental commitments beyond that must be based upon a

[1] Memorandum by Salisbury, n.d. [May 1887], F.O. 84/1863, P.R.O.
[2] Note by Salisbury, 18 May 1887, on memorandum by Mackinnon, 7 May 1887, F.O. 84/1863, P.R.O.
[3] Memorandum by Salisbury, n.d. [May 1887], F.O. 84/1863, P.R.O.

convincing case for special treatment, which in his view Mackinnon had not made, and any such commitment must be precisely stated to prevent the government's becoming entangled in responsibilities it had not intended to assume. So far as the subsidy to the shipping line was concerned, that was a matter for the Treasury.[1]

The permanent staff of the Foreign Office were more receptive to Mackinnon's overtures than was Salisbury. While they agreed that it was premature for the government to give any assurances of support until a company was actually formed, they advocated encouragement to Mackinnon rather than a cool response. As Anderson said, the proposed company would 'save our position on the East Coast' and for its service to a national purpose it could legitimately expect assurance that the government would assist it so far as was compatible with imperial interests and international engagements.[2] So far as the mail subsidy was concerned, stated Pauncefote, a contribution of £7,950 a year seemed a small price to pay to support British shipping and to prevent the Germans from monopolizing the coastal service with the consequent loss of British influence in east Africa.[3] The advice of these two influential advisers apparently swayed Salisbury. The Foreign Office response to Mackinnon encouraged him to proceed,[4] and the renewal of the mail contract was commended to the early and favorable attention of the Treasury.[5]

With this backing, Mackinnon acted energetically. His agent Edmund Mackenzie (brother of George) purchased the sea frontage on the western side of Momba Island at Mombasa and other property on the mainland opposite which could be used for such purposes as piers and customs houses, and for the terminus of the railway which they hoped to build into the interior. Acting on Kirk's earlier suggestion, Mackenzie employed General Mathews on loan from the Sultan to negotiate treaties with chiefs on the mainland. Kirk had commended Mathews as 'of all men living the very best to make these agreements'[6] and Mathews demonstrated that this confidence was not misplaced. He negotiated twenty-one treaties on behalf jointly of the Sultan and the Association, embracing

1 Memorandum by Salisbury, n.d. [May 1887], F.O. 84/1863, P.R.O.
2 Note by Anderson, n.d., on *ibid.*
3 Note by Pauncefote, 13 May 1887, on *ibid.*
4 F.O. to Mackinnon, private, 18 May 1887, F.O. 84/1863, P.R.O.
5 F.O. to Treasury, 19 May 1887, F.O. 84/1863, P.R.O.
6 Kirk to Mackinnon, 23 March 1887, Mackinnon Papers.

territories from Manga in the south to the Ozi River in the north and to the borders of the Masai country in the interior. Among the chiefs who affixed their marks was Mbaruk bin Rashid, a powerful Mazrui chief in the Mombasa area, who could be useful as an ally but who had frequently been in revolt against Barghash's authority.[1]

Mathews' activity was in accordance with a plan to establish the authority of the Association in the interior by a dual movement, Stanley moving from the west with his 'Emin Pasha' expedition and Mathews from the east. By these means the Association would secure the British position against all European rivals.[2] This scheme, however, immediately encountered obstacles resulting from the vivisection of Zanzibar by the Anglo-German agreement. The definition of the limits of Zanzibar had been primarily related to the interests of Germany rather than to the realities of Zanzibar's power and influence on the mainland. The agreement had denied the Sultan's authority beyond the ten-mile coastal strip, and had interdicted the extension of his rule beyond that area without the approval of Britain and Germany. This stipulation deprived the East Africa Association of a valuable asset, for the Sultan had considerable influence in the interior and it would have been useful to the Association to act in his name and under his flag.[3] But political considerations dictated that the flag of Zanzibar not be used in the interior. The Foreign Office repudiated Mathews' treaties so far as they applied to territories beyond the ten-mile strip.[4]

The prohibition of the use of Zanzibar's influence placed the full responsibility and expense for the extension of the Association's activity into the interior on the Association itself, for the government had no intention of involving itself in any expense in the British sphere of influence. Unless the Association acted, consequently, there would be no other authority to replace the Sultan's influence. In the meantime, the withdrawal of what power he had exercised contributed to disorder. When the governor of the Arab settlement at Unyanyembe died, the Sultan

---

[1] E. N. Mackenzie to —— 14 July [1887], F.O. 84/1866, P.R.O. The Mazrui (Mazaria) had been dominant at Mombasa before Said had asserted his authority in the area, and in 1824 had made the treaty with Owen accepting British protection.

[2] Kirk to Mackinnon, 23 March 1887, Mackinnon Papers.

[3] Holmwood to F.O., 10 July 1887, F.O. 84/1853, P.R.O.

[4] Note by Wylde, 30 August 1887, on Holmwood to F.O., 14 July 1887, F.O. 84/1853, P.R.O.

did not replace him for fear of offending Germany, and the ensuing wars for the succession disrupted the transportation system from the interior and shut off the valuable ivory shipments.[1] Wylde of the Foreign Office gloomily noted that 'it would take a wise man to prophesy what will happen in the British and German spheres now that the Sultan has practically withdrawn his rule. Civilization will undoubtedly do much but trouble may reasonably be expected'.[2] When that trouble came, the government desired that it would be faced by a private company, hopefully Mackinnon's Association. This policy of no risk, no cost, in fact was neither, since for the sake of avoiding immediate expense, the government risked far greater levies on the taxpayer if the company failed or if it became embroiled in wars in which the government was required to intervene, as was the case with the German East Africa Company when the blunders and insensitivity of company officials ignited the Abushiri rebellion in August 1888 which set the coast aflame and necessitated the dispatch of imperial German forces to fight a war which dragged on for over a year.[3] In 1887, however, fears of such future problems did not affect Salisbury. He continued to maintain that there were no strategic interests in east Africa which warranted governmental action; the area's importance was commercial, and the trader should bear the burden. He had, however, assured Mackinnon of assistance 'consistent with due regard for the Public Exchequer and for the ascertained rights of others',[4] and with this Mackinnon professed to be content.

With the concession signed, Mackinnon and the Association had to make a decision of basic importance as to the scope of the company's operations – whether it would confine itself initially to the coast and extend its operations gradually into the interior or to undertake from the outset an ambitious plan of opening up the interior. This decision would determine the extent of the capital requirements of the new company and until it was made, planning could not proceed. To aid in reaching a conclusion, Mackinnon sought and received permission to employ Holmwood when he

[1] Holmwood estimated the value of ivory which was not delivered because of these wars at £150,000. Holmwood to F.O., 10 July 1887, F.O. 84/1853, P.R.O.
[2] Note by Wylde, 30 August 1887, on Holmwood to F.O., 14 July 1887, F.O. 84/1853, P.R.O.
[3] G. S. P. Freeman Grenville, 'The German Sphere, 1884–1898', in Oliver and Mathew, *History of East Africa*, pp. 439–40.
[4] F.O. to Mackinnon, private, 18 May 1887, F.O. 84/1863, P.R.O.

was relieved as acting consul, to make a journey into the interior and report on the state of the country. Holmwood left Zanzibar in August 1887 and travelled as far as the Taveta district. His judgments of the inhabitants varied. He characterized the wa-Teita as 'among the very lowest types of the human race'. The highlands of the interior, however, were 'generally peopled by finer and more intelligent races', who would be more active if there were an outlet for their energies in foreign trade, as would be the case when the British company controlled the coast rather than 'half-civilised treacherous and unscrupulous Semitic adventurers'. The Arabs' 'evil reputation everywhere preceded them' and the peoples of the interior had developed hostility to any strangers arriving among them from the east.[1]

Holmwood had no reservations of the potentialities of the high plateau country around Taveta:

It is as impossible to describe as to exaggerate the perfect beauty of the scenery in every direction here, especially so when the great snow mountain is in view. . .

All the mixed beauty and grandeur of the Alps, the vastness of the Himalayas are then blended with the delicacy and softness of the finest parts of our English lake scenery with a harmony so perfect that once seen, it can never be forgotten even by the least impressionable. . .[2]

Not only was the country salubrious but its potentialities were great for wheat, corn, India rubber and a wide variety of other crops. With a railroad, this region could become a granary of vast importance for the supply of the needs of the British society.[3]

Holmwood's report was predictable in its general outline; he had begun the journey as an enthusiast and he found much to confirm his enthusiasm. To carry out his project for a railway, however, would require considerable capital, and a railway could not be contemplated without the establishment of order in the lands through which the railway would pass. This was a formidable undertaking, and Mackinnon was not convinced by Holmwood that returns would compensate a company for its outlay. Confronted with the necessity for a decision he drew back from a commitment of large resources. In this inclination to caution he was reinforced by his most respected advisers, George Mackenzie, his close associate in the shipping company and other ventures, and Sir John Kirk. Kirk and Mackenzie agreed that it would be folly to

[1] Holmwood to Salisbury, 28 May 1888, F.O. 84/1922, P.R.O.
[2] *Ibid.*
[3] *Ibid.*

K

embark on a vast scheme involving large amounts of capital without the most careful consideration. Great expenditures at the outset might produce no returns. Rather, the company should begin on a modest scale on the coast and move gradually into more expanded operations. Devotion to civilization and philanthropy was all very well, but it was of no effect unless it also served self-interest. Kirk wrote Mackinnon: 'My doctrine always has been that no philanthropic scheme can do good to Africa or to ourselves unless it has in it the elements of commercial success.'[1]

Unfortunately for the future of the East Africa Company, its founders were inconstant. Despite their early inclination to caution Mackinnon and Kirk were still susceptible to the lure of the grand scheme involving commitments in the interior, and their ambivalence and vacillation contributed to the downfall of a company whose role was never clearly defined. In the early months of 1888, however, Mackinnon proceeded with energy and success to raise the capital necessary to carry out the concession granted by the Sultan and to secure a charter for the new company. The capital for the new enterprise, designated the Imperial British East Africa Company, was set at £1,000,000, with the first issue to be £200,000, and within two months the first issue was oversubscribed. The original subscribers were given the privilege of selection of a court of directors of twelve members in addition to president and vice president and chairman and vice chairman. They were also entitled to pro rata percentages of one of four founders' shares. The Sultan was assigned one share, another was reserved as additional remuneration for the president, vice president, and court of directors, and one was held in reserve to reward those who had performed exceptional service for the company. These shares were of value only after a payment of a dividend of eight per cent to the stockholders, at which time each founder's share would receive ten per cent of the remaining net profit.[2] That eventuality never occurred.

The list of subscribers which Mackinnon and his friends had selected was impressive. Anderson at the Foreign Office commented that progress was highly satisfactory – 'good names and good subscriptions'[3] – and his comment seems an understatement,

---

[1] Kirk to Mackinnon, 17 January 1888, Mackinnon Papers.
[2] Mackenzie to Anderson, 8 March 1888, F.O. 84/1917, P.R.O.
[3] Note by Anderson, n.d. [March 1888], on Mackenzie to Anderson, 8 March 1888, F.O. 84/1917, P.R.O.

for included among the contributors were some of the most prestigious and substantial men in British business and public life. Among the subscribers were men who had been involved with east Africa for many years, including Kirk, Sir Lewis Pelly, and Holmwood. The humanitarians were prominently represented by Thomas Fowell Buxton, William Burdett-Coutts, husband of the celebrated Baroness, and Alexander L. Bruce, the son-in-law of Livingstone, who had devoted much of his fortune from breweries to missions in east Africa and to the African Lakes Company. Among the prominent businessmen were Mackinnon's long-time associate James F. Hutton, now also a director of the Royal Niger Company; Lord Brassey, who had been Civil Lord of the Admiralty in Gladstone's post-Midlothian administration, and had formerly been a director of the British North Borneo Company; Mackinnon's old friend and business associate, James M. Hall; Henry J. Younger, a partner with Bruce in an Edinburgh brewery; Robert Ryrie, a prominent London merchant; and George S. Mackenzie, a partner in Gray, Dawes, and Company, and a director of the British India Steam Navigation Company. Also included were General Sir Donald Stewart, who had recently retired as Commander-in-Chief of the Indian Army; General Sir Arnold B. Kemball, who after a long career in the Indian Army and in various diplomatic capacities in South Asia, had retired to become a business associate of the Duke of Sutherland; and Sir Francis de Winton, recently Administrator General of the Congo Free State.

The subscribers represented the spectrum of the upper reaches of Anglo-Scottish society. Business interest, philanthropy, independent wealth, distinguished public service were blended into a governing board which could command respectful attention from any government, Conservative or Liberal. Four were members of the House of Commons; Kirk was still influential with the permanent staff of the Foreign Office; Bruce, besides being illumined by the aura of Livingstone, was closely connected with his relative, the powerful Balfour of Burleigh, and Kemball was able to invoke the influence of the Duke of Sutherland in addition to his own.[1]

[1] See de Kiewiet, 'History of the Imperial British East Africa Company', p. 99. 'Nominated' directors were required to subscribe only £1,000 while 'regular' directors subscribed at least £5,000. This provision made it possible to include Stewart, Kemball, Pelly, Kirk, and de Winton, whose prominence was not matched by their fortunes.

With the Foreign Office's blessing of the concession and the speedy oversubscription to the company's capital by such influential people, the negotiations for a charter were largely formalities concerned with details rather than principles. The government by its authorization of the Borneo and Niger companies had already established the precedents; the petition for a charter for the Imperial British East Africa Company was primarily a matter for the lawyers, and evoked little attention in the press or Parliament. The first draft of a petition for a charter was submitted to the Foreign Office at the beginning of March 1888, and the charter was formally granted on 3 September 1888. It would probably have been awarded earlier had it not been for some confusion between Mackinnon and the Foreign Office which foreshadowed future relationships. For a month after the submission of the draft petition, Mackenzie, as the London spokesman for the promoters, waited for action by the Foreign Office, and the Foreign Office waited for a formal petition from the promoters. Each was irritated by the dilatoriness of the other. The onus for delay in fact rested on Mackinnon. He had told Mackenzie to press the Foreign Office, but at the same time had indicated that he did not wish to proceed until the Treasury had come to a decision on a continued subsidy for the mail contract to his shipping line. The Treasury, as was its custom, pondered the question at length and eventually decided to postpone action for a year,[1] and Mackinnon decided to go forward with the charter with only the guarantee of the moral support of the Foreign Office for the subsidy. But the delay in proceeding toward a charter indicated an ambivalence in Mackinnon and a serious defect in communication with his lieutenants – Mackinnon was in France during the early stages of the negotiations. At the same time, however, Mackinnon employed the best talent available in the drafting of the charter, and the document submitted to the government at the end of May was carefully drawn on the basis of the Borneo and Niger precedents and provided for every contingency including bankruptcy. An official of the Foreign Office commented that the chief official receiver in bankruptcy was listed among the petitioners and expressed the hope that his services would not be required.[2] The hope was not vindicated. Since the charter followed so closely on

---

[1] Notes on Mackinnon to Salisbury, 22 November 1888, F.O. 84/1933, P.R.O.
[2] Note, W. E. Davidson, 28 May 1888, on Mackinnon to F.O. [24 May 1888], F.O. 84/1921, P.R.O.

precedents it evoked little comment from the various government offices through which it had to pass. The only substantive issue raised was that of the flag. The German ambassador urged that the company not be permitted to hoist a distinctive flag in the territory of the Sultan, but only the Zanzibar flag, and the clause in the charter was altered accordingly.[1]

As with its two predecessors, the Imperial British East Africa Company was subjected by its charter to governmental controls. It was required to secure the approval of the Foreign Office for any agreements it negotiated. The Foreign Secretary could also intervene in any negotiations between the company and a foreign power. Essentially, therefore, the political activity of the company was subject to the surveillance of the Foreign Office. In its commercial operations, the company was subject to treaties which restricted duties on imports to Zanzibar to a maximum of five per cent. The company was further required to use its influence to discourage the slave trade.[2]

The board of directors of the new chartered company was impressive. Mackinnon was elected president and Lord Brassey vice president, and Buxton, Burdett-Coutts, Bruce, Mackenzie, Hutton, Pelly, and Kirk were among its members. With all of the influence and experience represented on the board, Mackinnon was clearly the dominant factor. He, his family, and friends held a substantial proportion of the shares; and the other members of the board at first looked to him for leadership as the moving spirit behind the company. This over-reliance on one man eventually contributed to the collapse of the company, but without the drive provided by Mackinnon the company might never have been born.

Mackinnon's influence should not be exaggerated. He insisted on being informed even of matters which might be considered petty – he could and did intervene when policy decisions were made; and he occasionally acted as if the Company were his personal property by making commitments without consultation with the directors. But from the beginning he was involved in the operation of the Company only sporadically. His life was spent more in his beloved Scotland or in the south of France than in London, and his periodic visits to the city could not substitute for day-to-day

[1] Notes, Pauncefote and Salisbury, 4, 5 June 1888, F.O. 84/1922.
[2] The text of the charter is contained in P. L. McDermott, *British East Africa* (London, 1895), Appendix 3, pp. 476–85.

supervision. The greatest burden was borne by George S. Mackenzie and Sir Arnold Kemball, particularly Mackenzie. Mackenzie's energy was indispensable for the execution of Mackinnon's ideas. He was active in prodding the Foreign Office to action in support of the Company and when the charter was approved, he was sent to east Africa to oversee the first stages of the Company's operations. On his return to London in 1889 he became an essential member of the board because of his first-hand knowledge and his ability.[1] Sir John Kirk called him by 'a long way the best informed' and 'most reasonable' of the Company's promoters.[2] Even those who were critical of Mackinnon and of the Company conceded that Mackenzie was the ablest businessman in the Company. As Mackinnon's health declined the sentiment was more frequently expressed that the Company would be more effective if Mackenzie were given his head. But as long as Mackinnon lived, Mackenzie deferred to the older man's views. Kemball also devoted much of his time to the affairs of the Company, and displayed the good business sense which had won him the confidence of the Duke of Sutherland. Lord Lorne, who was appointed in 1889, also faithfully attended meetings.[3] The other directors were relatively inactive, except for Kirk who was useful as an intermediary with the Foreign Office.

This concentration of power in a few hands was not unusual in the nineteenth-century chartered companies. But the East Africa Company was unique in the relationship of its founder to his creation – Goldie was centrally involved in the Royal Niger Company, Rhodes as managing director dominated the South Africa Company, but Mackinnon acted primarily as overseer at a distance. This relationship contributed to the woes of the Company. The weaknesses of Mackinnon, however, do not explain the demise of the Imperial British East Africa Company. It was born into a world in which, with the most effective of leadership, it could not long survive. It was vested with political responsibilities it could not achieve without expenditures far beyond its resources; it was restricted in its commercial operations by treaties which made it impossible to realize substantial revenues. East Africa had been a pawn in Anglo-German relationships; the East Africa

[1] Hobley, *Kenya*, p. 72; de Kiewiet, 'History of the Imperial British East Africa Company', p. 103.
[2] Kirk to Mackinnon, 12 January 1888, Mackinnon Papers.
[3] de Kiewiet, 'History of the Imperial British East Africa Company', p. 104.

Company also was used by the politicians for their own purposes, and in so doing they assured its early death. The basic deficiency of Mackinnon was not in the character of his management but in the naivete and romanticism which had led him to believe that the Company could combine commercial and political purposes to the advancement of both. Mackinnon had said that his Company would 'take their dividends in philanthropy'.[1] Its philanthropic returns were doubtful, the great yield to Mackinnon and his fellow contributors was acute frustration.

[1] Carton de Wiart, *Les grandes compagnies coloniales anglaises*, p. 239.

6

The Company begins operations, 1888–1889

During the months from the acquisition of the concession to the award of the charter the political environment of east Africa had changed substantially. Sultan Barghash, who had been ill for several months, died on 27 March 1888, hours after landing on his return from a visit to Muscat. His brother Khalifa, a British nominee, was duly proclaimed Sultan by the obedient Arab notables. Khalifa's virtues in the eyes of his British protectors were a reflection of the impotence of Zanzibar. Kirk, who had been asked for advice on the succession in anticipation of Barghash's death, described him as 'simple and open handed'. For five years he had been confined by Barghash, and his ignorance of the world was 'astonishing even for a Zanzibari Arab'.[1] Euan Smith who had been appointed consul general after the removal of Holmwood at the behest of Germany assessed him as 'a man of somewhat weak disposition, inclined to listen to the last comer and prone to enter into engagements without duly considering where they may lead him'. Euan Smith had no doubt of his ability to manage the new Sultan in the British interest. He prided himself in the knowledge of the 'Oriental mind' which he had acquired in his years of service in India. He wrote to Salisbury:

Seyyid Khalifa's main characteristics are common to all Orientals: love of ease, an earnest desire to be troubled as little as possible about anything, and love of money.[2]

These attributes undoubtedly made Khalifa susceptible to influence, but the direction in which that influence would be exerted was unclear at the time of his accession. Euan Smith's position in Zanzibar was a testament to the importance of Germany. Holmwood was gone, and Kirk, who had hoped to return to Zanzibar, had been retired, loaded with honor but without power

[1] Kirk to Anderson, 10 February 1888, F.O. 84/1915, P.R.O.
[2] Euan Smith to Salisbury, 8 April 1888, F.O. 84/1906, P.R.O.

to affect high policy.[1] Euan Smith had been Salisbury's selection, and the policy he was to execute was Salisbury's alone. There was no scope for the 'man on the spot' in the Kirk tradition, or even for the influential subordinate in Whitehall. East Africa continued to be ancillary to Salisbury's European policy which he pursued with a passion for secrecy which shut out even the Foreign Office staff. Kirk, who communed with these officials frequently in mutual frustration, commented that 'Salisbury is carrying out a personal policy. The officials seem to know nothing. The result is uncomfortable'.[2]

In 1888 Salisbury's policy continued to be to placate Bismarck as much as possible, though he was beginning to have doubts that the Chancellor could be conciliated. He complained to the British ambassador in Berlin:

. . .friendship with Germany is a more uncertain staff to lean upon than friendship with France. The Chancellor's humors are as changeable as those of the French Assembly and you can never be certain he will not try to levy a sort of diplomatic blackmail putting himself against you in some matter in which you are interested unless you do something to gratify some of his unreasonable antipathies.[3]

Despite his irritation, however, Salisbury was not ready in 1888 to abandon the policy of rapprochement with Germany. In east Africa this extended to cooperation short of the sacrifice to Germany of the island of Zanzibar itself.[4] Not even Bismarck could complain of Salisbury's devotion to the German interest. Count Bismarck expressed the Chancellor's gratitude:

I hope Ld. Salisbury knows how sincerely grateful we are to him for what he has done for us in the East African business. We understand that he has gone as far as it is possible to go to be of help to us and we are most anxious in return to do all we can to be agreeable to him.[5]

This deference to German wishes was exhibited in actions which had considerable effect on the future of the British East Africa Company. In June 1887 the German government had been worried that Stanley's Emin Pasha expedition might intrude

---

[1] Kirk to Mackinnon, 8 March 1887, Mackinnon Papers.
[2] Kirk to Mackinnon, 14 May 1887, *ibid.*
[3] Salisbury to Malet, secret, 11 April 1888, F.O. 343/2, P.R.O.
[4] Salisbury wrote to the British Ambassador, 'The abandonment of the Sultan of Zanzibar would never be tolerated by English public opinion.' Salisbury to Malet, 21 January 1889, F.O. 244/456, P.R.O.
[5] Malet to Salisbury, private and personal, 8 December 1888, F.O. 343/10, P.R.O.

British influence into the rear of the German sphere, and Salisbury had agreed to an understanding that Germany would be given a free hand in the territories to the south of Victoria Nyanza and that Britain would restrict the activity of its subjects to lands north of the line.[1] In April 1888 Euan Smith was instructed to cooperate in securing a concession from the Sultan to the German East Africa Company for control of the customs in the German coastal zone. The Sultan on Euan Smith's advice signed a document in April 1888, which, as the consul general admitted, he did not understand, essentially transferring control of the coast to the German company on terms very favourable to it. Euan Smith remarked, 'the Sultan will ere long learn by practical experience that he has virtually ceased to wield any power at all in the coast line, but this lesson will not be learned without much discontent.'[2] Anglo-German amity had dictated that he not be informed.

Foreign policy considerations also dictated a soft response to German activity in Witu and its environs. The delimitation agreement of 1886 had established the northern boundary of the British sphere at the Tana River. Just north of the river was the tiny district of Witu. The chief, Ahmed Fumoluti, who went by the ferocious name of Simba, had fled the neighboring island of Patta in 1862 after an unsuccessful rebellion against the Sultan of Zanzibar, and had gathered around him on the mainland a following of perhaps 3,000 men. With this force and the protection of the forests he defied the Sultan of Zanzibar. A British vice-consul who visited the area in 1884 described Witu as the 'Alsatia of the coast, which lived on the plunder of neighboring villages and the enslavement of their inhabitants'.[3] A German trader, Clemens Denhardt, and his brother negotiated an agreement with Simba in April 1885, and German naval power backed him in the assertion of Simba's independence. Barghash in June 1885 had planned to send a force to destroy Simba but was warned by Germany not to intervene, and this German protectorate was made formal in 1886 with the concurrence of Britain. A German Witu Company was formed with a nominal capital of 500,000 marks (£25,000) to exploit the Denhardts' concessions.[4] The effect of this protectorate

[1] Salisbury to Malet, 2 July, 1887, cited in McDermott, *British East Africa*, p. 13.

[2] Euan Smith to Salisbury, 26 July 1888, F.O. 84/1908, P.R.O.

[3] Report of Vice Consul John Haggard, 25 August 1887, cited in McDermott, *British East Africa*, p. 34.

[4] McDermott, *British East Africa*, p. 36. The Denhardts did not retain an

was to establish Germany on both the northern and southern flanks of the British zone, and Witu could be used, should Germany so desire, as a base for extension of influence into the interior or to the neighboring islands. Salisbury resisted the extreme German position that the delimitation agreement in effect had interdicted the spread of British influence beyond the Tana River and had allowed German free scope north of that boundary, but he also felt it politic to restrain the British East Africa Company in this area so long as there was danger of a confrontation with Germany. Thus when the German government inquired whether the British East Africa Company was seeking a concession of the island of Lamu, Salisbury reminded the Company that it could not undertake any such negotiation without the approval of the government.[1] Mackinnon replied with some acerbity that, while no such negotiation was contemplated, Barghash's original offer in 1887 had included all his remaining territories outside the British and German zones, including Lamu, and that the terms were known to both the British and German governments.[2] It would be more statesmanlike, Mackinnon suggested, for Germany to give up Witu and thus remove a thorn in Anglo-German relations rather than asserting an interest in Lamu, which clearly belonged to Zanzibar. Mackinnon's suggestion was not well received in the Foreign Office. Anderson condemned him as a dog-in-the-manger 'whose zeal for concessions was not matched by his capacity to exploit them' and suggested that if Lamu were to belong to either Britain or Germany it should properly go to Germany. But the outcome was an agreement by the two governments to avoid pressing issues relating to Witu and the off-shore islands. Bismarck at Salisbury's suggestion agreed to submit the question to arbitration, and the dispute was settled by a decision in August 1889 by the Belgian arbitrator, Baron Lambermont, that the Sultan was bound to neither party. The Sultan, legally free to act, followed the advice of the British consul, and signed a concession to the British East Africa Company.[3] But in the meantime, and indeed thereafter, both the German and British companies and the Denhardt brothers acting independently attempted to subvert any governmental actions contrary to their interests, and collisions

interest in the Witu Company, but continued to exert an influence over the Sultan of Witu.
[1] F.O. to Mackinnon, 1 December 1888, F.O. 84/1934, P.R.O.
[2] Mackinnon to Salisbury, 8 December 1888, F.O. 84/1934, P.R.O.
[3] McDermott, *British East Africa*, p. 45.

occurred. One such incident involved the Belesoni canal. The canal was clearly within the dominion of Zanzibar assigned to the East Africa Company in 1887. It had been constructed by Zanzibari subjects to provide access from the river Ozi to the Tana, thus avoiding a sandbar which prevented access to the Tana from the sea. At the instigation of Clemens Denhardt, however, Simba in the autumn of 1888 established a customs house on the canal. The German government denied responsibility on the basis that Simba and Denhardt were not associated with the German Witu Company. Salisbury on his part declined to intervene. The East Africa Company was told that it must protect itself in the area of its concession. Eventually, at the end of December 1889, in response to an ultimatum by the Company that it would send a force against the customs house, the German consul general advised Simba to withdraw, and he immediately complied.[1] On the other side, at the behest of Mackinnon, agents of the East Africa Company made treaties with Somali tribes who had already indicated loyalty to Denhardt and pursued private diplomacy with the Italians for the cession of Kismayu and other ports on the Benadir coast in an effort to restrict the Germans.[2]

The flaccid response of each government was interpreted by the opposing private company as a mask for connivance with the rival company. This does not appear to have been the case. Certainly with Salisbury the reverse was true. As the Belesoni canal affair made evident, the British government was not prepared to back its company when it was embroiled with African adversaries officially unconnected with a European power. Further, Mackinnon was allowed to pursue his private diplomacy without any clear guidance from the Foreign Office, and was allowed to think of himself as a quasi-independent force. Already inclined to make decisions without consultation with his colleagues, he was now encouraged to act without consultation with his government. This lack of control over Mackinnon by his colleagues or his government had serious consequences for the Company. The government could disavow his actions; the Company had to pay for his excursions in private diplomacy.

In the summer of 1888, however, the characteristic of the British East Africa Company which most concerned the govern-

---

[1] de Kiewiet, 'History of the Imperial British East Africa Company', pp. 142–6.
[2] *Ibid.* p. 141; John S. Galbraith, 'Italy, the British East Africa Company, and the Benadir Coast', *Journal of Modern History*, December 1970, 549–63.

ment was its lack of energy. By contrast, the German company to the south seemed to be moving forward rapidly with the impetus of a new director, Herr Vohsen. The German company's officers proceeded with dispatch to assume control of the ports and customs in the German zone, without any preparation of the Sultan's local officials or the population at large for the transfer.[1] The Germans, Euan Smith admitted, were detested by the people whom they treated with arrogance and brutality. Their subordinate officials were mostly retired army officers who were ill-equipped by nature or training to deal with 'the Oriental character'.[2] Their conduct might cause future difficulties with the peoples of the coast, he recognized, but at least they were doing something. By June 1888 they had surveyed the country from Dar es Salaam to Mpwapwa for a railway and were building houses for their staff, while in the British zone there was no sign of activity. 'The vigor and energy of the Germans are up to the present in marked contrast to the absolute want of initiative on the part of the English company', wrote Euan Smith to Salisbury.[3] Mackinnon and his fellow directors seemed listless except in pursuit of concessions for themselves. They had sought concessions from the Sultan for the farming of the Zanzibar and Pemba customs and for control of the customs in the Benadir coast north of Witu. Euan Smith extracted from the Sultan a secret commitment to give the Mackinnon company first refusal on the Zanzibar and Pemba customs,[4] but on Salisbury's instructions no action was taken on a proposed concession on the Benadir coast pending resolution of Italian claims in that area and a demonstration by the Company that it seriously intended to develop the concession it already had.[5] Salisbury later in the year also essentially vetoed the East Africa Company's assumption of the Zanzibar–Pemba customs with the revealing observations that while the arrangement might be good for Zanzibar and might check the slave trade and benefit Mackinnon's company, it was politically undesirable since it would give the government the burdens of annexation without the benefit.[6]

[1] Oliver and Mathew, *History of East Africa*, p. 438.
[2] Euan Smith to Salisbury, 29 July 1888, A/79, Salisbury Papers.
[3] Euan Smith to Salisbury, 1 June 1888, F.O. 84/1907, P.R.O.
[4] Euan Smith to Mackinnon, private, 25 April 1888, Mackinnon Papers.
[5] Salisbury to Euan Smith, 26 June 1888, F.O. 84/1904, P.R.O. For the Italian involvement, see Galbraith, 'Italy, the British East Africa Company and the Benadir Coast', pp. 549–63.
[6] Note by Salisbury, n.d., on telegram, Euan Smith to Salisbury, 16 September

From Mackinnon's perspective, what Salisbury described as inactivity appeared as mere prudence. Until the charter was approved it seemed unwise to begin operations, and the government's failure to come to a speedy conclusion on the mail contract was an additional reason for caution. Shortly after the charter was finally issued the German coast was aflame with revolt, and the repercussions extended into the British zone. The anger of the coastal people against the Germans had exploded into an uprising led by Abushiri ibn Salim al-Harthi which assumed such formidable proportions that direct German imperial intervention was required. Bismarck sought to mask the blow to German prestige by labelling the rising as an insurrection against the authority of the Sultan and imposing a blockade in the guise of action against the slave trade, invoking the cooperation of the British to make the blockade effective along the whole coast. Salisbury against his better judgment deferred to Bismarck's wishes.[1] In arriving at this decision, Salisbury did not consult with the East Africa Company despite the fact that its commercial interests would be greatly affected by the blockade.[2]

This was the environment when George Mackenzie arrived in Zanzibar as managing director in October 1888. It was Mackenzie's responsibility to organize the headquarters at Mombasa, to conciliate the local population, and to formulate a plan of action for commercial development. The first two he performed in a manner which moved the usually critical Euan Smith to unqualified praise of his deftness and sagacity.[3] He dealt with an explosive issue involving the harboring of runaway slaves at a Church Missionary station by the payment of $25 for each fugitive on the owner's granting a 'freedom paper', thus avoiding conflict with either the missionaries or the slave-owners.[4] In contrast to the brutal directness with which the Germans had intruded,

---

1888, F.O. 84/1913, P.R.O. Salisbury overruled his staff, who had recommended approval.

[1] Salisbury to Euan Smith, 13 October 1888, F.O. 84/1905, P.R.O.

[2] Note, Pauncefote, 2 November 1888, F.O. 84/1930, P.R.O.

[3] Euan Smith to Salisbury, 23 October 1888, Salisbury Papers A/79.

[4] MacDermott, *British East Africa*, p. 27. Mackenzie circumvented the legal problem that a British subject could not buy slaves by treating the slaves as lost property and inducing the owners to issue the necessary papers for compensation. He made this arrangement over the objection of Euan Smith who maintained that the slaves had not done anything to deserve their freedom. They were 'idle, indolent fellows merely anxious to avoid work'. Euan Smith to Salisbury, 20 November 1888, F.O. 84/1910, P.R.O.

Mackenzie sought to quiet opposition by assurances that the Company's advent would not undermine their interests or their institutions and by lavish distribution of gifts in presents and cash. Mackenzie's caution may have prevented a revolt in the British zone; but, as Euan Smith remarked, tranquillity reflected the fact that nothing had happened; and it was easy for people to accept an administrator who gave all and took nothing.[1] Frederick Jackson, who was in Mombasa at the time, felt that Mackenzie's gifts were interpreted as evidence of weakness and that the money would have been better spent on the employment of a force of Indian police which would have commanded respect.[2] Jackson assumed that the prime purpose of Mackenzie must be to establish an efficient administration. Mackenzie, however, was preoccupied with ensuring a peaceful transition. He was careful not to attack the vested interests of powerful men. This course meant essentially a continuation of the *status quo*, with much of the Sultan's administration remaining intact. During Mackenzie's first tenure as administrator, the Company had on its books 700 employees, but few of these were Europeans. A year after Mackenzie's departure, there were only about 40 European supervisors outside of Buganda, about half of whom were assigned to Mombasa in relation to customs administration, banking and postal services, and organization of caravans into the interior. Of the non-European laborers, as Jackson observed, what was observable was generally discreditable. Less than half were in evidence at all, the rest having received advances of three months' wages and decamped. Those who remained, observed Jackson, were quite useless.[3] Incompetence in the lower echelons of the Company's service was to be characteristic of its operations during its brief life; Mackenzie during his few months in Mombasa did nothing to correct this basic weakness.

Mackenzie's decision to cooperate with the existing order rather than to institute traumatic changes was a temporary expedient to ease the transition to Company rule; it was not intended to be a permanent policy. But during the years the Company 'controlled' the coast, it pursued the basic line he had laid down, and the Company continued to support officials from the previous era. Mackenzie's actions in the commercial sphere paralleled those in

---

[1] Euan Smith to F.O., 7 February 1889, F.O. 84/1976, P.R.O.
[2] Frederick Jackson, *Early Days in East Africa* (London, 1930), pp. 145–6.
[3] *Ibid.* pp. 146–7.

the administrative area. Instead of attempting to compete in trade with Indians, Arabs, and Swahilis, he chose to cooperate with them. He advanced money to Swahili groups to form a trading company to send a caravan into the Unyanyembe district to bring out ivory reported to be held up by the uprising on the German coastline. The Company contributed one-quarter of the capital, the Swahili the remainder.[1] Later, the Company would send out its own caravans to the interior, but the practices instituted by Mackenzie on the coast were never altered. At no time did the Company make an effort to challenge the position of local traders. This was a prudent decision, for the Company would almost certainly have suffered severe losses.

The coast was never the focus of the Company's attention. The future of trade was conceived to be around the Great Lakes and in other areas of the interior. Whether the mood was cautious or aggressive, the significance of the coast was as a means of access. Caravans across land from Mombasa would establish contact with the Lakes and Buganda. There were high hopes that by the Juba, the major river of east Africa, ivory might be brought out from the Boran Galla country, where there were reported to be great quantities. The Tana River could provide access to the country around Mount Kenya, where more ivory might be traded, and there might also be precious metals to be won. All this was highly speculative, and ignored such considerations as the Somali dominance over the Juba; but these were the assumptions on which the Company set its policy.

On the coast the Company hoped to make profits from customs, banking, postal services, and other functions. But with the exception of customs, no profits were forthcoming, and these were only a few thousand pounds per year. Restrictions surrounding the coastal concessions made additional revenue unlikely. In addition to the commercial treaties which restricted duties on imports to five per cent, there were other limitations on potential revenue. Subjects of foreign states were exempted from any taxation other than such customs duties. Under the concession, all costs of administration had to be borne by the Company; and by the Berlin Act of 1885 as well as by the Company's charter, the Company had to accept freedom of trade within its area of operations.

---

[1] Mackenzie to Euan Smith, 13 March 1889, F.O. 84/2000, P.R.O.

Compounding the problems of the Company was the disruption of trade produced by the war in the German zone and the blockade of the entire 'Zanzibari' coast. Despite these handicaps, Mackenzie began the construction of a cart route which he intended to extend along the entire sea front of the British concession and made plans for a telegraph parallel to the road and for the establishment of a cable connection between Mombasa and Zanzibar.[1] Even in the most favorable of times, however, as Kirk himself recognized, the prosperity of the Company depended upon the establishment of a route of communication from the coast to the Lakes area. Here again the difficulties were compounded by the Anglo-German agreement. The traditional caravan trials were principally in the German zone; the company must now create routes of its own through a country where what was known was discouraging. Holmwood had reported that the route he had taken was unsatisfactory because of the wide expanses of sterile waterless land between Taru and Maungu. Mackenzie now had to organize an expedition to report on an alternative passage. The expedition hopefully would link up with Stanley as he proceeded from the west with his Emin Pasha Relief Expedition. The first choice of the directors was Captain Frederick Lugard, who had been recommended by Euan Smith, but Lugard had committed himself to the African Lakes Company[2] and Lieutenant Swayne of the Royal Engineers was selected. The first contingent set out from Mombasa on 18 October 1888, bound for Baringo just north of the equator to the north-east of Lake Victoria. Swayne was a poor choice; if his associate Frederick Jackson is to be believed he was obsessed with the thrills of big-game shooting to the point of monomania. He would run about the camp with a heavy gun and when tired, point it at an object about the height of an elephant's vitals and shout, 'Am I steady, Jackson, am I steady?'[3] Mackenzie removed him from the leadership of the expedition and put Jackson in charge. Swayne, however, was not discharged; instead he was sent on another expedition to the territories between the Tana and the Juba Rivers to conclude treaties with the chiefs in that area.[4]

Jackson's original commission was to establish a chain of stations along the road to Baringo. At Baringo the directors expected that

[1] Euan Smith to Salisbury, 17 October 1888, F.O. 84/1910, P.R.O.
[2] Margery Perham, *Lugard: the Years of Adventure* (London, 1956), p. 70.
[3] Jackson, *Early Days in East Africa*, p. 147.
[4] Mackenzie to F.O., 1 April 1889, F.O. 84/1992, P.R.O.

there would be sufficient ivory for barter to pay the expenses of the expedition. After making the base at Baringo secure he was to proceed with the remainder of his party to Wadelai, where it was expected Emin Pasha would be waiting to receive him. Because of the apparent hostility of the Kabaka of Buganda and reports of that state's great military power, Jackson was instructed to avoid Buganda. On receiving further word from Stanley, Mackenzie modified the instructions to provide that Jackson should proceed directly to the south-east shore at Lake Victoria to meet Stanley who was reported to have arrived in that vicinity with Emin. Neither set of instructions revealed any understanding of the nature of the difficulties the caravans would encounter, the resources necessary to establish trading stations in potentially hostile country, or of the character of the indigenous societies. The directors, impressed with the tales of the formidable Masai, proposed to conciliate them by paying tribute in exchange for a guarantee of protection for the caravans. Such a suggestion assumed a social organization which had no relation to the Masai. The instructions were ludicrously unrealistic.[1] No leader however talented could possibly have executed such a commission. Jackson had under his command 500 men, many of doubtful devotion, sufficient to carry out a reconnoitering expedition but grossly inadequate to establish a chain of stations from the coast to the Great Lakes. He penetrated through the Masai country without any armed encounters and without paying any tribute. But he sought in vain for Stanley in the vicinity of Lake Victoria and then turned north in obedience to his instructions. During his journey, which had the dual purpose of negotiating treaties and acquiring ivory, Jackson learned that Stanley had already found Emin and was on his way toward the coast. Further, and most distressing, he found that in February 1890 Carl Peters had appeared at his camp at Umia's, on the periphery of Buganda, and had committed the indecency of reading his personal letters. These included Stanley's communication and a plea from Mwanga to come to his assistance against the Muslims who had driven him from his capital and promising much in return, including acceptance of the Company's flag, a monopoly of trade and a guarantee of religious freedom. Peters had taken advantage of this intelligence

---

[1] Instructions to Swayne, 11 October 1888, Mackinnon Papers, quoted in de Kiewiet, 'History of the Imperial British East Africa Company', pp. 112–13. These were also essentially the instructions on which Jackson proceeded.

to rush to Buganda where he offered his service to Mwanga, who in the meantime had been restored to the throne, and induced the Kabaka to sign a treaty. Mwanga, however, was not willing to go beyond agreeing to allow Europeans to trade and to permit German settlement.[1] When Jackson arrived a month later he found Mwanga pleasant but no longer interested in British protection, and the French Catholic priests exerting their influence against Britain and Protestantism. The brief opportunity presented by Mwanga's extremity had been lost.

Jackson's expedition was successful to the extent that it provided valuable knowledge of the interior and its peoples; but it did not acquire ivory and other goods in quantities sufficient to pay for its expenses. The capital of the Company, depleted by expenditures for piers at Mombasa, road building, telegraph wire, and other purposes, was drained further by this and other ventures into the far interior which served a political as well as a commercial purpose.

In the last months of the Company, when it was tottering into bankruptcy, the directors alleged that, in its involvement in Buganda, the Company had acted in the governmental interest. The assertion was true, but it was misleading. In the early months of the Company's existence, there was a basic conflict among the directors as to the policy to be pursued in the interior. Reconnoitering expeditions such as Jackson's were generally acknowledged to be desirable but a major investment of resources was another matter. Some directors, notably Pelly and Burdett-Coutts, believed that the most prudent course for the Company was to 'stand quietly and firmly for the present, and let all the German and other storms blow themselves out'.[2] They opposed the aggressive expansion of the Company's claims pursued by Mackinnon, particularly when this expansion was at the Company's own risk, with no support from the Foreign Office. Finally, Pelly and Burdett-Coutts, disturbed at what they considered Mackinnon's rashness, obtained an interview with Sir Philip Currie, the Permanent Undersecretary, to seek a statement of the Foreign Office's position. Currie's performance was all that his superior could have desired; Salisbury himself could not have acted more adeptly. Currie suggested to the two directors that the Company's

---

[1] Bair, 'Carl Peters and German Colonialism', p. 199.
[2] Pelly to Mackinnon, 13 March 1889, Mackinnon Papers, quoted in de Kiewiet, 'History of the Imperial British East Africa Company', p. 162.

best interests would be served by pushing on to the Lakes area before the Germans arrived. To their anxious inquiry as to how much support they might expect, he offered sybilline responses which they interpreted to be suggestive of governmental sympathy and support, but they received no concrete guarantees, and Currie was frank enough to make it clear that the government was not prepared to support the Company to the extent of confronting Germany.[1] With this tepid encouragement Pelly and Burdett-Coutts, remarkably, withdrew their opposition to Mackinnon's expansionism. But Mackinnon himself had needed no encouragement from government to pursue his plans and had been prepared to carry out his scheme even with opposition on the board. From the origin of the Company he had conceived of its being the agent of a grand design similar to that which he had projected in the 1870s. The earlier idea of joint action with Leopold had faded but in 1889 Mackinnon's imagination had been fired by another dreamer of great dreams who had energy to carry them out, Cecil Rhodes.

During the time when Mackinnon and his associates had been planning to use Emin Pasha to establish British control of the Lakes area, Rhodes had been promoting his plans for expansion to the north from the Cape. With the amalgamation of his interests and those of a London group headed by Lord Gifford and George Cawston, a coalition had come into being with great power both at Whitehall and at Government House, Cape Town. The focus was Matabeleland and Mashonaland, but the founders of the British South Africa Company had ambitions far beyond. From the beginning they contemplated ousting the Portuguese from Mozambique and expansion north to the borders of the Congo Free State and to the Lakes. In these greater ambitions they linked themselves with Mackinnon. Both companies had interests in the area of the Great Lakes and these common interests drew them together into plans for a cooperative endeavor which would associate Rhodes' northward movement and Mackinnon's westward expansion to produce a great British trade empire extending over the 'unappropriated' and some of the appropriated lands of Africa.

Specifically, Rhodes was brought into contact with Mackinnon through his interest in the acquisition of the African Lakes Company as a means of gaining access to Lake Nyasa. The Lakes

[1] de Kiewiet, 'History of the Imperial British East Africa Company', p. 164.

Company was the spoiled darling of the humanitarian elements in Scottish society, who discounted its ineffectiveness because of its avowed idealism. In fact, the Lakes Company did little to advance either commerce or Christianity. John Kirk as consul general had frequently commented on the inertia of its representatives and their lack of judgment when they occasionally were stirred to action.[1] But these facts were ignored, for the Company wore the mantle of Livingstone, and British politicians deferred to it for fear of arousing Scottish humanitarian ire. Among its strong supporters were Balfour of Burleigh and A. L. Bruce, the latter being a link with the East Africa Company.

When Rhodes and his fellow-promoters began to discuss the buying-up of the Lakes Company, they consulted with Kirk as the greatest authority on east Africa and also became associated with Euan Smith, who was home on leave from his post in Zanzibar. Kirk and Euan Smith brought the South Africa interests into contact with Mackinnon. By the summer of 1889, even before the British South Africa Company was formally chartered, discussions had reached an advanced stage for using the Lakes Company as the lynch pin to bring together the British South Africa and East Africa companies with a common boundary. Euan Smith was an eager go-between, and kept all his options open by informing Salisbury of all that took place. The first plan was to absorb the Lakes Company and then to recreate it in a new incarnation with Mackinnon as one of the directors in addition to Sir Donald Currie of the Union Steamship Line and representatives of the British South Africa Company. Balfour was the first selection to be chairman of the reborn Lakes Company, provided that Salisbury did not consider his acceptance as a conflict of interest with his responsibilities in the Salisbury ministry.[2] The plan was not carried out in its original form, in large part because of unexpected difficulties in digesting the old Lakes Company, but the alliance between Mackinnon and Rhodes continued for the acquisition of the Lakes area for Britain and for their respective companies.

The ambitions of Mackinnon and Rhodes were not translated into precise plans. The edges of the two companies' empires were

---

[1] See, for example, Kirk to Anderson, 3 April 1884, F.O. 84/1688, P.R.O. Kirk noted that the Company had started no industry and done nothing to promote agriculture but in its eagerness to acquire ivory had given guns to 'all the renegade mission boys and native loafers to shoot elephants and thus have enriched a lot of vagabonds'.

[2] Euan Smith to Salisbury, 15 June 1889, A/79, Salisbury Papers.

fuzzy as is frequently the case with grand designs. But Mackinnon's sphere clearly included a common boundary with the Congo Free State and control over Uganda. His plans also extended to Equatoria Province, though the disappointment with Emin made this less feasible. Kirk, on whom Mackinnon relied for information and advice on international politics affecting east Africa, was convinced that there was danger that Peters' activity would be converted into another German coup. The German government was ambitious, and Mackinnon considered Salisbury to be craven. The German plan, Kirk understood, was to capture control of the lands west of Lake Nyasa and to establish a boundary for their sphere from the east side of that lake to the Congo State frontier. The results would be that the nascent British South Africa Company would be cut off from Lake Tanganyika, the Germans would control the 'Stevenson Road' between Lake Nyasa and Lake Tanganyika, the East Africa Company would not be able to communicate between Lake Nyasa and Victoria Nyanza. This plot Kirk thought could not be thwarted by Rhodes, who was 'not a very practical man' and was chiefly interested in the Matabele country.[1] If any effective response was to be made it must come from the East Africa Company.

Kirk's advice strengthened Mackinnon's own suspicion that a deal might be impending between the two governments to settle the boundary by a line drawn across Lake Tanganyika to the boundaries of the Congo Free State in such a manner that British east and central Africa would be separated and the East Africa Company would be denied its boundary with the Congo Free State. It was this preoccupation with securing the Lakes area for Britain which led him to instruct Stanley to make treaties with chiefs between Lake Victoria and Lake Tanganyika in order to forestall the Germans, and he hoped that Alexander Mackay and other British missionaries in Buganda would similarly engage in treaty making so that a line from the south end of Lake Victoria to the north end of Lake Tanganyika could be defended against German expansion.[2]

Mackinnon's passionate quasi-diplomatic activity in 1889–90 was incompatible with prudent use of the Company's limited

[1] Kirk to Mackinnon, 26 July 1889, Mackinnon Papers.
[2] Nicol to Stanley, 5 November 1889, enclosing Mackinnon to [Nicol ?], 1 August 1889, enclosure in Salisbury to Malet, 6 May 1890, F.O. 244/471, P.R.O.

resources. The Company suffered not so much from Mackinnon's feebleness as from his ambition. In 1889 he was involved in plans for mastery of the Lakes, in negotiations with the Italians for the lease of the Benadir coast, with the Denhardt brothers, now at odds with the Witu Company, to use their influence with Simba to transfer his loyalty to the British East Africa Company, and with the Witu Company to try to buy out their concession.[1] These negotiations were exciting for him, but they were costly to the Company, since he neglected the mundane business of Company organization but insisted on being consulted.

Mackinnon was not alone responsible for the lack of clarity in the definition of the Company's plans and policies. Though in his negotiations with the Italians regarding the Benadir coast he had acted on his own initiative, he, with justification, believed himself to be acting on behalf of Imperial interests in his efforts to thwart the Germans in the interior. Salisbury, however, for reasons of public policy, would not provide Mackinnon with a clear indication of how far the government desired the Company to go. The limits were determined only when they were overstepped. Beyond the complications introduced by governmental interests, however, the Company suffered throughout its life from the nature of its origins. It had been founded to promote great national ends and to make a profit. The first objective subverted the second.

Confusion within the board of directors as to the nature of the enterprise and lack of communication between Mackinnon, frequently in Scotland or in France, and the London members of the board greatly complicated the task of the administrator on the spot in east Africa. George Mackenzie might in time have become effective, but he had been sent to east Africa only for a brief period to establish the Company at Mombasa with minimum of resentment from the local population. At the end of six months, having accomplished this task, he returned to England, and a successor had to be selected. Mackinnon's offer to Stanley of the chief administratorship left the issue in limbo, for Stanley was still somewhere in the interior at the time Mackenzie's six months' tour of duty was over. To serve in the interim pending Stanley's decision the directors appointed J. W. Buchanan as acting administrator. Buchanan took his position as a temporary appointee seriously and declined to take any action beyond the ordinary routine of Company business. Consequently the leadership which

[1] Euan Smith to Salisbury, A/79, Salisbury Papers, Christ Church, Oxford.

was needed to develop the concession was absent. This, combined with the continuing disorganization caused by the blockade, contributed to an inertia which was the subject of critical comment by government officials. Gerald Portal, who was acting consul general while Euan Smith was on leave for his health, fumed at Buchanan's lack of initiative,[1] and in Whitehall, Anderson commented that the Germans, while they might be overbearing, at least had 'pluck and energy'.[2] The statement was an ironic one, for the activity in the German zone at the time was governmental, not private, since the German East Africa Company had foundered.[3]

In January 1889 the German government sought to snuff out the Abushiri rising by appointing Lieutenant Hermann von Wissman as head of a military expedition supported by credits of two million marks, voted by the Reichstag. Bismarck had tried to emulate the British by using a company as a means of avoiding governmental responsibility and levies on the taxpayer. He had attempted to enhance the company's prospects for success by leaving out such restrictions incorporated in British charters as prohibitions of the trade in alcohol and mandates to assist in the abolition of the slave trade,[4] and he had failed. The German company's representatives in east Africa had acted with an arrogance and ruthlessness which ignited a rebellion. Even Lord Salisbury, whose moral instincts were not easily roused, was moved to comment that 'after what has taken place on the German Coast, it is impossible to maintain that any concession to them is done in the cause of civilization'.[5] But the German company did not have the power to restore order, and direct governmental authority replaced private agency.

The German experience did not affect British policy. The failure of the German East Africa Company was attributed to defects in the German character, not to the unsoundness of the policy of using chartered companies to avoid public expense. Furthermore, the Treasury refused to compete with French and

---

[1] Portal to Salisbury, confidential, 22 June 1889, F.O. 84/1979, P.R.O.
[2] Note by Anderson, n.d., on *ibid.*
[3] It was not officially buried until November 1890, but it was moribund from the end of 1888 and its political and administrative functions were assumed by the government.
[4] R. F. Eberlie, 'The German Achievement in East Africa', *Tanganyika Notes and Records*, September 1960, p. 183.
[5] Note by Salisbury, n.d. [January 1889] on back of envelope, F.O. 84/1983, P.R.O.

German heavy subsidies to vital steamship lines by providing similar governmental assistance for British shipping. Mackinnon had sought a guarantee of a mail subsidy to the British India Steam Navigation Company as a necessity for the success of his chartered company, but despite the urgent importunities of the Foreign Office the Treasury remained adamant against such assistance. The Treasury position infuriated the staff of the Foreign Office. This 'blind, unreasoning opposition'[1] meant that British shipping would be driven from east Africa by subsidized French and German competitors.[2]

After almost two years the Treasury finally gave way but even then its surrender was not complete. It agreed only to a contract for two years with twelve months' notice thereafter, providing a mail subsidy, and it accompanied its sullen acquiescence with a lecture to the Foreign Office on elementary principles of economics:

It has been, and is, My Lords' conviction that it is unsound commercial policy to seek to assist British enterprise in its struggle with foreign rivals, out of the pocket of the general taxpayer and they believe that a firm adherence to this principle has been more than justified by the past history of British commerce and especially of the British carrying trade.[3]

Governmental policy was essentially to use the East Africa Company for political ends at no expense to the taxpayer, even though these ends might be in opposition to the Company's commercial interests. As Euan Smith admitted, Wissman's appearance on the coast would have repercussions in the British zone. If he succeeded, the prestige of the Sultan on which Mackinnon depended for the preservation of order would be destroyed, and the Company would have to raise a substantial force of its own. If he failed and the Germans withdrew, the British Company would have to fight the coast people who would seek to oust it as well.[4] In neither instance was the British government prepared to offer material support despite the fact that the turmoil was created in large part by Anglo-German policy.

Judged from this perspective, criticisms of the Company by officials in Whitehall and Zanzibar for its inability to establish a thriving administration in the first few months of its existence

[1] Note by Anderson, 28 January 1889, on telegram, Euan Smith to Salisbury, 25 January 1889, F.O. 84/1984. P.R.O.
[2] Note by Anderson, n.d., on Mackinnon to Pauncefote, 11 February 1889, F.O. 84/1988, P.R.O.
[3] Treasury to F.O., 28 August 1889, F.O. 84/2002, P.R.O.
[4] Euan Smith to Salisbury, 5 March 1889, A/79, Salisbury Papers.

might seem unfair. But officials did not view it thus. They saw only that the company had not asserted its authority at Mombasa by establishing its own customs administration to replace that of the Sultan and that it had not proceeded as rapidly as they had hoped to open up commercial routes to the interior and along the coast. Mackinnon protested that it was unreasonable to expect the Company within a few months after its chartering to carry out all the projects which impatient local government officials desired, and that caution was necessary, particularly in view of the uncertainties created by governmental decisions, past and prospective. But he admitted that delay in appointment of a permanent administrator had contributed to inaction. When Stanley decided not to accept Mackinnon's offer, the directors began the search for an alternate. The qualifications they laid down were, in addition to the usual attributes of a competent administrator, 'a practical knowledge of handling and governing orientals', and they believed that only a person with experience in India could qualify. They first approached Colonel Kenneth Mackenzie, who had spent many years as an administrator in Hyderabad,[1] but he declined. No other paragons with the requisite experience were receptive to dealing with the 'Orientals' of east Africa and the board was forced again to call on George Mackenzie for temporary duty.

During the months Mackenzie had been away, little progress had been made in the development of an effective east African administration since Buchanan had not been inclined to take any initiative in his capacity as an acting administrator, and what efforts he had made had been largely frustrated. The Company had attempted to hire for its police force the Sultan's Persian Guards who had been involved in an abortive mutiny, but this application had been rejected by acting consul general Gerald Portal because the Sultan might resent the transfer.[2] Approximately 100 Indians were recruited for the Company's military service, but there were complications over pensions from the Indian government which some of them would forfeit.[3] Then, the Company sought permission from the Colonial Office to recruit several hundred Zulus as policemen-soldiers on the assumption that their vaunted military qualities would make them effective not only to overawe the coast people but to deal with the Arabs in

[1] Mackinnon to F.O., 8 August 1889, F.O. 84/2000, P.R.O.
[2] Telegram, Portal to Salisbury, 23 July 1889, F.O. 84/1984, P.R.O.
[3] Mackenzie to Salisbury, 17 July 1889, F.O. 84/1999, P.R.O.

Buganda should conditions make it necessary.[1] The Foreign Office thought the idea excellent but the project was quashed by the Governor of Natal who suggested subtly that neither Company nor Foreign Office knew their Zulus, that no warriors would leave without their wives and that they would not be effective in a foreign environment.[2] The problem of recruitment of a police force was not resolved until the middle of 1890, and then after months of frustrating negotiations with Sir Evelyn Baring in an effort to employ Sudanese. Despite the fact that the German government had been permitted to recruit soldiers in the Sudan for Wissman, Baring refused to grant similar authority to the British East Africa Company. Only after strong representations from Mackinnon against a policy which seemed to classify a British company but not Germany as a foreign state did the British government press Baring to reverse his decision, the Egyptian government consequently allowed the recruitment of 200 soldiers.[3]

The incident of the Sudanese soldiers was illustrative of the deference to German wishes which characterized Salisbury's policy and which had led the British government to participate in the blockade of the Zanzibar coast. Mackenzie arrived in Zanzibar as the blockade was drawing to a close. It had been ineffective both with regard to its avowed purpose of restricting the slave trade and its actual object of denying supplies to the insurrection on the mainland, and it had been expensive. But eventually Abushiri's forces were crushed, and he was caught and hanged in December 1889. The rising had been costly to Germany not only in expenditures but in the disorganization of plans for the exploitation of the German sphere. The revenue collected in the German zone between August 1888 and August 1889 was only about one quarter of the annual returns during the last years of Zanzibari administration.[4] In contrast, customs duties in the British zone rose fifty per cent. The contrast reflected the disruption of the German area more than the prosperity of the British, for the amount of revenue accruing to the British company was small. Collections had been only about \$32,000 to \$35,000 (£7,000 to £7,700) in Barghash's day, and had risen to a little over \$50,000 under Company administration. But the Company was committed

---

[1] Note by P. Currie, 28 November 1889, F.O. 84/2007, P.R.O.
[2] C.O. to F.O., 18 December 1889, F.O. 84/2009, P.R.O.
[3] McDermott, *British East Africa*, pp. 154–5.
[4] Portal to Salisbury, 21 October 1889, F.O. 84/1981, P.R.O.

to pay the Sultan $56,000 a year and had to pay the entire cost of administration as well.[1] Clearly there must be a sizeable increase in revenue if the Company were to survive, but such an increase could not come from the coastal zone. In addition to limitations imposed on import dues by convention, the Company found it impossible to levy other taxes – on the coast largely because of legal problems and in the interior by the absence of a money economy and by the lack of sufficient power to collect tribute. There was little prospect for profit in trade on the coast in competition with Arab, Swahili, and Indian merchants who were more knowledgeable and more efficient than the Company's representatives, and the Company made little effort to do so. The concentration of the Company's European employees was on the customs administration and on the organization of caravans into the interior. The personnel whom the Company employed in these roles were usually drawn from the British Isles, in particular from Scotland, and few had had any previous experience in Africa. What little business background they brought with them was acquired in the British Isles, and they acquired their knowledge of African conditions in the most painful way – by experience. In the learning process, they frequently failed to document the Scottish national reputation for business acumen. Many of the Company's 'raw Scots lads' who were the object of ridicule in time demonstrated great ability and reached positions of distinction in the British service.[2] The period of apprenticeship, however, was at Company expense.

The deficiencies of the Company's employees should not be overstated; with the best of personnel it probably could not have succeeded for in addition to all the encumbrances laid upon it by governments was the basic fact that there was no commodity in east Africa from which it could derive quick profits to offset its heavy capital expenses, aside from the ivory trade of the interior. The potentialities of the Company area of activity largely lay in agricultural development which would be a slow process and which could occur only after transportation facilities were established to bring the farmers to the land. There was no gold to be mined, no palm oil to provide quick profits. Even the ivory trade of the Lakes area on which the Company reposed high hopes could not realize rich returns so long as it depended on human porterage,

---

[1] Euan Smith to Salisbury, 23 December 1889, F.O. 84/1922, P.R.O.
[2] Oliver and Mathew, *History of East Africa*, p. 410.

which was not only expensive but slow. The average time required for a caravan to march from Mombasa to Buganda was about three months.[1] A railway was an obvious necessity, the directors recognized, but a prodigious investment of capital was necessary and before construction could begin detailed knowledge was required of routes and costs.[2] In the meantime the Company had to carry on its commerce in the traditional manner. To promote both commerce and exploration, and to thwart any political threat from Germany the Company resolved to send another expedition to Buganda, and the choice fell on Frederick Lugard. The appointment would have fateful consequences for Lugard and for the British Empire.

[1] *Ibid.*

[2] The directors in October 1889 considered a portable railroad, the De Canville system, 'but decided it was not stable enough for the requirements of East Africa'. Kemball to Mackinnon, 2 October 1889, Mackinnon Papers.

7

The Anglo-German treaty and its aftermath

The early experience of the British and the German governments with their chartered companies in east Africa had been disheartening. The German company died in the convulsions of the Abushiri rising; the British lived on, but with a lack of vitality which dismayed government officials in Zanzibar and Whitehall. The German company had been intended to bring glory to the Empire and profits to itself; it achieved neither. The British company had been conceived as a means of representing British strategic interests and the advancement of commerce; in both respects it seemed to be accomplishing little.

The political and economic significance of east Africa in the late 1880s and 1890s was not on the coast but in the Lakes area and particularly in the Kingdom of Buganda. From the time of John Hanning Speke's visit in 1862 Buganda had fascinated many Britons. King Mutesa had been described in a traveller's accounts as a ruler of rare enlightenment with a great desire to 'improve' his country and himself by the adoption of European ways. He had, it was true, been converted to Islam[1] but on learning from Englishmen of the truths of Christianity had professed a desire to have missionaries sent to his country. Through Stanley this wish was communicated to the Church Missionary Society which sent its first mission to Buganda in 1878. Mutesa's concern was not with the respective truths of Islam and Christianity; the first missionaries found him much more interested in learning of the power of Britain and in promoting an alliance. His secular ambitions were made manifest by his dispatch of a mission to Britain to talk to the government and observe the wonders of technology. Mutesa indeed was a disappointment to the missionary society. After

[1] There has been a dispute among historians as to whether he was an actual convert. Among those who assert that he was not is Sir John Gray, 'Mutesa of Buganda', *Uganda Journal* I, 1 (1934), 1–49. But arguing that he was, is M.S.M. Kiwanuka, *Muteesa of Uganda* (Nairobi, 1967), pp. 28–30.

acknowledging his acceptance of Christianity, he had relapsed. When he became ill in 1879 he acted on the advice of his non-Christian advisers and had hundreds of people killed as a sacrifice for his recovery. 'Mutesa,' wrote Alexander Mackay, 'is a pagan – a heathen – out and out.'[1] This setback, however, did not cause the missionaries to withdraw or the government to lose interest in promoting closer relations with Buganda.

This interest continued despite the persecution of the missionaries by Mutesa's successor Mwanga, the murder of Bishop Hannington, and the turmoil surrounding Mwanga as various factions under the banners of Islam, Protestantism, and Catholicism sought to control the throne. But to the board of the British East Africa Company and to missionary groups, Buganda was still the 'pearl of Africa' which must be British. To Mackinnon and his co-promoters the establishment of a secure trade with Buganda was essential to the prosperity of the Company. To Mackinnon, the possession of this kingdom and its adjacent territories was essential also to the realization of his plans for joint control with Rhodes and the South Africa Company for a vast empire reaching from the Zambesi to the Upper Nile. To the agents of the Church Missionary Society it was a prize of great value to be won in the battle with Catholicism and Islam, and it must be British to be Protestant. To others not concerned with commerce or conversion, Buganda, its neighbor Bunyoro, and the Great Lakes were invested with an aura of mystery, associated with the quest for the sources of the Nile.

As the key to the Upper Nile, Buganda also had great significance to the British government. By 1890 Salisbury's previous indifference had disappeared. He had decided that Britain would remain in Egypt for the foreseeable future, and the possession of Egypt involved the corollary that no other great European power should control the Upper Nile.[2] In 1890 the only threat seemed to come from the German sphere in east Africa, though not, he thought, from governmental initiative. Salisbury did not doubt that Bismarck was sincere in his professions of disinterest in further adventures in the interior of east Africa. But less certain was the government's ability to control those ardent spirits in the German

[1] Oliver, *The Missionary Factor in East Africa*, p. 77.
[2] Robinson and Gallagher, *Africa and the Victorians*, p. 290; G. N. Sanderson, 'England, Italy, the Nile Valley, and the European Balance', *Historical Journal* VII, I (1964), 94–119.

society such as Carl Peters who by their actions might create a situation in which the government would feel itself compelled to support them. The Foreign Office heard from Berlin that the Colonization Society was intent on throttling British enterprise and that Carl Peters was to be the instrument. The plan was to hem in the British sphere on all sides by asserting German sovereignty to the north between the Tana and the Juba and then gaining control over Buganda and the region between the Lakes and the Congo Free State. From the Upper Nile, an expedition would sweep north of the Congo State to the Cameroons, thus establishing a German zone from the Indian Ocean to the Atlantic. The plan was so ambitious as to border on the fantastic, but the Foreign Office had no doubt of the intent. If Peters carried out his mission, perhaps Bismarck's professed distaste might turn to support as it had on an earlier occasion.[1]

Euan Smith had been Salisbury's personal choice to succeed Kirk and Holmwood, whose unadaptability to the Anglo-German concordat had required that they be replaced. But by the end of 1889 Euan Smith had begun to manifest the same suspicions of German intentions as his predecessors. At the beginning of January 1890 he heard from Vohsen, now a director of the moribund German East Africa Company, that there was a plan to amalgamate that company with the Witu Company. This union, in conjunction with the recently announced German protectorate on the coastline from Kipini to Kismayu, would place the Germans in a strong position to carry out an enveloping movement from the north and south of the British sphere to shut off the British company from Buganda and the Lakes. Euan Smith had no doubt that this opportunity would be exploited and that this action would have at least the covert support of the government. These reports coincided with the intelligence that Peters, whose expedition had been reported massacred, was in fact not only alive but actively prosecuting some sinister objectives in the interior. The consul general suspected that these false reports had been a cover for ulterior German plans.[2] Euan Smith could not know that Peters, acting on information from purloined letters, was en route to Buganda in February 1890, but his discussions with Vohsen and with Wissman convinced him that a large project was afoot.

---

[1] This story is told in a confidential memorandum by Anderson, 10 September 1892, printed for use of cabinet, 13 September 1892, F.O. 84/2258, P.R.O.
[2] Euan Smith to Salisbury, private, 28 January 1890, A/80, Salisbury Papers.

This conviction was strengthened by a conversation with Emin Pasha in mid-March. In the months since his meeting with Stanley, the fortunes of Emin had plummeted. Stanley's contemptuous references to him had embittered him, and he had accepted an offer of Wissman to join the German service. His loyalty to his new employers was not complete, however, for he communicated to Euan Smith – in strictest confidence, he requested – Wissman's plans to send an expedition to the south end of Victoria Nyanza with Buganda as its ultimate destination. There they would receive a welcome from the French missionaries, who detested the British, and the alliance could establish German ascendancy in Buganda. On orders from Berlin the expedition was suspended,[1] but the threat remained that it could be reactivated.

Suspicion was not directed only one way. From the German viewpoint the actions and statements of representatives of the British East Africa Company were not in accordance with the friendly professions of the home government. In particular, letters from Mackinnon and his agent W. J. Nicol addressed to Stanley, which were found when Abushiri was captured, indicated an acute hostility to Germany and a plan to shut off the Germans from the interior just as Euan Smith suspected the Germans intended to shut off the British.[2]

Adding to the unsettled state of affairs was the death of Sultan Khalifa in February 1890. His successor Seyyid Ali who was installed without opposition, however, was an old man in poor health. The identity of the next sultan was of considerable importance, and among the possibilities was the son of Barghash's sister, Madame Reute, who had married a German. The young man was an officer in the German army.[3]

The reaction at Whitehall to this combination of rumors and events was that action must be taken to come to a settlement with Germany which would put an end to the disruptive actions of private individuals. But pending such an agreement, it was imperative that the British company move to checkmate the Germans in the interior. Euan Smith heard at the beginning of March that Mwanga had regained his throne with the help of some Europeans – Belgians, it was reported – and that the Kabaka had

---

[1] Euan Smith to Salisbury, secret, 18 March 1890, F.O. 84/2060, P.R.O.
[2] F.O. to Euan Smith, 18 February 1890, F.O. 244/470; Salisbury to Malet, secret, 6 May 1890, F.O. 244/471, both in P.R.O.
[3] Portal to Barrington, 25 March 1890, F.O. 84/2077, P.R.O.

M

dispatched two emissaries to Zanzibar. Here was a great opportunity to establish British influence in Uganda, stated Anderson.[1] The East Africa Company must act to secure Uganda[2] for itself and for Britain.

In the judgment of Euan Smith, with which Salisbury agreed, the Company was a poor instrument to perform this function. Mackenzie, who continued as acting administrator, was an able man, but his administration had the weakness attached to temporary rule, and he had few qualified assistants. Furthermore, the resources made available to him were pathetically small. Euan Smith estimated that for every rupee Mackenzie spent, the Germans spent 2,000 – the consul did not mention that the sources of the one were private and of the other governmental. The only way the Company could check the Germans, he suggested, was for it at whatever cost and without delay to build a railway to Lake Victoria. 'Money, energy, determination and knowledge are the principal desiderata to effect these aims.' With the great interest of the British people in east Africa there should be no difficulty in Mackinnon's raising the money, particularly with Stanley's eloquence at his disposal. If the East Africa Company were so lethargic as not to act immediately, he suggested that perhaps the Company should be asked to step aside and let other, more energetic, imperialists undertake the task. In particular, Cecil Rhodes seemed a likely choice. He and his associates in the British South Africa Company were opening up a rail route from the south into the heart of Africa, and Euan Smith had no doubt that Rhodes would eagerly accept the responsibility of saving the Lakes area by driving a line to Uganda from Mombasa.[3] With the daring which irresponsibility made possible, the consul ignored the vast differences in the problems of financing a line from the settlements of south Africa to a reputedly rich gold area and those in an area which possessed little in resources that could be immediately exploited. He also with no evident embarrassment contrasted the vigor of agents financed by the German government with the feeble efforts of an unsubsidized private company.

Euan Smith's eagerness for Mackinnon to invest his and other private investors' money in a railroad which would serve a political at least as much as a commercial purpose is an impressive com-

[1] Note on Euan Smith to Salisbury, 3 March 1890, F.O. 84/2060, P.R.O.
[2] Anderson had in mind not only Buganda but the surrounding territories.
[3] Euan Smith to Salisbury, private, 31 March 1890, A/80, Salisbury Papers.

mentary on the official mind. But beyond the effrontery of his proposal was its impracticality. Surveys and construction of a railway would take years at best; the threat which he sought to counter was immediate. Furthermore, no private company would compete with the government of Germany in providing resources, and the British government would not and could not enter the race itself. As W. H. Sanderson of the Foreign Office acknowledged after reading one of Euan Smith's panicky appeals, no government could ask Parliament for money to send out a British Major Wissman to the Lakes to take and hold the country. If the German government really was intent on gaining control of the Lakes at the expense of alienating Britain it could not be prevented by any initiative in east Africa. Sanderson pessimistically predicted that Uganda and the Lakes would fall to Germany. There would be an outcry from the missionaries, but there was nothing that Britain could do.[1]

Sanderson was overly gloomy. There was much which could be done in Berlin and London, and the German government was not committed to a course of expansion into Uganda. The government which controlled Germany after the downfall of Bismarck was committed to a policy of wooing Britain, not humiliating it, and the relations between the two states between 1889 and 1891 were cordial – 'the honeymoon of the flirtation between Britain and the Triple Alliance'.[2] They sought an accommodation which would be presented to the German public as a diplomatic victory but which would not embarrass the Salisbury government. Consequently they kept Wissman on a rein.

This relaxed relationship between London and Berlin made the crisis less acute than Euan Smith imagined, but the directors of the company tried to respond to the urgency he and other officials had communicated. They decided to send a well-equipped caravan to Uganda with the object of negotiating treaties with the Kabaka and other African chiefs which would acknowledge British supremacy. Frederick Lugard was selected as the leader of the expedition.

To the time of his appointment, Lugard had experienced a series of rebuffs which could have destroyed the spirit of a lesser man.

[1] Note by Sanderson, 2 April [1890], on telegram, Euan Smith to Salisbury, private, 1 April 1890, A/80, Salisbury Papers.
[2] W. Hermann, *Dreibund, Zweibund, England* (Stuttgart, 1929), p. 25, quoted by C. J. Lowe, *The Reluctant Imperialists* (2 vols., London, 1967), I, 155.

After near-tragedy in his disillusionment with a fickle love he had sought service in Africa, first with the African Lakes Company and then with Rhodes' South Africa Company. His months of service with the Lakes Company ended with mutual recriminations, and his negotiations with the South Africa Company broke down with what Lugard considered to be a repudiation by Rhodes of a promise of employment.[1] While he was in this depressed state he was rescued by Horace Waller who had been his firm friend and admirer during his difficult times in the Nyasa country, and by Kirk. Through these two, Lugard's qualifications were brought to the attention of the board, though the precise role he would play in the company's operations was not clear.[2] He proceeded to Africa with George Mackenzie in November 1889 on a ship on which Euan Smith was a fellow passenger, returning to his consul generalship. During this voyage the three frequently discussed the importance of action to secure Uganda, and Mackenzie concluded that Lugard with his experience in transport and the command of men would be an excellent choice to take charge of the first caravan.[3]

Again the East Africa Company displayed the indecisiveness which constantly irritated the Foreign Office, and again the hesitation was for reasons which to the directors were substantial. First, at the time of Lugard's arrival Stanley's status remained in doubt, for Mackinnon's offer to him of the management in east Africa remained open, and there was a possibility that he himself might lead the Uganda expedition. When Stanley removed himself from consideration and went off to Egypt to write his book on the relief expedition he gave advice to Mackinnon which contributed to further hesitation. He indicated that to assure control of Buganda a formidable expedition would be required involving not less than 500 white men with 2,000 porters, and an expenditure of not less than £100,000. Furthermore, he believed that such an undertaking was not desirable until a railway was constructed.[4] Such advice from a giant of African exploration was enough to deter any board of directors, however energetic, for if Stanley's estimates were correct the cost of occupying and controlling Buganda was beyond the resources of the Company.

[1] For details, see Perham, *Lugard: the Years of Adventure.*
[2] *Ibid.* p. 168.
[3] Alexander to F.O., 3 January 1890, F.O. 84/2072, P.R.O.
[4] Stanley to Mackinnon, 6 February 1890, Mackinnon Papers.

While the directors contemplated their course of action, Lugard at Mackenzie's behest made a preliminary reconnoitering expedition through the Taru desert as far as the Sabaki river. During this journey he received two urgent letters from Mackenzie informing him that great events were impending in Buganda which necessitated a drastic change in plans. Lugard must immediately strike westward to Buganda.

The news which had caused Mackenzie such excitement was in part true, in part obsolete, in part exaggerated, and in part false, but Mackenzie knew that there had been a rising in Buganda which had unseated Mwanga and that the Kabaka had in vain asked for help from Jackson. He had also heard that Mwanga had been restored with the help of the Christian parties. Mackenzie also was keenly aware that Peters was somewhere in the interior – he had been last reported in the Kavirondo country near Lake Victoria, and Peters was just the man to capitalize on the unstable state of Buganda. Furthermore Wissman, it was rumored, was ready to drive toward Buganda to annex it for Germany.[1] This was essentially the same intelligence which had caused Euan Smith such alarm. Indeed, the consul general was the principal source on whom Mackenzie depended. The Foreign Office, also responding to this information at the same time as Mackenzie was writing to Lugard, had asked the Company to state immediately what steps it proposed to take. Mwanga in his present state of insecurity might accept the overtures of the first white men to arrive with offers of support.[2] These importunities of the Foreign Office were irritating to the directors. Kirk observed that what the government was asking was for the Company to contend against the German Empire, with neither material nor moral support from Whitehall. Without some guarantees from the government, the Company was almost certain to end in ruin. Reason dictated that rather than accept that prospect, it ask the government to assume responsibility itself.[3] Mackinnon, acting on Kirk's advice, asked Salisbury for some assurances that the government had no secret understanding with Germany which would embarrass the Company and would support the Company if it negotiated a treaty with Mwanga. Given such stipulations, Mackinnon promised rapid action;

[1] Perham, *Lugard: the Years of Adventure*, pp. 179–80.
[2] F.O. to I.B.E.A., immediate, 2 April 1890, F.O. 84/2078, P.R.O.
[3] Kirk to Mackinnon, 6 April 1890, Mackinnon Papers

without them, he warned, the Company could not challenge Germany:

In all directions we are overborne by German officials and startled by new German plans, and I feel so disheartened by the apparent luke-warmness of the support which we receive from H.M.G. in the work we have been trying to do for our country that I begin to realize that the prospects of usefulness which encouraged us to undertake the work are so rapidly disappearing that I feel great difficulty as to our plans for the future.[1]

Salisbury declined to make any commitment. The only response of the Foreign Office was to inform the Company that the German government had given an assurance that no expedition was contemplated and that Germany had no intention to interfere in the 'hinterland' of the British sphere of influence.[2] The Company decided to proceed.

Again there was delay, and again for good reason. Instead of responding to Mackenzie's appeal and making a dash for Buganda, Lugard decided that he must return to Mombasa. He was suffering from an old wound and his caravan was depleted and the men unwilling to set out on an arduous journey for which they had not been originally employed. If he had been so rash as to make the attempt under these circumstances his gamble would likely have ended in failure, perhaps in death, and he acted with prudence in deciding against following orders. He arrived in Mombasa on 11 May 1890, almost one month after he had received Mackenzie's letter.[3] More time had been lost; if the German menace had been as Euan Smith imagined it, the issue would have been settled.

As it was, the Company was able without immediate penalty to indulge in the luxury of confused counsels and divided authority. Mackenzie continued to have confidence in Lugard and desired that he should lead the Uganda expedition as soon as he was able. The directors agreed, but on terms which Lugard would find unacceptable. Mackenzie's second term as acting administrator had been extended beyond the original expectation and the board appointed as his successor another director, Sir Francis de Winton. De Winton's record was impressive. He had served in a variety of important posts, including that of Administrator of the Congo, and he seemed to be a man with the requisite qualities of

---

[1] Mackinnon to Salisbury, 8 April 1890, Mackinnon Papers.
[2] F.O. to I.B.E.A., 9 April 1890, F.O. 84/2078, P.R.O.
[3] Perham, *Lugard: the Years of Adventure*, pp. 182–3.

leadership for whom the Company had been seeking. But the directors had decided, apparently at de Winton's own behest, that he must assume as one of his first responsibilities the overall command of the Uganda expedition. Lugard should set out with an advance party, but the main caravan would follow with de Winton in command, and when the larger body overtook Lugard's party, de Winton would be in charge of the combined expedition. The result was a bitter quarrel between de Winton and Lugard, during which more precious time elapsed. Lugard finally agreed to the directors' original plan and set out with the advance party for Lake Victoria, there to await the arrival of de Winton. In the meantime, the directors had changed their minds again. They had been impressed with Lugard's Sabaki report, and decided that he should take sole command and that de Winton should remain on the coast. They telegraphed de Winton to this effect at the end of June, but he decided not to obey the instructions. The eventual outcome was that de Winton was peremptorily instructed in November to follow the orders he had received in June.[1] Lugard had won; the price was the humiliation of the chief administrator. The failure of de Winton may have been in part personal. Euan Smith thought him unequal to the great responsibilities assigned him. He was, the consul general maintained, lacking in vigor, perhaps because of his age (55 at the time!), and he was too humane and well-meaning for a job which required an iron will and a touch of ruthlessness.[2] But this assessment may be more revealing of Euan Smith than of de Winton. The consul general had often expressed his admiration for Germanic efficiency and contrasted the drive of von Wissman with the passivity of his British counterparts. His judgments on de Winton certainly reflected at least in part his own stereotypes of effectiveness. De Winton was also fated to be associated with Lugard, whose admirers heightened his achievements by contrasts with the allegedly bumbling de Winton. But, most important, de Winton was the victim of confusion and indecisiveness in the Company's ruling board. The institutional weaknesses of the Company were translated into the personal deficiences of the chief administrator.

The Company in turn has been faulted for a lack of decisiveness when in fact the causes of uncertainty were in large part related to the attributes of the government rather than to those of the

[1] The story of this quarrel is told in Perham, *Lugard*, pp. 183–91.
Ibid. p. 188.

Company. Salisbury communicated little of his strategy and tactics even to his subordinates; to the Company he conducted relations almost as with a foreign power; what little he communicated was couched in language which offered no firm guarantees. The directors of the Company were left with the uneasy feeling that they were being used and that the Company to Salisbury was an instrument of high policy which was expendable whenever 'higher interests' might dictate. This fear was certainly a deterrent to decisive action with massive commitment of capital. Mackinnon found a sympathetic audience in Victoria and other members of the royal family. The Queen was captivated by the heroic deeds of the explorers and by the noble objects of Mackinnon, Stanley, and Rhodes in such glittering contrast to the small-mindedness and timidity so characteristic of Whitehall. After a dinner party attended in early May by Mackinnon and Stanley, as well as Salisbury, she gushed in her diary of the inspiration she had received from an evening with great souls.[1] Three weeks before, Mackinnon had written to her private secretary, Sir Henry Ponsonby, of his despondency over the government's treatment of the Company:

I have felt discouraged and disheartened by the passive and evasive attitude of our Foreign Office. They inform us of the opportunity presented by the revolution in Uganda and of the aggressive activity of Germany and ask what we propose to do in the circumstances. But when we in reply ask whether they will support us if we succeed in making treaty arrangements with the ruler of Uganda before the proposed Wissman–Emin expedition arrives, or whether there is any private arrangement with Germany which would render our efforts unavailing the answer is too vague to be reassuring.[2]

Mackinnon assured Ponsonby that the Company would continue its efforts to save as much of east Africa as possible for Britain even without government support. But, he asserted, the prospects were discouraging. Mackinnon's suspicion of Salisbury and the failure of government to provide clear guide-lines were undoubtedly a factor in Mackinnon's decision to carry out a high policy of his own. He had already tasted the excitement of diplomatic negotiations; his associations with Leopold and with Rhodes whetted his appetite. Mackinnon wanted assurance of a continuous strip of British-controlled territory from the Cape to

---

[1] Buckle, *Victoria*, I, 601–2.
[2] Mackinnon to Ponsonby, 14 April 1890, in *ibid.* pp. 595–6.

Cairo, which would enable the East Africa and South Africa Companies to link up, and he feared that Salisbury would allow the Germans to break the communication by accepting the extension of the German sphere to the Congo Free State. An agreement with Leopold for the lease of a strip through the Congo Free State might forestall such a danger.[1] He found in Leopold an eager collaborator; the Belgian King had not forgotten the dream of a foothold on the Upper Nile and was happy to participate in a negotiation which might help him to achieve it. In these ambitions they were, remarkably, encouraged by Salisbury himself.

Precisely when the scheme of a Leopold–Mackinnon treaty was first considered is not clear. Stanley believed that it emerged from discussions which he had had with Mackinnon in April 1890, which were followed by conferences with Leopold in Brussels.[2] This fitted the facts as Stanley saw them, for at the time Mackinnon met Stanley in Cannes, he was brooding about Salisbury's refusal to grant him an interview and the possible meaning of this aloofness.[3] Mackinnon's state of mind, however, was not the only consideration. Another interested party was the British South Africa Company. In the spring of 1890, the ambitions of Cecil Rhodes were at high tide. He hoped to seize access to the Indian Ocean from the weak control of Portugal, and he expected to extend the Company's influence through the Nyasa country northward to a junction with the East Africa Company. The South Africa Company was drawn into negotiations with Leopold primarily because it coveted the rich prize of Katanga and was unsure it could wrest the copper region from Leopold's grasp. Rhodes hoped to capitalize on the uncertainties of the Congo State's south-eastern boundaries to negotiate a treaty with Msiri, who had established his dominance in the area,[4] attaching him to the South Africa Company. Rhodes, with that irresponsible aggressiveness which he was displaying at the same time toward the Portuguese, was confident of success, but his associates in London were less sanguine. Cawston, who was not only a financier but a map maker, was convinced that Msiri's kingdom was within the Congo's boundaries and without waiting for Rhodes' agreement he proceeded to Brussels at the beginning of February to test the

---

[1] Anstey, *Britain and the Congo*, p. 227.
[2] Stanley, *Autobiography*, pp. 412–13.
[3] Mackinnon to Salisbury, 8 April 1890, E, Salisbury Papers.
[4] See A. Verbeken, *Msiri Roi de Garenganze* (Brussels, 1956).

possibilities of an alternative means of acquiring Katanga. He knew that Leopold was laboring under the heavy expenditures imposed by the Congo. Perhaps the King would be willing to sell his rights in Katanga or if he could not do so without violating his treaty with France, giving it the right of reversion, he might rent the area for a percentage of the profits.[1]

Urgency was given to Cawston's visit by the fear that if the future of Katanga remained unsettled, Germany might intervene to shut out the South Africa Company. While Rhodes was in London during the summer of 1889 awaiting the grant of a charter for the new company he, Cawston, and Kirk discussed plans for a railway to the north, which Kirk thought should proceed across the Zambesi at Wankie, just below Victoria Falls and thence to Ujiji on the eastern side of Lake Tanganyika. The line would either pass through or near the copper area. This plan was threatened by the reported intention of Germany to build a railway to the Congo with the object of acquiring control over Katanga.[2]

By early 1890 the nervousness of the South Africa Company directors about German intentions had not abated; indeed they had been intensified by remarks which Salisbury had carelessly or deliberately let drop in conversations with the Duke of Abercorn.[3] Mackinnon, perhaps stimulated by Kirk, who was the link between the two companies, was also exercised, and he and Cawston by the beginning of March 1890 had developed a plan to thwart the German menace by negotiating parallel agreements with Leopold. When Leopold visited London on 29 March 1890, Cawston presented him with a draft convention which would give the British South Africa Company a right of way for a railway west of Lake Tanganyika in exchange for an agreement by the Company to recognize a boundary favorable to the Free State and other concessions, including the right of the Free State to construct a railway through Company territory.[4] These discussions were held with the knowledge of the Foreign Office and with its implied approval.[5] Mackinnon in his negotiations with Leopold acted in concert with Cawston.

[1] Cawston to Rhodes, 6 February 1890, BSAC Misc. ii, Rhodes House.
[2] *Ibid.*
[3] Abercorn to Cawston, 11 March 1890, BSAC Misc. ii, Rhodes House.
[4] Report by Cawston on interview with Leopold, 24 April 1890, F.O. 84/2081, P.R.O.
[5] Notes on *ibid.*, by staff of the F.O.

As the negotiations began, the nature of the problem shifted. Mackinnon and Cawston heard by the beginning of April that an effort would be made by Salisbury to settle the Anglo-German boundary. They received this news with no sense of relief. Salisbury had previously appeased Germany by the sacrifice of east African interests; he might do so again, and the price on this occasion might be the severance of the all-British route to the north.[1] Cawston and Mackinnon therefore intensified their efforts to make an arrangement with Leopold. Mackinnon sought both to strengthen the British case against German pretensions and to provide insurance in the form of a route through the Free State. In support of the first, he submitted to the Foreign Office the treaties which Stanley asserted he had made with the chiefs in the country west of Lake Victoria.[2] Also, he enlisted the support of the Church Missionary Society to secure a declaration from Salisbury that all of Uganda, 'including its tributaries', was within the British sphere and that this status was not subject to negotiation.[3] Meanwhile, he continued his discussions with Leopold. By 14 May he was able to report to Salisbury that an agreement with Leopold giving the Company access to Lake Tanganyika was impending, and several days later Leopold presented to the Foreign Secretary the draft of an agreement for approval. Salisbury noted that the document 'should be copied and returned with our approval to the King'.[4] The official communication from Salisbury to Leopold followed this instruction. The King was informed that the Foreign Office would have no objection to the arrangements which Mackinnon and Leopold had reached.[5] The agreement provided that the Free State and the East Africa Company would recognize a line between their respective spheres running from Lake Albert up the Semliki River to Lake Edward, and from there to the northern end of Lake Tanganyika. The Company agreed to recognize the sovereign rights of the Congo Free State over the left bank of the Nile as far as Lado and Leopold recognized the sovereignty of the Company over a

[1] Abercorn to Cawston, 5 April 1890, BSAC Misc. II, Rhodes House.
[2] Vincent to F.O., 2 May 1890, F.O. 84/2081, P.R.O. These treaties, Stanley had said to Mackinnon, were only verbal; Stanley to Mackinnon, 6 February 1890, Mackinnon Papers. Consequently, the documents presented to the government could hardly have been copies of the originals, and were worthless. Perham, *Lugard: the Years of Adventure*, p. 259.
[3] Hutchinson to Mackinnon, 19 May 1890, Mackinnon Papers.
[4] Note, Salisbury, 19 May 1890, F.O. 84/2082, P.R.O.
[5] Salisbury to Leopold, 21 May 1890, F.O. 84/2082, P.R.O.

five-mile strip within the Free State between Lake Tanganyika and Lake Edward.[1]

Salisbury's approval of the agreement was an illustration of the hazards of personal diplomacy. The intent of the understanding was in accordance with his objective of safeguarding the British interest without antagonizing Germany, but in his preoccupation with Anglo-German relations, he had neglected to take into consideration an agreement in 1884 by which France had acquired the right of preemption if the Free State gave up any part of its territory. His principal advisor on African affairs, Sir Percy Anderson, had been absent in Berlin conducting preliminary negotiations when Salisbury had given his approval, and on his return pointed out that the Mackinnon agreement contravened the French–Free State Treaty and could cause serious complications with France. Consequently, he advised that the agreement would have to be modified to eliminate any reference to the East Africa Company's acquiring sovereignty over any part of the Free State.[2] Mackinnon was not willing to redraft the treaty, arguing that it was imperative that it be ratified immediately, but proposed that an annexure might be appended making it clear that no actual cession of territory was involved. Salisbury accepted this suggestion, and the Foreign Office drew up a document to this effect.[3] On the understanding that this arrangement was satisfactory, Mackinnon and Count de Lalaing on behalf of Leopold exchanged ratifications.[4]

Leopold II was never a man to miss an opportunity to extract concessions. Salisbury was obviously worried about the effect of the agreement on Anglo-French relations. Leopold, therefore, portrayed himself as motivated only by a desire to facilitate an entente between Britain and Germany. In his treaties with the two British companies, he had offered a route through the Free State as a means of breaking the deadlock in the Anglo-German boundary negotiations. The least Britain could do under these circumstances was to press the British South Africa Company to sign its agreement and to give prompt governmental blessing to that treaty.[5] Leopold's anxiety for an understanding with the South

---

[1] Agreement, Congo State and I.B.E.A., 24 May 1890, F.O. 84/2082, P.R.O.
[2] Robert O. Collins, 'Origins of the Nile Struggle', in Gifford and Louis, *Britain and Germany in Africa*, p. 143.
[3] Minute, Anderson, 4 June 1890, F.O. 84/2082, P.R.O.
[4] Mackinnon to Salisbury, 7 June 1890, F.O. 84/2083, P.R.O.
[5] Leopold to Salisbury, 22 June 1890, F.O. 84/2084, P.R.O.

Africa Company was based on a fear that the Company coveted Katanga and other areas which he claimed for the Free State; the Company's delay in accepting the boundary stipulated in the agreement was precisely for the reasons which produced Leopold's anxiety.[1] The Foreign Office was not inclined to put pressure on the South Africa Company, and consequently the decision was taken to approve the treaty between Leopold and Mackinnon without waiting for the conclusion of a settlement with the South Africa Company.[2]

The approval of the 'Mackinnon treaty' made it possible for Anglo-German boundary negotiations to be concluded without opposition from a man whom Salisbury had come to detest as an obsessive Germanophobe whose lack of energy had weakened the British bargaining position and whose rigidity against concessions to Germany could stimulate public opinion against an alleged sellout. At the beginning of the boundary negotiations, Salisbury wrote to Goschen, the Chancellor of the Exchequer:

The great difficulty here [in the East African problem] is the character of Mackinnon. . . He has none of the qualities for pushing an enterprise which depends on decision and smartness. He has got the finest harbour on the coast – has had it for five years – yet there is not even a jetty there. His hopes of trade depend on his enabling the caravans to get over a waterless belt of fifty miles which separate him from the profitable country. Yet, though he has had a mass of railway material there for a long time, he has not yet laid a yard of it. He has no energy for anything except quarrelling with Germans.[3]

Salisbury was hardly fair to Mackinnon – the suggestion that the key to a thriving trade was the construction of a mere fifty miles of railway indicated either ignorance or deliberate misrepresentation, probably the former. Salisbury in 1890 knew and cared little about east Africa: his concern was the preservation of the Upper Nile as a protection for the British position in Egypt and beyond that an

---

[1] Rhodes and the South Africa Company were anxious to make treaties which would bring Katanga within their sphere, and the Company and Leopold were involved in a race for control of this rich copper area. See Minutes by Anderson, 27 May 1891, F.O. 84/2166, P.R.O.

[2] Note by Salisbury n.d., on Leopold to Salisbury, 22 June 1890, F.O. 84/2084, P.R.O.

[3] Salisbury to Goschen, 10 April 1890 in Cecil, *Salisbury*, p. 281. 'Any terms we might get for him [Mackinnon] from the Germans by negotiation he would denounce as base truckling to the Emperor.' See also, W. Roger Louis, 'Great Britain and German Expansion in Africa, 1884–1919', in Gifford and Louis, *Britain and Germany in Africa*, p. 17.

agreement which would be as little harmful as possible to the government's position.[1] His German counterparts also had little interest in east Africa for itself, but even more than Salisbury, were under the compulsion to demonstrate their effectiveness as defenders of German interests and prestige. The master diplomat Bismarck had been deposed in March 1890, and his successors and the Emperor who had discharged him had to appear as champions at least as zealous as he, whatever their private judgments.

The relative strengths of the British and German positions and the essential objectives of the two powers have been the subject of debate. On the one hand it has been contended that Salisbury's sudden decision to offer Heligoland as a means of producing a comprehensive settlement had no relation to concern for Uganda and the Nile. These areas, it is argued, were beyond contest so far as Germany was concerned, and Salisbury's offer of Heligoland resulted from a fear for the British position in Zanzibar.[2] In rebuttal it has been pointed out that the object of the negotiations was the elimination of irritations not only in east Africa but throughout the continent, and that Salisbury continued to believe that Britain needed German friendship from bitter experience with the mischief which Bismarck had been able to do with regard to Egypt. The new government, further, might threaten the Upper Nile from the base of the German protectorates at Witu and in the Tana–Juba area.[3] Whichever interpretation is accepted, it is clear that Salisbury was intent on conciliating Mackinnon and Rhodes and their companies short of producing a rupture of the discussions with Germany. The most critical problem was the reconciliation of Rhodes' and Mackinnon's ambitions for a north-south communication through the Lakes area with the German insistence on the extension of their hinterland to the borders of the Congo Free State. After preliminary discussions between Anderson and Dr Krauel of the German Foreign Office on questions involving the two governments in west, south-west, and east Africa, Salisbury took personal charge of the negotiations in conferences at Hatfield with the German Ambassador, Count

[1] Cecil, *Salisbury*, p. 281.
[2] D. R. Gillard, 'Salisbury's African Policy and the Heligoland Offer of 1890', *English Historical Review*, October 1960, pp. 631–53.
[3] G. N. Sanderson, 'The Anglo-German Agreement of 1890 and the Upper Nile', *English Historical Review*, January 1963, pp. 49–72. Professor Gillard provided a rebuttal in 'Salisbury's Heligoland Offer: The Case Against the Witu Thesis', *English Historical Review*, July 1965, pp. 538–52.

Hatzfeldt.[1] From the beginning, the only serious issue in dispute regarding east Africa was the delimitation of the respective zones in the Lakes area;[2] Buganda and Bunyoro were tacitly accepted as being in the British sphere, though there was some concern that if the negotiations were unduly prolonged this understanding might be jeopardized. A thwarted Germany might find a powerful ally in the Roman Catholic missions which were known to be hostile to the establishment of British control in Buganda, and in Cardinal Lavigerie, the moving spirit behind the Brussels Anti-Slavery Conference which was in session at the time.[3] Lavigerie had been an embarrassment to Britain since he had first proposed an anti-slave-trade crusade in the summer of 1888, for his ideas were considered at best futile and likely to be mischievous. At the conference itself, the Cardinal's contribution was even more annoying to the British government, for he had been devoting his efforts to try to induce the conference to declare Uganda as outside the British sphere. This prospect of a Roman Catholic–German alliance contributed to Salisbury's desire for a speedy settlement.[4] Again the principal domestic irritation came from Mackinnon and the East Africa Company. The Foreign Office had given explicit instructions to the Company that Stanley's 'treaties' with the chiefs to the west of Lake Victoria should not be made public.[5] But at the very time that this admonition was given, Henry Morton Stanley was telling a mass audience at the Albert Hall of his great accomplishment during the Emin Pasha expedition in winning possession for Britain of the territories east of the Free State by the negotiation of these treaties. He confided to his listeners that he understood that the treaties had been deposited with the Foreign Office on behalf of the East Africa Company. The *Pall Mall Gazette* of 8 May appeared with the headline 'Central Africa for England. Stanley's Treaties with the Native Chiefs'.[6] Stanley followed up his Albert Hall revelations with similar speeches to other enthusiastic audiences, including the

[1] Hatzfeldt to Salisbury, personal, 3 May 1890, File G, Salisbury Papers. There is other correspondence in these papers regarding private conversations.

[2] Hatzfeldt to Caprivi, 29 April 1890, 30 April 1890, *Die Grosse Politik* VIII, 1675.

[3] For an account of the conference, see Suzanne Miers, 'The Brussels Conference of 1889–1890', in Gifford and Louis, *Britain and Germany in Africa*, pp. 83–118.

[4] There is considerable correspondence on this theme in F.O. 84/1927, P.R.O.

[5] F.O. to I.B.E.A., 8 May 1890, F.O. 84/2081, P.R.O.

[6] *Pall Mall Gazette*, 8 May 1890.

London Chamber of Commerce. Salisbury interpreted Stanley's advertisement of the treaties as a maneuver to embarrass the government in its efforts to settle its differences with Germany, and he suspected that Stanley had acted with the connivance of Mackinnon. His annoyance was manifest when he dictated an answer to a parliamentary question by James Bryce in which he emphasized that Stanley's 'engagements' had been made on his own behalf and without any authority from government.[1] Mackinnon denied that he had had advance knowledge of Stanley's campaign to enlist public opinion in support of the Company's ambitions and expressed regret to Salisbury that some of Stanley's remarks had been intemperate, but he reminded Salisbury that the explorer had no connection with the Company and spoke only for himself.[2] In these professions of innocence, Mackinnon was no doubt being technically honest, but he was certainly not displeased by Stanley's campaign which might forestall the sellout of British interests which he suspected was impending. In fact, negotiations at the time were stalemated because of Salisbury's strong advocacy of the claims of the two British companies.

After his initial indignation, the Foreign Secretary on reflection saw the opportunity to turn embarrassment to advantage. On 13 May he called Hatzfeldt to Hatfield to make a dramatic proposal for a final settlement. He lamented to the ambassador that Stanley's speeches were stirring up public opinion to a point that the government's life could be endangered. This approach was effective, for Hatzfeldt had himself become concerned about the outburst of 'colonial Chauvinism' in the press, and feared prolonged negotiations entailed greater risks. Consequently when Salisbury made a proposal for the settlement of all of the differences in East Africa, Hatzfeldt was receptive. Then Salisbury threw into the bargain the offer to transfer Heligoland to Germany, and a settlement suddenly seemed imminent. The German government for years had coveted this island because of its proximity to the Kiel Canal, and the prospect of acquiring it warranted substantial concessions in east Africa, though not as substantial as Salisbury proposed. His offer of 13 May embraced the following elements: the territory north-west of Lake Nyasa would be partitioned; south-west of Lake Victoria, the boundary would

---

[1] Note by Salisbury on question in Parliament, Mr Bryce, 9 May 1890, F.O. 84/2081, P.R.O.
[2] Mackinnon to Salisbury, 23 May 1890, File E, Salisbury Papers.

extend to the north end of Lake Tanganyika; Germany would renounce its protectorates over Witu and adjacent districts, Britain would acquire a protectorate over the island of Zanzibar in exchange for the transfer of Heligoland, and Britain would support permanent German control over the section of the coast acquired in the concession from the Sultan.[1]

The effect of Salisbury's boundary proposals would have been to interpose a British wedge between German East Africa and the Congo Free State and to establish the hoped-for link between the two British companies without the necessity of a corridor through the Free State. It would have meant, in effect, a virtual German surrender of east African claims in exchange for the cession of Heligoland, and this was too much for the German government to accept, though it much desired a settlement.[2]

The great prize for Germany was Heligoland. The Foreign Secretary, Adolph von Marschall, wrote that 'the possession of Heligoland is of supreme importance to us and is by far the most serious matter in the whole negotiation'. Chancellor Caprivi and the Emperor shared this judgment. They believed that without Heligoland the Kiel Canal would be useless to the German navy.[3] For that island much could be sacrificed. They attempted to cover their eagerness, but without success. Salisbury knew that they coveted the island, and his ambassador in Berlin gave him accurate information on the German state of mind.[4] He was, therefore, playing shrewdly on German fears when he suggested that the discussions be adjourned for perhaps five to ten years, since the prevailing public emotion in Britain and Germany was so strong as to make a satisfactory agreement difficult. East Africa, he told Hatzfeldt, was of great symbolic significance. It was the country of Livingstone, of great British explorers, and of devoted British missionary activity. Stanley and others had roused not only public opinion but even members of the government against even the appearance of surrender. East Africa in the Great Lakes area was like 'the El Dorado of the 16th century'. It might be worthless but it exercised a tremendous attraction. After there was more experience with what it was really like, this lure would probably fade, and practical men could proceed to a reasonable

[1] Hatzfeldt to Marschall, 14 May 1890, in Dugdale, *German Diplomatic Documents*, II, 33–4.
[2] Telegram, Marschall to Hatzfeldt, 17 May 1890, in *ibid*. II, 35.
[3] Same to same, 29 May 1890, in *ibid*, II, 37.
[4] Malet to Salisbury, 24 May 1890, File A/63, Salisbury Papers.

N

settlement.[1] This maneuver had the predictable effect. The German government was alarmed that the prize was slipping away and its willingness to make concessions for the sake of immediate agreement was increased.[2]

Under these conditions, Salisbury, if he had been prepared to stand firm on his proposals of 13 May, might have won still more from Germany than he extracted. But Salisbury was beset with problems of his own which made an early settlement desirable. The public ferment which he sought to use to advantage was also a threat to his government and to his own diplomatic objectives. The campaign led by Stanley against 'surrender' had affected not only the newspapers and missionary organizations; it had created serious opposition even within his own cabinet. At a meeting on 3 June the majority of the cabinet in effect endorsed the Mackinnon–Stanley position by advocating that Britain stand fast not only for the Stevenson road but for the territories encompassed by Stanley's treaties, which would involve the redrawing of the boundary about thirty miles south of the line at 1° south latitude to which he and Hatzfeldt had tentatively agreed.[3] After a conversation with Hatzfeldt on 4 June, Salisbury expressed himself as optimistic that this adjustment could be made. The cabinet also expressed apprehension at the strategic implications of the loss of Heligoland, and it was not until Salisbury and a cabinet committee had obtained assurances from the Admiralty on this score that cabinet opposition was withdrawn.[4]

The frontier issue was resolved by a compromise, the Germans conceding the 'Stevenson road' in exchange for Salisbury's withdrawing British claims south of 1° south latitude. The last remaining obstacle was removed when Mackinnon reluctantly agreed to the southern boundary.[5] With the great issues settled in east, west, and south-west Africa, all that was left were technical details, and on 1 July 1890 the omnibus treaty for the settlement

[1] Salisbury to Malet, 21 May 1890, F.O. 244/471, P.R.O.
[2] Telegram, Marschall to Hatzfeldt, secret, 29 May 1890, in Dugdale, *German Diplomatic Documents*, II, 37–8; same to same, secret, 21 May 1890, in *ibid.* p. 39.
[3] Robert O. Collins, 'Origins of the Nile Struggle', in Gifford and Louis, *Britain and Germany in Africa*, p. 144.
[4] Salisbury to Victoria, 4 June 1890, in Buckle, *Victoria*, I, 610–12. Victoria did not withdraw her opposition so easily. She chided Salisbury for his handing over loyal subjects to 'an unscrupulous, despotic government' and grumbled that 'next we will propose to give up Gibraltar'. *Ibid.* p. 612.
[5] F.O. to Mackinnon, 9 June 1890, F.O. 84/2083, P.R.O.

of Anglo-German differences in Africa was formalized. So far as east Africa was concerned, the agreement was favorable to the British, as even the ardent expansionists admitted. Germany recognized British primacy on the Nile. Britain and its East Africa Company were made secure in their possession of Uganda, and Germany ceded Witu, thus removing a major irritation on the coast. French objections to Britain's assumption of the protectorate over Zanzibar were removed by a recognition of a French protectorate over Madagascar and concessions in west Africa.[1] Mackinnon congratulated Salisbury on a 'highly satisfactory arrangement which maintains the dignity, influence, and interests of the Empire to a degree which ought to satisfy the whole nation.'[2] Mackinnon's old friend Hall wrote:

> Lord Salisbury has certainly done well for the BEA Co. and his Country, and greatly beyond what our most sanguine hopes attained to.
>
> Stanley deserves well of the Co. – he did much to stiffen Lord Salisbury's back and help him with the German government as well. I only hope he won't now in the exuberance of his satisfaction tempt the Germans to think we have a great deal too much the best of the bargain.[3]

Sir John Kirk grumbled that the Germans had been able to reach the borders of the Free State because they could now drain the trade from the Congo through their East African territories,[4] but he expressed complete satisfaction so far as the agreement affected the interests of the British east Africa Company.[5] Harry Johnston called the convention 'an absolutely satisfactory arrangement'.[6] The directors of the South Africa Company who had feared that Salisbury would 'dance to the German fiddle' were also pleasantly surprised. A. L. Bruce, who had been convinced that Anderson was pro-German and would sacrifice British African interests, expressed his 'thankfulness' for an agreement which was so much better than he had expected, even though it did not include the 'all-Red' belt. Stanley, he thought, must have

---

[1] Stanley considered the Anglo-French agreement of 5 August 1890 as a coup for the French, for they had exchanged valueless rights in Zanzibar for valuable concessions. *Evening Standard*, 15 August 1890. See A. S. Kanya-Forstner, 'French African Policy and the Anglo-French Agreement of 5 August 1890', *Historical Journal* XII, 4 (1969), 628–50.
[2] Mackinnon to Salisbury, 20 June 1890, File E, Salisbury Papers.
[3] Hall to Mackinnon, 20 June 1890, Mackinnon Papers.
[4] Kirk to Salisbury, 22 June 1890, File E, Salisbury Papers.
[5] Kirk to Salisbury, 18 June 1890, in *ibid*.
[6] H. H. Johnston, *The Uganda Protectorate* (London, 1904), I, 231,

been effective in confronting the government with outraged public opinion.[1]

This uniform satisfaction might seem remarkable in view of the ardor with which Mackinnon and his friends had pursued the ambition of a British-controlled connection between Lake Victoria to Lake Tanganyika. The explanation, of course, lies in their expectation that Salisbury's endorsement of the Leopold–Mackinnon treaty guaranteed them an alternative route. In their preoccupation with Uganda they did not take any action to utilize the corridor, and the Company soon was overwhelmed with other problems of such magnitude that its rights under the treaty became of no significance. Leopold, however, had lost neither interest nor energy, and when he claimed his part of the bargain was outraged by Salisbury's refusal to admit that there had been any legal agreement at all and his denial that his endorsement had committed the British government.[2] Mackinnon found himself in the uncongenial role of seeking to dissuade Leopold from carrying out their agreement,[3] for the Company's hopes of survival were dependent on the goodwill and, far more important, on the financial assistance of the government.

The treaty also promoted false hopes for profit in other parts of the interior. The Company had chafed at the German possession of Witu as a barrier to the use of the Tana River, which was navigable for many miles and could provide easy access to ivory and perhaps to even greater riches as yet unknown.[4] The Sultan of Witu was assumed to be a German puppet whose opposition would collapse with the withdrawal of his protectors. In this judgment, the Company's agents reflected no understanding of the ferment with which they had to contend. The Sultan of Witu was significant largely because he had become a nucleus for anti-European sentiment and resentment at subservience of the Sultan of Zanzibar to European dictates. The transfer of power occurred at approximately the same time as Euan Smith imposed upon the

[1] Bruce to Grey, 2 July 1890, File 189/9, Grey Papers, Durham.

[2] These later developments are treated in several books. See for example, Robert O. Collins, *The Southern Sudan, 1883–1898* (New Haven, 1962); G. N. Sanderson, *England, Europe, and the Upper Nile* (Edinburgh, 1965); and Robert O. Collins, *King Leopold, England, and the Upper Nile, 1899–1909* (New Haven, 1968).

[3] Note by Sir Percy Anderson, 21 March 1891, F.O. 84/2159, P.R.O.

[4] Joseph Thomson, *Through Masai Land*, pp. 531–2, cited by de Kiewiet, 'History of the Imperial British East Africa Company', p. 242. Thomson reported that there were great amounts of ivory near Lake Rudolf.

Sultan the necessity of issuing a decree for the abolition of slavery in Zanzibar, a measure which de Winton, the Company's administrator, correctly predicted would cause widespread unrest among the Arab population in Zanzibar and on the coast.[1] De Winton's fears were dismissed by Euan Smith as evidence of ignorance of the 'Oriental' character. The Arabs, Euan Smith said, respected dignity and power and a firm hand: 'The Arabs on our coast line differ at heart in no respect from those further south; they can be ruled by fear alone – whether of punishment or of detection.'[2]

The proof of this assessment, Euan Smith pointed out, was that *'absolutely nothing'* had occurred.[3] Both Euan Smith's judgment and his sources of intelligence were sadly defective. At the time he made this pronouncement, a rebellion was about to break out on the coast with the Sultan of Witu as one of its prime movers.

Between the conclusion of the treaty and the formal assumption of a British protectorate over Witu,[4] six Germans were killed by the soldiers of the Sultan of Witu, Fumo Bakari, son of Ahmad (Simba). A British naval expedition was sent to the area to punish the culprits, and the ease with which they put down resistance left a false impression that the population had been cowed.[5] Fumo Bakari fled, and died soon after, but resistance continued. When the Company assumed the administration of Witu in 1891, it was confronted with continual guerrilla warfare with which it was unable to cope. Under the circumstances, possession of Witu was an unrelieved liability, and the Company withdrew at the end of July 1893, leaving the problem of pacifying the area to the Imperial government which used Zanzibari troops under British command to put down resistance.[6]

Attempts to exploit the Juba as a highway for trade were likewise unsuccessful. Mackinnon had engaged in long and harrowing negotiations with representatives of Italy with the object of assigning control over the so-called 'northern ports' of Brava, Merka, Mogadishu, and Warsheikh in the lands of the Somali peoples and

---

[1] Euan Smith to Mackinnon, private, 19 August 1890, Mackinnon Papers.
[2] Euan Smith to Mackinnon, strictly private and confidential, 2 September 1890, Mackinnon Papers.
[3] *Ibid.*
[4] A British Protectorate was announced in November 1890 over Witu and the territories between it and the Juba River, the islands of Manda and Patta, and all other islands in Manda Bay; *London Gazette*, 25 November 1890.
[5] Euan Smith to Mackinnon, private and confidential, 3 January 1891, Mackinnon Papers.
[6] McDermott, *British East Africa*, p. 228; Lyne, *Apostle of Empire*, pp. 109–11.

giving the company the administration of Kismayu at the mouth of the Juba.[1] These ports were recognized as under the jurisdiction of the Sultan of Zanzibar, whose garrisons protected them, but in the country beyond, the writ of Zanzibar did not run. 'The fanatical and hostile population of treacherous Somalis',[2] as Euan Smith described them, refused to permit Europeans to intrude into their trading systems. The Company through its steamer, the *Kenia*, attempted to break the Somali monopoly over the Juba trade in ivory, but without success. It encountered not only the hostility of the Somalis who made passage on the river unsafe except for Arab, Swahili and Indian traders at Kismayu who had long acted as middlemen for the Somalis.[3]

Officials on the spot discovered that conditions of life in Somaliland could not be decided by drawing lines on maps on board the yacht *Cornelia*. They had little understanding of the Somali people with whom they had to contend – the Ogaden on the coast and the Majerteyn in the interior – whom they categorized as 'treacherous and quarrelsome, more given to brigandage and blackmailing than to lawful industry'.[4] Further, they considered them cowardly, since they would not stand and fight. But they knew that these people could not be quelled without exercise of force greater than the Company could command.

The Company employed a variety of means in its efforts to break Somali resistance, all involving expenditures which depleted its resources. The garrison at Kismayu was the largest Company force outside Uganda – over 400 men, principally Askari. The Company also supported a colony of runaway slaves several miles up the Juba to provide protection against the Ogaden Somali and subsidized local chiefs to keep them friendly.[5] But the chiefs would not stay bought at the original prices and kept demanding higher payments as the price for continued 'loyalty'. Outlays for all these purposes cost the Company several thousand pounds per year, and there was no compensating revenue, for all of the customs receipts went to the Sultan of Zanzibar as 'rent'.[6] When the

---

[1] For a detailed discussion, see Galbraith, 'Italy, the British East Africa Company, and the Benadir Coast, 1888–1893', *Journal of Modern History*, XLII, 4 (December 1970), 549–63.

[2] Euan Smith to Salisbury, 2 July 1888, A/79, Salisbury Papers.

[3] de Kiewiet, 'History of the Imperial British East Africa Company', p. 236.

[4] These are McDermott's words, *British East Africa*, p. 242, but they represent the prevailing view among local officers.

[5] de Kiewiet, 'History of the Imperial British East Africa Company', p. 237.

[6] McDermott, *British East Africa*, p. 241.

Company gave up Witu, the Foreign Office assumed jurisdiction over the entire territory between the Tana and Juba rivers, and the Company was left with only Kismayu and a ten-mile radius around it under the concession from the Sultan. The possession of Kismayu was thus made practically valueless, for the whole purpose of the concession had been to tap the trade of the interior.

The high hopes which the Company's directors had entertained for a profitable trade with the interior were thus all shattered. Rather than being a source of wealth, the hinterland consumed the Company's capital. The Tana and the Juba were never highways of commerce. Uganda, which had been conceived to be a pearl of great value, had proved to be no pearl at all. Within three years of the Anglo-German agreement the East Africa Company had collapsed, though its official death was not recorded until several years later.

8

The Uganda debacle, 1890–1893

Uganda was the death of the East Africa Company. The capital expended on reaching it and in establishing British control exhausted the Company; and the government which had exhorted the Company to action was unable or unwilling to take the necessary measures to rescue it from ruin, even though the end of the Company imposed upon the government responsibilities which it had sought to avoid through the charter. As bankruptcy approached, the mutual indictments which had characterized Company–government relations almost from the outset became more strident. Spokesmen for the Company contended that the Foreign Office had appealed to the patriotism of the directors to save Uganda for Britain and caused the Company to abandon the cautious program of consolidation on the coast which commercial considerations dictated, and then had refused to take any responsibility for the consequences. George Mackenzie, after the Company's liquidation, asserted that its interest had been sacrificed for the sake of the Empire. In the autumn of 1889 he had proposed that the Company first concentrate on the rapid development of the ports and the development of a coastal steamship service with activity in the interior being restricted to a survey for a railroad to Lake Victoria. The international threat, he asserted, reversed the priorities and the emphasis was shifted to the interior:

The action of the Germans and Italians in forcing the Coy prematurely to extend their original boundaries alone prevented the recommendations being carried into effect in their entirety. Had the Directors not acted as they did British East Africa today would be but a barren possession.[1]

The government continued to maintain that mismanagement, not government pressure, had been the ruination of the Company. Privately the permanent staff of the Foreign Office had to admit that the race for Uganda and the expense of holding it had im-

[1] Mackenzie to Anderson, 9 September 1895, F.O. 84/1383, P.R.O.

posed a great strain on the Company and that the Salisbury government had pressed the Company to take energetic action. Sir Percy Anderson in 1892 when he gave the incoming Liberals a précis of the Uganda issue, stated that if there had been no threat from Germany in 1890, and if Buganda had been friendly to British missionaries, the Company undoubtedly would have continued to follow the advice of Kirk and others who advocated development near the coast, and a gradual advance into the interior.[1] Carl Peters and the German Colonization Society by this interpretation were in a sense the agents of destruction of the British Company. The Liberal government which took office in 1892 accepted a somewhat different version of the events of two years before. Lord Rosebery, the new Foreign Secretary, and Sir William Harcourt, the Chancellor of the Exchequer, were at odds as to the proper government policy toward Uganda, but they agreed that the Company stood condemned for ignoring the advice of Kirk and occupying Buganda, several hundred miles from the coast, without having the resources to make the occupation effective. The role of government in these proceedings was ignored.[2]

These descriptions of the events leading to the occupation of Buganda all assume a coherence in the Company's leadership which was not in fact in evidence. The Company was not committed to a policy of caution before it responded to governmental exhortations. Instead, its directors were beset by doubts as to what its policy should be. The Lakes and Buganda were an attraction, even to Kirk; and Mackinnon had never entirely recovered from his earlier enthusiasm. Consequently, even without governmental pressure, the Company in 1889 was expending capital and energy in expeditions to Buganda. Before Peters appeared, Jackson's caravan had already arrived at the Lakes; it would have been followed by others. This activity did not have the unanimous support of the directors. Not only Mackenzie but Pelly and Burdett-Coutts expressed reservations against premature expansion but deferred to Mackinnon. The threat of a German coup and the government's importunities to the Company to act to forestall it, however, impelled the Company to much more intense activity in the direction of Buganda than even

---

[1] Confidential memorandum, Anderson, 10 September 1892, printed for use of cabinet, 13 September 1892, F.O. 84/2258, P.R.O.

[2] Secret memorandum, Harcourt, 22 September 1892, CAB 37/3/24, P.R.O.

Mackinnon had advocated. Before the spectre of German action in Buganda appeared, Mackenzie had been directing his attention to establishing a secure route from the coast to Machakos, 350 miles inland, utilizing the Sabaki route, and it was for this purpose that he had sent Lugard on his expedition to establish stations along the way to protect caravans. But the shift to immediate action in Buganda caused the abandonment of this plan and the concentration of available resources on securing Buganda. Lugard's stations were abandoned, and Mackenzie's plans for cautious development were set aside.[1] Mackinnon and the board of directors were thus justified in the assertion that they had subordinated commercial considerations to political necessities.

The new sense of urgency manifested in London was not immediately translated into action. Jackson, isolated in the interior, could not be made aware of the change in policy and consequently missed the opportunity to capitalize on Mwanga's desperation after his temporary overthrow at the end of 1889 by negotiating a treaty establishing the Company's protection over Buganda. Lugard was unable to carry out instructions sent him in April 1890 to lead his Sabaki expedition on a dash for Uganda to forestall Carl Peters. In this emergency, George Mackenzie felt it necessary to try whatever expedients were available and enlisted the assistance of Charles Stokes despite his awareness that Stokes' only loyalty was to himself. Stokes had been a lay missionary of the Church Missionary Society but in 1886 had left the Society to begin a career as a trader in arms and ivory. He had married the daughter of a Nyamwezi chief, and through this association had been able to assure himself of a plentiful supply of porters. His gun-running activities would eventually lead to his death,[2] but in 1890 his influence with Mwanga through the weapons he provided made him a possible asset to the Company if he felt it advantageous to cooperate. Mackenzie in May asked Stokes to try, either with Jackson or on his own, to secure a treaty with Mwanga accepting British protection.[3] Stokes, however, was supplying the Catholic party with arms and did not find it in his interests to work for a settlement which could ruin his business. He apparently made no

---

[1] Mackenzie to Villiers, 22 September 1891, F.O. 84/2175, P.R.O.
[2] On Stokes, see Oliver, *Missionary Factor*, pp. 135–6, 139, and Perham, *Lugard*, *passim*. His death is dealt with by W. Roger Louis in 'Great Britain and the Stokes Case', *Uganda Journal* xxviii, 2 (1964), 135–49.
[3] Mackenzie to Stokes, 21 May 1890, F.O. 244/472, P.R.O.

effort to act on behalf of the British cause – in July he entered the service of Germany on a one-year contract.[1]

At the time of the Anglo-German convention, Mwanga was determined to try to remain independent of European control. But he ruled a country seething with factionalism which could explode at any time into a renewal of civil war. Though expressed in religious terms, these divisions represented great tensions within the society exacerbated by the intrusion of outside influences into the Baganda society – first the Arabs and then the Europeans. Many of the converts were deeply committed to their new faith – voluntary martyrdom is an impressive testament to conviction – but the symbols of Islam and Christianity were used by factions primarily concerned with the issues of the here rather than the hereafter.[2] The 'Protestants' of the 'Inglesa' party might know little of Protestantism and the Catholic 'Fransas' may have been unschooled in the doctrines of Rome, but they knew that they hated each other only slightly less than they did the Muslims whom they in a brief coalition had defeated in restoring Mwanga to power. The symbols of religion obscured a basic division based on conflicting interests and ambitions. In the convulsions in Buganda after the death of Mutesa, the 'Arab' party derived much of its strength from the fear of the extension of European influence and European values, and Mwanga when he had initially accepted Muslim support had been similarly motivated. Bunyoro's backing of the Muslims after Mwanga had shifted to the Christian party had nothing to do with doctrine, much with the ambitions of its ruler, Kabarega, to restore his kingdom to its earlier greatness by capitalizing on the internal weaknesses of rival Buganda. The Fransa and Inglesa chiefs, on the other hand, saw the future of Buganda as within the sphere of European influence but were divided as to which of the European powers should be their protector. In 1890 'Protestantism' had as its symbol the flag of the British East Africa Company, while the opposition to British rule coalesced behind the Catholic crucifix.

The hostility of the two Christian parties was aggravated by the nature of the land settlement which they had made after they defeated the Muslims and restored Mwanga to power. This un-

[1] Vincent to F.O., 6 November 1890, F.O. 84/2094, P.R.O. Perham, *Lugard*, p. 184, states that Stokes was employed by the Germans and wearing a German uniform when Mackenzie sought to enlist his support in May. This does not appear to have been the case.

[2] Low, *Buganda in Modern History*, pp. 35–8.

written understanding provided that the territorial chieftainships and the offices of the Kabaka's government would be divided equally between the Inglesa and the Fransa factions. If a chief changed his allegiance, he forfeited not only his office but his land. This division was not long acceptable to the stronger Catholic faction or to their missionaries who saw it as a barrier to their work of conversion, and an agreement made to promote peace became a source of renewed conflict which would lead to war.[1] An uneasy truce remained in effect for several months only because of the fear of each of the 'Christian' factions that if they attacked each other they would in their weakened state be overrun by the Muslims. Ernest Gedge, whom Jackson had left to watch the scene when he returned to the coast, reported to the directors that conditions were so volatile that a small incident could cause a 'religious' war.[2] Mwanga, though he favored the Fransa party, could not govern with their support alone. With the withdrawal of Germany from any contest to British claims, Mwanga was consequently in a weak position to resist the importunities of the British Company.

This was the condition of Buganda when Lugard arrived in December 1890 with a caravan composed of 3 Europeans, 66 Sudanese and Somali soldiers, and 285 Swahili including porters and *askari*.[3] He had won his battle with de Winton and was now in unchallenged command of the Uganda expedition. He was indeed subject to no restrictions aside from his resources and the instructions he had received from de Winton when he had set out from Mombasa. He was to negotiate a treaty with Mwanga recognizing the Company's suzerainty and was to attempt to reconcile the Inglesa and Fransa factions, but the manner in which he accomplished this mission was necessarily left to his own discretion. Lugard accomplished the first of his charges a few days after his arrival when he imposed upon an unwilling Mwanga a treaty by which the Company was recognized as the protector of Buganda. The Kabaka acquiesced only because of the advice of the French priests who were influenced by Lugard's promise to protect their religious liberty and by the fear of a renewal of war, and Mwanga's attitude was eloquently expressed by the clause he and his chiefs insisted on adding that the treaty would be nullified

[1] Oliver and Mathew, *History of East Africa*, pp. 420–1.
[2] de Kiewiet, 'History of the Imperial British East Africa Company', p. 209.
[3] Perham, *Lugard*, p. 206.

'if another white man greater than this one shall come up after-wards'.[1] The imposition of the treaty was a remarkable display. of courage and self-confidence for Lugard who had only about 100 reliable men at his disposal in a country in which each of the contending factions had armed forces in the thousands.

Having achieved his first objective, Lugard set out to the Kingdoms of Ankole and Toro, adjacent to Buganda, and negoti-ated similar treaties with their chiefs.[2] Treaties, however, were not sufficient. The peace of Buganda rested upon an uneasy equili-brium. Lugard's personal influence was not a substitute for military power, and the requisite resources to overawe Buganda could not be provided by a Company already laboring under the strain of providing even for Lugard's meager force. Further, despite his efforts to convince the Fransa of his good will he could not escape the identification of himself and the Company with the Protestant faction. Bishop Tucker, who arrived in Buganda a few days after Lugard, commented that the Protestants had identified themselves with the Company so completely that they had com-promised themselves in the eyes of their fellow-countrymen and that they would undoubtedly be massacred were the Company to withdraw.[3] This contention was to be an important factor in determining British policy when the Company announced its intention to evacuate Buganda.

Lugard attempted to unite the Christian factions by an attack upon the common enemy, the Muslim party and its backers in Bunyoro, and the Ganda forces won a victory in May 1891, but the common cause did not contribute to unity. In the campaign, the Inglesa had induced Lugard to allow them to fly the Com-pany's flag, thus re-emphasizing the identification which other Ganda abhorred,[4] and the elimination of the Muslim menace enabled the 'Christians' to resume their feuds. Open war broke out in January 1892.

The immediate issue was a decision by Mwanga upholding the acquittal of a member of the Fransa party of the charge of murder of an Inglesa, who allegedly had committed a theft. Though this judgment was in accordance with Buganda law, Lugard refused to accept it, and the incident became the occasion for a war in

[1] Perham, *Lugard*, p. 232.
[2] Oliver, *Missionary Factor*, p. 142.
[3] Alfred, Bishop of East Africa, to Buxton, 30 July 1891, Mackinnon Papers,
[4] Perham, *Lugard*, p. 256.

which the Inglesa with the support of Lugard's forces and his Maxim gun routed the Fransa.

Lugard's conduct in the weeks before the war was affected by his receipt of instructions at the end of December 1891 to evacuate Buganda immediately. Withdrawal was contrary to Lugard's being. He, like so many other 'men on the spot', identified himself with his mission; his own ambitions and the cause became fused. He had been sent to pacify Buganda, and he had interpreted his instructions broadly. During the time between his defeat of the Muslims and the outbreak of civil war he had been busy in extending British influence to the kingdoms bordering on Buganda on the justification that the security of Buganda depended on the control of the periphery. On this principle he smashed a Bunyoro army and drove them from Toro, where he reinstated a scion of the royal house as a client king, protected by a line of forts. He garrisoned these forts with Sudanese whom he recruited from the remnants of Emin's garrison who had continued to subsist on the shores of Lake Albert. He also extended the protection of the Company to the border Kingdom of Ankole. By these measures he hoped to check the power of Bunyoro and to throttle the arms traffic.[1]

These were large and expensive commitments for which he had neither received nor sought any authorization from the London board.[2] But he had committed himself to a course of action, and he would not now passively accept a decision which undid the work he had accomplished and risk the loss by Britain of the fairest provinces of the Lakes area. This revulsion against an act of scuttle undoubtedly caused him to press for an immediate settlement in Buganda by which the Company's authority throughout the kingdom was made manifest, thus confronting the directors and Whitehall with a *fait accompli*.[3]

---

[1] For a detailed discussion, see Perham, *Lugard*, pp. 260–87.

[2] The directors may have instructed Lugard to negotiate treaties with Toro and Ankole for the acceptance of the Company's protection. In his Report no. 2, Lugard stated that he was acting in accordance with his instructions in so doing; de Kiewiet, 'History of the Imperial British East Africa Company', p. 218. But it is clear from his diaries that his decisions were largely his own, and certainly the directors never contemplated his hiring a force of approximately 600 Sudanese with several thousand camp followers. Lugard estimated that the cost of maintaining them was about £5,000 per year; *The Rise of Our East African Empire*, II, 640.

[3] Oliver and Mathew, *History of East Africa*, p. 422.

The instincts of Lugard and the realities of life as seen by the directors were in conflict. While he had been preoccupied with the establishment of an orderly and secure British province they had been dominated by financial crisis. The capital of £240,000 subscribed by the original founders was gone. The directors in August 1889 had tried to raise additional capital by offering shares to the public,[1] but of the £750,000 offered, only about a third had been applied for.[2] The investing public might be gullible enough to invest in speculations on possible gold mines in Rhodesia, but there was no comparable lure in east Africa. Even the most unwary investor could see in the balance sheets evidence of impending demise. By the end of 1890, expenditures had risen to an annual rate of approximately £120,000 for the administration of the coast, caravans to the interior and on interior stations, and this outlay was not substantially defrayed by revenues.[3] The customs concessions with Zanzibar involved a commitment to an annual payment to the Sultan of $56,000 which virtually eliminated all profit to the Company. An application for a commutation of these payments to a lump sum as the German government had done was rejected by the government on the basis that such a settlement would necessitate cession of the coastal belt to Britain. The Sultan had transferred his authority to the German government, not to a company, and Whitehall was not interested in accepting the responsibility which would accrue to it by a parallel transaction. Among other embarrassments which it would involve, the Foreign Office asserted, was the existence of slavery in what would then be a British territory.[4] The government in effect had again informed the Company that economic interests must be subordinated to 'high policy' – which in this instance meant the avoidance of responsibility and expense. Mackinnon and his co-directors were outraged at what they regarded as callous indifference to the Company's plight. Other governments had provided substantial subsidies to commercial enterprises serving the public interest. Germany had provided the equivalent of several hundred thousand pounds to support its now defunct East Africa Company. Italy had guaranteed its company in east Africa a return of six per cent on a capital of £800,000. Belgium had voted a subsidy of £80,000 per

[1] *The Times*, 14 August 1889.
[2] McDermott to Barrington, 13 January 1892, F.O. 84/2239; Summary of capital and shares, 7 August 1895, B.T. 31/5594/38949, both in P.R.O.
[3] Minutes, Court of Directors, 15 March 1891, Mackinnon Papers.
[4] McDermott, *British East Africa*, p. 336.

year toward the maintenance of Leopold's Free State and had advanced substantial sums for railway construction. But the British East Africa Company not only received no assistance but was shackled by governmental decisions, past and present. It could not impose customs duties beyond the limitations of the commercial treaties, its powers of taxation were severely circumscribed, and now it was prevented from making a financial arrangement with the Sultan simply because of a government edict.[1] The Company, on the advice of its legal counsel that it had the right to negotiate commutation on the same basis as the Germans, decided to defy the government and open direct negotiations with the Sultan but were peremptorily instructed to desist.[2] The Foreign Office offered a sop to the Company by prevailing on the Sultan to agree to a revised concession cancelling his right to half the surplus revenue beyond the amount guaranteed him, on the condition that the Company not press any claim to commutation during his lifetime.[3]

Such palliatives were of little benefit to the East Africa Company. Mackinnon and the board by the beginning of 1891 recognized that their enterprise was foundering and could not long survive without substantial governmental support. They now all agreed that the Company could not prosper without exploiting the resources of Uganda and the surrounding territories and that it could not profit from Uganda without a railway.

Mackinnon had long been a believer in railways as the essential arteries of commerce. In the 1870s and early 1880s he had advocated the construction of lines in the Congo Free State, hopefully by a syndicate of which he was a member, as a supplement to the river system. His competence as well as his interest had been recognized when the government had commissioned him and Mackenzie in 1886 to devise a plan for Persian railways.[4] From the formation of the East Africa Company, he had recognized that profitable commerce with the interior was not likely so long as transportation was by human porterage. A railway was essential,

[1] Euan Smith estimated that the German settlement with the Sultan would involve a loss to Zanzibar and a saving to Germany of about £1,000,000 over the remaining 47 years of the concession. Euan Smith to Salisbury, 16 January 1890, F.O. 84/2059, P.R.O.

[2] Bentley to F.O., 31 January 1891, F.O. 84/2155. Note by Anderson on *supra*, n.d., F.O. 84/2156; F.O. to I.B.E.A., 9 February 1891, F.O. 84/2156; Bentley to F.O., 17 February 1891, F.O. 84/2157; all in P.R.O.

[3] McDermott, *British East Africa*, pp. 337–8.

[4] See ch. 2.

but a railway required vast capital outlay. Early in 1890 the Company shipped materials sufficient for the construction of thirty miles of light railway[1] and in August the first few miles of the railway were opened with much ceremony, but the difficulty of getting labor and the expense involved in further extension stopped construction after only six miles had been laid.[2] For surveys, land purchases, materials, and construction, the Company estimated that it had expended £50,000 on the railway. This included the costs of Jackson's and Lugard's caravans which involved a net outlay of £6,563,[3] but even without assigning these expenditures to the railway, the outlay was large, and it was clear to Mackinnon and the directors that further construction should not be undertaken without guarantees of governmental support. They expected that such assistance would be forthcoming. This assumption rested on more than wishful thinking. During the Brussels Anti-Slavery Conference, Sir John Kirk had been an active advocate of the Belgian proposal that the conference endorse railway construction in Africa as a substitute for the use of human beings which contributed to slavery and the slave trade. He did so both because he genuinely believed that railways would indeed undercut one of the economic bases for slavery and because he hoped that a resolution of this nature by an international conference would be useful in inducing Parliament to vote for financial assistance to the East Africa Company to build a railway to the Lakes. In his correspondence with Mackinnon he emphasized that he was promoting the Company's interest in so doing; he saw no conflict with his responsibility as the government's representative, and the Foreign Office raised no objection so long as there was no commitment for the government to accept responsibility for railway construction. Article III of the Brussels Act provided:

The Powers exercising sovereignty or protectorate in Africa, in order to confirm and to give greater precision to their former declarations, undertake to proceed gradually, as circumstances permit, either by the means above indicated, or by any other means which they may consider suitable, with the repression of the Slave Trade; each State in its respective Possessions and under its own direction. Whenever they consider

[1] Mackinnon to Salisbury, 26 March 1890, F.O. 84/2078, P.R.O. The railway had a two-foot gauge.
[2] Bentley to Mackinnon, 17 February 1891, Mackinnon Papers. See Sir Gerald Portal's account of his ride on 'the Central African Railway' in his *The British Mission to Uganda* (London, 1894), pp. 28–31.
[3] Summary of cost of railway, Mombasa, 6 May 1891, Mackinnon Papers.

O

it possible they will lend their good offices to the Powers which, with a purely humanitarian object, may be engaged in Africa upon similar mission.[1]

There is no clear evidence as to precisely when Salisbury gave Mackinnon expectations of moral support in an approach to Parliament for funds. It may have been before the Anglo-German convention, when Mackinnon asked the Foreign Office for financial assistance for a railway from Mombasa to the Lakes,[2] for by the fall of 1890 Mackinnon and the Company's board were engaged in active investigations on the costs of such a railway. But the Foreign Office put itself officially on record in support of a subsidy in December 1890 in a letter to the Treasury which portrayed the Company's services in as flattering terms as had Mackinnon himself. The Foreign Office draft in fact derived much of its argument from a statement by Mackinnon on the justifications for a subsidy.[3]

Following Mackinnon's line, the Foreign Office asserted that the Company had served the cause of civilization, commerce, and philanthropy. For no selfish purpose it had maintained peace and order in the British sphere as well as paving the way for the gradual civilization of the peoples of the interior. In this high calling it had received no financial assistance from the taxpayers in contrast to its German counterpart, yet it had survived: 'Its success has been a remarkable contrast to the failure of the neighbouring German Company which has necessitated the direct intervention of its Government, involving heavy expenditures out of Imperial funds. . .'[4]

Because of the operations of the Company, the Foreign Office asserted, the Imperial government had been able to avoid any expense or responsibility in its sphere, but the resolutions of the Brussels Conference to which Britain was a party now imposed upon the government a commitment which it was unrealistic as well as unjust to expect the Company to assume. Britain had an obligation to assist in the suppression of the slave trade by land. Experience had shown that cruisers off the coast alone could not throttle the traffic. The most effective way to stop the trade was to make it unprofitable, and roads and particularly railroads would

1 Edward Hertslet, *The Map of Africa by Treaty*, II, 492.
2 Mackinnon to F.O., 7 June 1890, F.O. 84/2083, P.R.O.
3 Mackinnon to Salisbury, 17 December 1890, F.O. 84/2097, P.R.O.
4 F.O. to Treasury, 20 December 1890, F.O. 84/2097, P.R.O. Salisbury noted on the document, 'a very good draft'.

eliminate the use of slaves and other human labor as carriers. The construction of the railway to Victoria Nyanza would be a fulfill-ment of a British commitment. The Company did not have the resources to undertake the project, and even if it did, the under-taking could not be justified on commercial grounds alone. A subsidy from the government of £24,000 a year would be a modest recognition of the public character of the railway. The investment would produce great humanitarian dividends; it might even in the long run save the Exchequer considerable expenditure, for if the slave trade was stopped at its source the expensive slave trade squadron would no longer be required. If Britain did not accept the responsibility, the Foreign Office warned the Treasury, it risked international odium. The German government was planning a railway and if Britain remained inactive, the slave traders might move into the British sphere – the resulting scandal would be catastrophic to any government.[1]

This appeal to high principle and to the risks of obloquy was in accordance with the strategy Kirk had devised during the Brussels Conference. It was shrewdly conceived to harmonize humanitarian and fiscal considerations in its argument that the railway would eliminate the necessity for the sea-borne slave watch and its suggestion that if the Company succumbed the government would have to assume a heavy financial burden, as Germany had done. But it was not in the nature of the Treasury to be swept up by great enthusiasm for Imperial expenditures as a means of saving money. Its record had been uniformly to the contrary. As Salisbury complained in another connection, 'when the Treasury lays its hand upon any matter concerning the future development of the British Empire, the chances of an Imperial policy are small'.[2] Beyond the Treasury there was Parliament which could be de-pended upon to be obstreperous in response to any proposal for a subsidy to a chartered company. But Salisbury had committed himself and was prepared to fight the issue through. In the development of the government's position he sought the advice of Kirk and Harry Johnston, and by January 1891, with their con-currence, had decided that he would propose a guarantee of a percentage on the capital expended for the railway.[3]

The expenditure which would be required had not yet been

[1] F.O. to Treasury, 20 December 1890, F.O. 84/2097, P.R.O.
[2] *Truth*, 21 February 1895.
[3] Memorandum by Salisbury, 13 January 1891, F.O. 84/2156, P.R.O.

determined at the beginning of 1891, but each successive cal-
culation raised the estimate, and all were beyond the resources of
the Company. When the railway was first discussed in 1889 the
directors had thought that approximately £200 per mile would be
sufficient, but Sir Francis de Winton, on the basis of reports on the
topography between the coast and the Lakes, had predicted that the
total expense would be approximately five times that amount for
a railway with the two-foot gauge which was contemplated.[1] On
further calculations, the directors further raised this estimate to a
cost of about £1,000,000 for a two-foot gauge and at least £1,500,000
for a gauge of one meter for the approximately 540 miles between
Mombasa and Lake Victoria.[2]

From the standpoint of the Company's directors, the case for
governmental support for the railway was unanswerable. As John
Kirk observed, railways in east Africa served long-range national
purposes. Eventually they would be the means of expanding
trade.[3] But private companies could not wait; either they balanced
costs with revenue within a few years or they went bankrupt, an
eventuality which the directors foresaw as imminent unless the
government intervened.

At the beginning of 1891 the Company faced the consequences
of having attempted to achieve national ends with private means.
It had expended tens of thousands of pounds on expansion into the
interior with little return. Its resources were now depleted, and its
fate was dependent upon the generosity of a government which to
that point had used the Company for political purposes without
regard to the drain imposed on its finances. There was an element
of irony in the fact that the hope for salvation was Lord Salisbury.
The Foreign Secretary who before the Anglo-German Convention
of 1890 had stood strongly against any direct governmental
involvement was now committed to back the Company in its
financial plight. Mackinnon, with bitter recollections of his
relationships with Salisbury since the 1870s, was not convinced of
the genuineness of the conversion. On every occasion when the
Company had sought relief from Salisbury it had been rebuffed.
The latest occasion was the refusal to support the commutation
of payments for the coastal lease. There was no basis for optimism,
Mackinnon thought, that the outcome of the discussions on the

---

[1] Kemball to Mackinnon, 8 August 1890, Mackinnon Papers.
[2] Mackinnon to Salisbury, 17 December 1890, F.O. 84/2097, P.R.O.
[3] Kirk to Mackinnon, 2 February 1891, Mackinnon Papers.

railway would be different from previous experiences. Even with a guarantee for the railway, the Company's future looked bleak.[1]

Mackinnon's mental state was in part a reflection of objective reality – the Company was in serious financial trouble. It was also a manifestation of his own deterioration. He was sick and dispirited; his will to fight had been drained away. More and more he left the affairs of the Company to the board in London; he found refuge for more extended periods in the south of France, away from the cold and damp of Britain and away from the debilitating encounters with governmental officials which had taxed his energies over the years. As a young man he had been exhilarated by the battles he had fought and won in building a great shipping line. But he was no longer young; and his experiences with Whitehall had been uniformly dismal. He had not entirely given up; but he had the attributes of a man who fought only because struggle was ingrained in his nature, not because he hoped to succeed.

During the first few months of 1891 Mackinnon's despondency seemed to be excessive in view of the encouraging response of the government to the Company's overtures. Not only had Salisbury promised his support, but the Treasury had abandoned its usual negativism and endorsed the principle of a subsidy to the Company with remarkable alacrity. Within two months of Salisbury's request for Treasury support he had received it. The justification for this departure from established principle was the saving in expense for the slave patrol which would be effected if the railway undercut the inland slave trade. There were five cruisers in the slave trade squadron patrolling the east African coast which cost the Exchequer approximately £100,000 per year and an additional £8,000 to £10,000 was paid in bounties. The prospect of eliminating these heavy costs, the Treasury agreed, justified a guarantee to the railway. It stipulated that the subsidy should take the form of guarantee of interest for twenty-five years of two per cent on capital not to exceed £1,250,000; the maximum levy on the public purse would thus be only £25,000 per year. To qualify for this guarantee, the Company must provide evidence that the full amount of the capital needed had been subscribed and that the bulk had actually been paid up. All profits over five per cent would be divided equally between the government and the shareholders until all payments under the guarantee had been recovered by the

[1] Euan Smith wrote to Salisbury of Mackinnon's despondency, 2 February 1891, File A/80, Salisbury Papers.

state. The managing director of the railway would also have a veto on raising of capital beyond the amount specified by the guarantee.[1] It is doubtful that the Treasury was convinced by the argument that the railway would eliminate the need for the naval squadron. The Brussels Act had given the opportunity to support railway construction in the guise of fulfilling Britain's commitment to extirpate the slave trade, and Salisbury had put the full force of his office and his personal influence behind the application for a subsidy. George Goschen, the Chancellor of the Exchequer, was in the great tradition of watchdog of the Treasury; he had on occasion dissented from Salisbury on fiscal issues, but he was not prepared to oppose the prime minister on the railway guarantee, especially since the deviation from general policy could be justified in terms of economy as well as humanitarianism and the public interest.

The Treasury's terms were somewhat less generous than the Company had hoped – Mackinnon had proposed a guarantee of three per cent or a subsidy of £30,000 to £40,000 for twenty-five years.[2] But the Company was in no position to haggle. The terms were quickly accepted. Negotiations were immediately begun with Rothschild's with a view to raising the necessary £1,250,000,[3] and several engineers were employed to examine reports and maps of the country between Mombasa and Victoria Nyanza and make an estimate of the cost for the railway. One expert recommended a gauge of a meter or 3ft 6in for effective transportation over long distances, and concluded that the total cost of construction of such a railway over a distance of 570 miles would be not more than £1,804,195, and might be substantially less.[4] A second report by Major General E. G. Williams, Deputy Governor of Indian Railways, also provided an estimate of a total outlay of £1,800,000.[5] These reports followed precedent in providing higher cost estimates than their predecessors but the differential was not so great as to be discouraging. The company's concern was now with the fate of the subsidy proposals in Parliament, where there was certain to be substantial controversy, not only from the opposition but from the government ranks themselves.

[1] Welby to F.O., 10 February 1891, F.O. 84/2156, P.R.O.
[2] F.O. to Mackinnon, 12 February 1891, F.O. 84/2156, P.R.O.
[3] Special meeting of the Court of Directors, 16 February 1891, Mackinnon Papers.
[4] Fowler to Lorne, 4 April 1891, Mackinnon Papers.
[5] Memorandum by Williams, 20 April 1891, Mackinnon Papers.

Much of the reputation of the Treasury as a guardian of the public purse derived from the attitudes of Parliament toward expenditures beyond those required for the 'necessary' functions of government. The veneer of humanitarianism covering the railway guarantee was not likely to deter the critics, nor was the argument that expenditures would actually save money. Parliaments had rarely been impressed by the contentions that long-range savings would result from immediate outlays, and the government approached the House of Commons with considerable trepidation.

An earnest of things to come was when Henry Labouchere, that perennial gadfly of governments of whatever party, asked at the end of April whether any assurance had been given the Company that a guarantee would be granted and whether Parliament would be consulted before any definite commitment was made. He was informed that Parliament would indeed be consulted;[1] the government in fact had no choice in the matter, since a supplementary appropriation would be required.

Labouchere in himself was of little significance. Much of his effectiveness had been lost over the years. His penchant for hyperbole and his tendency to scatter his shots rather than to concentrate on the accurate and systematic demolition of selected targets had made him a celebrity more than a force. But he frequently represented the extreme fringe of formidable forces, and in this case he had substantial backing because the proposed subsidy ran contrary to traditional economic policies. On the Liberal side, such influential members as Sir William Harcourt were prepared to fight against what they interpreted to be a 'bail-out' for a sinking chartered company, and on the government benches of the House of Commons there was considerable disquiet over the government's decision to ask Parliament for money. As Goschen recognized, there was little possibility of a favorable vote without much more detailed knowledge of the engineering problems involved and the consequent costs. 'In short,' he told Sir Lewis Pelly, 'the House of Commons would reject a Bill unsupported by a Survey.' The decision was made to 'test the feeling' of the House by requesting passage of a supplementary estimate of £20,000 for a preliminary survey.[2]

[1] Question by Labouchere, 24 April 1891, *Parliamentary Debates*, CCCLI, col. 1321.
[2] Pelly to Mackinnon, 24 June 1891, quoted in de Kiewiet, 'History of the Imperial British East Africa Company', p. 283.

The government's ability to act was crippled, however, by the fact that the session was drawing to a close with a mass of unfinished business still before it. The leader of the house, William Henry Smith, had given a pledge not to introduce 'fresh contentious matter' during the remainder of the session, but when the proposed vote was brought before the House he was ill; he died shortly thereafter. The government decided that in the absence of Smith it would present the issue as being 'non-contentious' but that if Harcourt and his allies should insist to the contrary, the matter should be dropped for the session, since to press it would protract the sittings of Parliament and encourage the opposition to be obstructive on other, more urgent matters. Consequently, when Harcourt on 20 July asked that debate be postponed because the proposal was contentious, the government withdrew, with the stipulation that in so doing it did not imply any change in its decision to carry out the obligations imposed upon it by the Brussels Conference.[1]

The blow to the Company was softened by the assurance given Pelly by W. L. Jackson, Financial Secretary to the Treasury, that the government would press for a vote at the next session. Jackson suggested that in order to avoid delay, the Company advance whatever money was necessary to begin the survey with the understanding that the government was morally committed to reimburse it,[2] and the directors decided to proceed on that assurance.[3]

Throughout the discussions with the government the Company's representatives had insisted that the construction of the railway served Imperial purposes more than Company interests. This was an overstatement. But it was true that the race for Uganda at the behest of the government had accelerated the financial drain on the Company. By the summer of 1891 over £300,000 had been spent, and the paid-up capital had been almost exhausted.[4] Four days before the government's withdrawal of its bill to support the railway survey, the board had decided that the Company could no longer sustain Lugard in Uganda and that it must at least temporarily retire and consolidate its position on the coast. They con-

---

[1] *Parliamentary Debates*, CCCLV, 20 July 1891, cols. 1759–60; *The Times*, 21 July 1891.
[2] Memorandum of interview by Sir Lewis Pelly at Treasury with W. L. Jackson, M.P., and Sir R. Welby, confidential, 20 July 1891, F.O. 84/2173, P.R.O.
[3] Memorandum, 31 July 1891, Mackinnon Papers.
[4] de Kiewiet, 'History of the Imperial British East Africa Company', p. 286.

sidered the possibility of borrowing money to continue in Uganda but discarded the idea because it would add a further fixed charge for interest and impair the prospects of public support when they should seek a loan for railway construction or for some other purposes in the future.[1]

At the end of July Mackinnon, Lorne, and Kirk visited Anderson at the Foreign Office to inform him that the Company had decided to withdraw from Uganda. This intelligence did not surprise him. Through Kirk and others he had heard over the last few months of the Company's desperate financial plight, and he knew that the balance sheets confirmed the contention that the Company could not retain Uganda at the current level of expenditure. He had consequently devoted thought to possible alternatives which could retain British control without direct governmental intervention. Given the unavailability of resources, private or governmental, to exercise the functions of government, Anderson considered that the most feasible course was to use Mwanga as the agent of Imperial policy by attaching him permanently to Britain and giving him strong reasons of self-interest for 'good behavior'. The treaty which Lugard had negotiated expired in December 1892; it should be replaced by another, long-term, agreement; and Mwanga should be given a subsidy so long as he performed in accordance with British wishes.[2] These suggestions seemed to Salisbury to be the most acceptable palliatives. He proposed that Mwanga receive a yearly subsidy of £5,000 – the amount was reduced to £1,000 on the advice of General Mathews, then in London, who thought that any payments above that sum would only contribute to greed and other vices and make Mwanga less effective. Beyond that, Salisbury asserted, the significance of the withdrawal of Lugard's force from Uganda must be masked for as long as possible. The ostensible explanation might be that it was being moved eastward to provide protection for the impending railway survey.[3] Salisbury's views were incorporated in a letter from the Company to Lugard, which instructed him to seek an extension of the treaty for at least five to ten years, hopefully in perpetuity. He should select some suitable officer from volunteers who would be willing to serve as resident at his own risk, since he would have no forces at his disposal; and Mwanga should be

[1] Kemball to Mackinnon, 24 July 1891, Mackinnon Papers.
[2] Note by Anderson, 31 July 1891, F.O. 84/2171, P.R.O.
[3] Note by Salisbury, n.d., in *ibid*.

offered a gratuity of between £1,000 and £2,000 per year. As soon as he had made these arrangements he should immediately withdraw from Uganda and the Lake district and return to Mombasa. The directors assured Lugard that the withdrawal was only temporary and that the Company would reoccupy Uganda as soon as its financial condition permitted. Mwanga and the other chiefs should be so informed.[1] At the same time the directors instructed de Winton in Mombasa to reduce his total expenditure to a maximum of £40,000 per year.[2]

The pretence that the evacuation of Uganda would be only temporary, whatever value it might have in relations with Mwanga, did not delude anyone else. Anderson and Salisbury recognized that once the Company left Uganda it would never return, and the directors considered the promise an expedient which might be useful in bargaining purposes rather than a statement of genuine intent. The prospects for the Company appeared highly doubtful even to the most optimistic members of the board. The expense of Uganda, the deferral of governmental aid to the railway and the restrictions imposed upon the taxing powers of the chartered company on the coast meant continuing deficits. Perhaps the gloomiest of all were Mackinnon and Kirk, and each fed the despondency of the other. The latest delay in governmental action simply confirmed in Mackinnon's mind the futility of any partnership with government. He decided that he would abandon the mail line to Zanzibar; he was tired of the periodic wrangles with the Treasury which demeaned the Imperial purpose he had sought to promote. As for the East Africa Company, he could not yet emotionally accept the prospect of its imminent demise but he saw no real hope that it could long continue. Kirk shared this black outlook. The government's hasty withdrawal before the Opposition's objections in the last session of Parliament he interpreted to be an indication that the politicians had for all practical purposes abandoned any intention of financial assistance to the railway, perhaps even to a survey, despite the promises which had been made. Anderson's readiness to accept withdrawal from Uganda was still further evidence, he thought, that the British government set little value in retaining its influence in the area and was merely concerned to forestall criticism at home. Under these circumstances, the Company should set its policy in terms of

1 McDermott to Lugard, 10 August 1891, F.O. 84/2174, P.R.O.
2 de Kiewiet, 'History of the Imperial British East Africa Company', p. 286.

securing the best terms for liquidation. It must drastically economize, for once its capital was used up, its bargaining power was gone.[1] The other board members who were actively involved in the business of the Company, Mackenzie and Kemball, agreed with much of Kirk's assessment, but they were not yet resigned to inevitable liquidation. Kemball had no doubt that Parliament would honor the Treasury's provisional guarantee of support for the railway subsidy, but the fundamental problem would remain that unless substantial new capital was forthcoming the Company could not long continue. With the assurance of a railway, the directors might be in a position to call upon shareholders for the necessary additional money. Without it, they and their fellow investors would be 'throwing good money after bad'. He had hoped that the Company's near-insolvency might be used as a means of forcing the government to provide financial support. The Company, he concluded, had committed a tactical error in accepting a vote for a preliminary survey rather than insisting on a commitment to subsidize actual construction.[2]

The preponderance of the board in the last months of 1891 supported Kemball's position that if the government provided a guarantee for railway construction the Company might yet be able to survive. Even Kirk acknowledged that the completion of a railway could be the salvation of the Company, though he professed to consider the necessary government assistance to be out of the question.[3]

Kemball had become a major force in the Company's leadership. He had overcome Kirk's passivity and he proceeded to flay laggard members of the board to take an active part in the affairs of the Company. And he seems to have been instrumental in rousing Mackinnon to one last effort. His strategy was to incite public opinion to such a pitch of indignation that the government would feel compelled to back the railway subsidy vigorously. The government's passivity he considered to be morally reprehensible, and he was certain that this opinion was widely shared. If the withdrawal of the Company from Uganda could be publicized as a sacrifice of Protestantism in Uganda and perhaps even the lives of the missionaries and their adherents, there was certain to be an outcry not only from the missionary movement but from the

[1] Kirk to Mackinnon [9–10 August 1891], Mackinnon Papers.
[2] Kemball to Mackinnon, 14 September 1891, Mackinnon Papers.
[3] Kirk to Mackinnon [9–10 August 1891], Mackinnon Papers.

general public, which no government could ignore. If this indignation could be focussed on Parliament in demands for the
railway subsidy as necessary for the continuation of Company rule,
the opposition would crumble and the railway might yet be built.
It was an excellent strategy which combined humanitarian appeal
with effective propaganda to mobilize public opinion. If his
assumptions as to the options available to the government had been
correct, his campaign might well have achieved its object.

The first step was easy – to excite the Church Missionary
Society to action. Kemball sought not only its moral support but
financial assistance to enable the Company to remain in Uganda
until the critical vote was taken. No approach to the Society was
necessary, since General George Hutchinson, its lay secretary until
1889 and still a prominent member, sought Kemball out. Rumors
of the Company's intention to retire had reached Hutchinson
through Bishop Tucker and from many other sources, including
articles in the press. Lugard's sister, having seen an item to this
effect in the newspaper, had rushed to Horace Waller to inform
him of the disaster which impended because of the government's
failure to pass the vote for a subsidy, and Waller predictably went
into action to promote a deputation to the Foreign Office demanding that it fulfill its obligations by supporting the Company.
Hutchinson when he first talked with Kemball in August was not
able to commit the Society to anything more than expressions of
sympathy since its wealthy patrons were almost all away on the
continent until October. To Hutchinson's professions of goodwill
Kemball replied that these sentiments were much appreciated, but
that the Company had gone beyond the stage where benevolent
expressions were of value. It was now in the position of the
Irishman in charge of a fort who knew of fifty reasons for not
evacuating and only one for doing so – that his stock of powder and
ammunition was exhausted. Without some outside help during the
next few months the Company would have to leave Uganda, at
least for a time.[1] Kemball's warning had a gratifying response. In
mid-September Hutchinson promised Mackinnon that a strong
letter would be sent to Salisbury appealing to him to take the
necessary action to keep the Company in Uganda, since withdrawal would be a devastating blow to the Protestant missions. He
also stated the Society's readiness to try to raise funds of perhaps
£10,000 to £15,000 if the Company would commit itself to stay in

[1] Kemball to Mackinnon, 14 August 1891, Mackinnon Papers.

Uganda at least until the end of 1892 and, if the government provided the railway guarantee, until the end of 1895.[1] With this assurance Mackinnon announced that he personally would contribute £10,000 to continuing the Company's administration in Uganda if the Society would raise a minimum of £15,000 toward the £40,000 necessary to delay withdrawal at least until the end of 1892.[2] By the beginning of November Kirk was able to assure the Foreign Office that the necessary funds had been raised or guaranteed and that the Company would remain in Uganda till the end of December 1892.[3] At the same time the Foreign Office was deluged with petitions from branches of the Church Missionary Society throughout England, from the Anti-Slavery Society, and from other humanitarian groups, expressing dismay at reports of the contemplated abandonment of Uganda.[4]

This apparent resurgence in the Company's fortunes acted like a tonic on Mackinnon. Much of his old vitality returned. He was again busy with plans for boats on the Lakes, exhortations to humanitarian friends, communications to Lugard, the transport service between the coast and the Lakes pending the completion of the railway, and many other matters relating to the future of his Company. He was still deeply conscious of the necessity for rigorous economy. As he advised Lugard, for the immediate future there must be retrenchment from the previous level of £120,000 per year to no more than £40,000. But after many months of despair there now seemed to be basis for hope that the Company would survive as the British presence in east Africa. Again the hopes proved unfounded.

The Company's campaign was based upon two assumptions: that the British public would not permit withdrawal from Uganda and that the only agency which could represent Britain in Uganda was the Company since the government would not assume the responsibility and expense involved in direct rule. The first assumption was correct; the second was mistaken; the Company's record of failure and the evidence of its desperate financial con-

---

[1] See C.M.S. to Mackinnon, 18 September 1891, Mackinnon Papers.
[2] Note by Anderson, 29 October 1891, F.O. 84/2177, P.R.O.
[3] Note by Villiers, 2 November 1891, F.O. 84/2178, P.R.O. The order was sent by telegraph on the same day; Bentley to F.O., 11 November 1891, F.O. 84/2178, P.R.O. The fund-raising was not as easily accomplished as was then anticipated, but with the assistance of Baroness Burdett-Coutts and other influential backers, the Society raised £16,000 by the beginning of 1892.
[4] Some of these petitions are contained in F.O. 84/2176 and 2177, P.R.O.

dition convinced the government that some alternative must be found. That conviction was strengthened by the testimony of Gerald Portal, who had replaced Euan Smith as consul general in Zanzibar. Portal, a well-connected young man,[1] had risen rapidly in the diplomatic service and in the esteem of Salisbury. In Egypt he had so much impressed Lord Cromer that Cromer considered him a likely successor.[2] Only thirty-two at the time of his appointment as consul general, Portal had achieved a close confidential relationship with the prime minister, who received his opinions with great respect even though Salisbury had occasion from time to time to suggest that they were couched in terms which were excessively downright. Portal considered his predecessor Euan Smith to be a bungler and the Sultanate an anachronism, and within a few months of his arrival had recommended the dissolution of the protectorate on the death of the reigning Sultan and its replacement by efficient British administration.[3] Portal soon came to a similar conclusion with regard to the East Africa Company. The Company, he advised the Foreign Office, was on its death bed from a combination of 'penuriousness, false economy and reckless extravagance', and the government should allow it to expire rather than prolonging its agonies by misplaced efforts at assistance.[4] Salisbury noted that Portal was somewhat importunate, and that 'to help a Company into liquidation before its time is not regarded as a friendly act'.[5]

Salisbury's disinclination to euthanasia, had they known of it, could scarcely have been encouraging to the directors. As it was, they were preoccupied with organizing a movement to lobby Parliament into a favorable vote for the survey bill and eventually for the railway guarantee. They opened their campaign in January 1892, in the expectation that the survey bill would be brought before the House of Commons sometime in February. A detailed argument on the importance of the railway to the national interest was sent out to eighty-eight chambers of commerce with the request that they press members of Parliament to vote for the

---

[1] His mother was the daughter of the second Earl of Minto.

[2] Introduction by Cromer in Gerald Portal, *The British Mission to Uganda in 1893* (London, 1894), p. xvii.

[3] Salisbury to Portal, 8 March 1892, File A/80, Salisbury Papers. Salisbury pointed out that the issue was not simply one of efficiency and that for a variety of reasons they must continue the protectorate.

[4] Portal to Anderson, 26 February 1892, F.O. 84/2229, P.R.O

[5] Note by Salisbury on *ibid*.

survey and for financial guarantees.[1] The board also employed A. J. Mounteney Jephson, a member of Stanley's Emin Pasha expedition, to tour the country giving speeches exhorting his listeners to express their backing for the railway, and sought newspaper support.[2] The campaign had a mixed response. Some chambers of commerce sent resolutions to the Foreign Office:[3] others were wary of endorsing the principle of government subsidies for private enterprise,[4] and others apparently did not respond at all. Some newspapers expressed themselves favorably, but the general response to the Company's appeal was subdued;[5] there was no evidence of widespread feeling that the railway was of vital importance.

When the issue of a grant of £20,000 toward a survey came before Parliament again at the beginning of March, the arguments for and against were essentially those presented in the previous session, though the government's position had been somewhat strengthened by the final ratification of the Brussels Act at the beginning of January,[6] which gave the railway subsidy the coloration of an anti-slave trade measure. The opposition were not deluded by this argument; they recognized that the proposal involved a major departure in Imperial policy and expressed themselves to that effect. James Bryce argued that the grant of a subsidy was the first step down a road which ended in annexation;[7] Labouchere repeated the theme in more polemical language.[8] When the proposal was brought to a vote, however, the leadership of the Liberal party chose to abstain, and the measure carried, 211 to 113.[9] Neither the vote nor the anticipations of the spokesmen had any relationship to George Mackenzie's lyrical description of the occasion as 'perhaps the most important debate affecting the question of slavery since the cause of the African Negro was so gloriously and successfully championed 60 years ago by Brougham, Buxton, Clarkson, Macaulay, Wilberforce, and others'.[10]

[1] Directors to chambers of commerce, 5 January 1892; Bentley to Mackinnon, 7 January 1892, both in Mackinnon Papers.

[2] de Kiewiet, 'History of the Imperial British East Africa Company', pp. 288–9.

[3] See F.O. 84/2242, P.R.O.

[4] See, for example, Robert A. Lockhart, chairman, Edinburgh Chamber of Commerce, to Bentley, 8 January 1892, Mackinnon Papers.

[5] See, for example, *Pall Mall Gazette*, 27 February 1892.

[6] Kirk to Mackinnon, 5 January 1892, Mackinnon Papers.

[7] *Parliamentary Debates, Hansard*, 3 March 1892, p. 1862.

[8] *Ibid.*, 4 March 1892, pp. 51–2.   [9] *Ibid.* p. 91.

[10] George S. Mackenzie, 'British East Africa and the Mombasa Railway', *Fortnightly Review*, April 1892, p. 566.

The decision of the Liberal leadership to abstain was greeted by government supporters as an act of cowardice. Gladstone's statement that he would not support the bill but yet would not oppose it evoked derisive laughter from the government benches.[1] But the Opposition was caught in a dilemma. Far more than the Conservative party, the Liberals were deeply divided on the posture they should adopt toward the Empire. Gladstone's constitutional aversion to the expansion of British responsibilities clashed with the imperial outlook of Rosebery, widely regarded as the heir apparent, whose views on the significance of Uganda and its importance to the Nile Valley closely corresponded to those of Salisbury.[2] Between these extremes there were many gradations. Harcourt was as cold as Gladstone to expenditure for imperial purposes but not necessarily to expansion itself, as his admiration for Cecil Rhodes made evident. Confronted with the contradictions within its ranks, the party chose to defer rather than to oppose. The consequence was that it came into office with no declared policy. The Salisbury government tottered to a fall in August 1892 and Gladstone formed his fourth ministry, with Rosebery at the Foreign Office and Harcourt as Chancellor of the Exchequer.

During the months since the survey vote, the Company had continued in a comatose condition. In its straitened circumstances it had lost the energy to carry out commercial development; it remained in suspended animation pending some basic decision with regard to the future. The vote of £20,000 for a survey was encouraging, but did not automatically ensure the construction of a railway, and time was running out. The emergency infusion provided by the Church Missionary Society and Mackinnon would not be repeated. It was useless to attempt to raise funds by offering additional shares to the public. Without a railway, or at least a firm assurance that it would be constructed, there was no market for the shares of a near-bankrupt company, but without additional capital the Company could not survive long enough for a railway to be built. Sir John Kirk registered his conclusion on the future of the Company under such circumstances when he expressed the desire to dispose of his shares for whatever they would bring and retire from the board.[3] There were two possible out-

[1] *Parliamentary Debates, Hansard*, 4 March 1892, p. 91.
[2] Robinson and Gallagher, *Africa and the Victorians*, pp. 311–12.
[3] Kirk to Mackinnon, private, 2 May 1892, Mackinnon Papers. He did not carry out this intention, perhaps because the shares would have brought little return.

comes for the Company, in the view of the directors. They might sell its chartered rights either to Britain or to Zanzibar and then either go into liquidation or continue as an ordinary commercial company, or the government might conceivably grant a subsidy sufficient to keep the Company alive. In January 1892 they had developed a strategy to prepare for either contingency. One line of approach was suggested by Kirk. The Sultanate of Zanzibar might be prevailed upon by the British government to buy the Company's mainland concession.[1] Kirk's advice was incorporated in a 'private' communication which the assistant secretary of the Company, P. L. McDermott, addressed to Eric Barrington, Salisbury's secretary. McDermott proposed unofficially that the Sultan resume control over the mainland and pay the Company a 'fair proportion' of its capital outlay – perhaps two-thirds of an estimated expenditure of £525,000, either in cash or in three per cent annuities. The annual charge to Zanzibar for installment payments over fifty years would be £10,500, and this would be more than compensated by the revenue from customs of about £17,500. The East Africa Company would then be free to devote itself entirely to commercial operations.[2]

Mackenzie made a similar overture to Portal in Zanzibar through the Company's administrator, E. J. Berkeley. Portal's further observation had merely confirmed his earlier impression of the ineffectiveness of the Company: 'their administration is I consider, thoroughly bad.' Its officers, with the exception of Berkeley and Lugard, were misfits whose low pay matched their contributions.[3] But he responded favorably to Mackenzie's suggestions. It would be in the best interests of the government, he thought, for Zanzibar to buy out the Company and for Britain to assume direct administration of Uganda. The transition might be effected in one year by which time Zanzibar would be better able to bear the strain of expansion to the coast and the Parliament could be prepared for the expense of direct administration. In the meantime the Company should continue with whatever assistance was necessary to keep it in Uganda.[4] Salisbury was receptive to the idea, but in the last months of his government he was not inclined to take any action, and the Foreign Office response to the Company's overture was not enthusiastic. Anderson commented that it

[1] Kirk to Mackinnon, 23 January 1892, Mackinnon Papers.
[2] McDermott to Barrington, 13 January 1892, F.O. 84/2239, P.R.O.
[3] Portal to Salisbury, 15 August 1892, Portal Papers, s.106, Rhodes House.
[4] Portal to Anderson, 3 September 1892, in *ibid.*

P

was practically a proposal to give a monopoly to a trading company in return for which it would have no responsibility.[1] But the Foreign Office took no official notice of a private communication and the proposal remained dormant, to be revived at a later date in a somewhat altered form.

The issue of the future of the Company was joined to that of the future of Uganda, and this was brought into high relief by a succession of events in 1892. In May the Company notified the government of its decision to retire from Uganda at the end of the year,[2] and shortly thereafter a public furore broke out over allegations by the French government that Lugard had been party to the massacre of Catholics in Buganda. The charges were eventually demonstrated to be exaggerated or baseless,[3] but the effect of the sensation which they engendered was to focus attention on Uganda as a national question. Neither opposition nor government could any longer consider the issue only in terms of the substantive effects of Company withdrawal. Now they had to contend with national honor, prestige, religion – to the emotion-laden appeals which are the joy of the demagogue and the despair of the statesman. An additional ingredient was provided by Portal, who warned Rosebery that the withdrawal of the Company from Uganda would mean anarchy and bloodshed.[4]

The incoming Liberal government was therefore required to confront a far more explosive problem than that faced by its predecessors. The majority of the Parliamentary membership and the preponderance of the cabinet were true in the faith of anti-annexationism and their six years of opposition had not taxed their principles with responsibility. But now they were forced to make a decision which could have grave consequences for the continuance of their government in office. The bulk of the Liberal press remained doctrinaire in its opposition to governmental involvement in Uganda, but a government which followed this advice risked the indictment that it had 'scuttled'; the memory of Khartoum and its political consequences had not entirely faded.

Shortly after the election public pressure began to be exerted on the new administration to commit itself to the retention of

---

[1] Note by Anderson, 18 January 1892, in *ibid.*
[2] Bentley to F.O., 7 May 1892, F.O. 84/2248, P.R.O.
[3] For a detailed discussion, see Perham, *Lugard*, pp. 327 ff.
[4] For a detailed discussion, see D. A. Low, 'British Public Opinion and the Uganda Question: October–December 1892', *Uganda Journal*, September 1954, pp. 81–100, reprinted in his *Buganda in Modern History*, pp. 55–83.

Uganda, and this pressure steadily mounted during the autumn and winter of 1892. In this campaign the Company's directors were involved but they did not direct it. Indeed, the 'Keep Uganda' campaign was not entirely harmonious with the Company's objectives, for 'British' rule could mean the replacement of the Company in Uganda rather than its continuation.

The active phase of the campaign began at the end of September, when a delegation from the Church Missionary Society appealed to Rosebery against withdrawal and received a sympathetic hearing. At about the same time, Lugard arrived in England to participate in the fight to save Uganda and to defend himself against accusations that he had permitted atrocities against Buganda Catholics. With the same energy he had displayed in the conquest of Uganda, he travelled throughout England and Scotland exhorting chambers of commerce and various public meetings appealing for expressions of opposition to evacuation.[1] Lugard, the Church Missionary Society, and others contributed to a massive manifestation of public opinion seldom equalled in the nineteenth century. From all over Britain petitions poured in to the Foreign Office demanding retention. Newspapers reported the enthusiasm of public meetings attended by all classes for a 'forward policy' in Uganda.[2] Beyond Britain were the colonies, and the Colonial Office reported that abandonment would raise a 'terrible cry' overseas against a government allegedly hostile to the colonies. This indignation, one official pointed out, could be a powerful electioneering weapon in an age in which someone in every village had friends or relatives in the colonies.[3] These manifestations at home and overseas strengthened the position of Rosebery against those of his colleagues who favored withdrawal.

The deadline of 31 December 1892 set by the Company for its evacuation of Uganda gave the new cabinet little time for maneuvering to minimize the political consequences of any action it might take. It was evident to the cabinet that Mackinnon and the Company's board were attempting to utilize public excitement to blackmail the government into subsidizing the Company as a means of maintaining the British presence in Uganda. Mackinnon in effect had admitted that this was his intention when in notifying

[1] Perham, *Lugard*, pp. 421–7.
[2] Low, *Buganda in Modern History*, pp. 55–83.
[3] Meade to Ripon, 15 September 1892, Addtl. MSS 43556, Ripon Papers, British Museum.

the Foreign Office of impending withdrawal he had added that he clung to the hope that 'it may be in the power of Her Majesty's Government to avoid the serious danger of national reproach that must accompany retreat from an area which the European concert declare to be under British influence'.[1] Mackinnon and the directors pressed hard on the theme that the country would be a scene of carnage if the Company withdrew. As soon as the pacifying influence of the Company was withdrawn the rival factions would fly at each other's throats, and in all likelihood the Muslims would take advantage of the war between Christians to eliminate both the weakened Catholics and Protestants and their missionaries as well. With such an emotional approach they sought to force the Gladstone ministry to take action contrary to what they believed to be its natural craven inclinations.[2] They hoped to extract from the government not only a subsidy to remain in Uganda but a basic financial arrangement which would keep the Company alive for at least another five years. There were two ways by which the Company's operations on the coast could be supported without commitments from the Exchequer. The Sultan might agree to a pledge of the Company's revenue from customs, including his rent, as collateral for a loan to be raised by public subscription or he himself might lend the necessary £200,000 to cover five years of the Company's operations.[3]

This was the last desperate gambit. If it failed, the only recourse was to surrender the charter on the best terms that could be obtained. Whatever sympathy Salisbury might have displayed for such a proposal, there was none from a Gladstone administration. The Company hoped for support from Lord Rosebery, who in his determination to hold Uganda stood out against the majority of his colleagues. But Rosebery's preoccupation was not with prolonging the life of a chartered company but with the protection of the approaches to Egypt and the danger that France by occupying Uganda might then extend its influence to Equatoria on the Upper Nile.[4] The new Colonial Secretary, the Earl of Ripon, held

[1] Mackinnon to F.O., 17 May 1892, F.O. 84/2249, P.R.O.
[2] This line of strategy is outlined in a letter from Kemball to Mackinnon, 15 July 1892, Mackinnon Papers.
[3] Memorandum by Mackenzie, 27 July 1892, F.O. 84/2255, P.R.O.
[4] This was the concern of the Intelligence Department of the War Office and of Sir Percy Anderson. Intelligence Dept., W.O. to F.O., 23 August 1892, F.O. 84/2257, P.R.O. Rosebery was not immediately convinced by this argument. He noted that 'I do not think very highly of this memorandum'. But he was

the orthodox Liberal opinion that Salisbury's African policy had involved Britain in far too great responsibilities from which there would be little material benefit, and his advisors agreed with him.[1] What had been done could not be undone, but Uganda and the railway question were still open issues. He did not entirely discount the alarmist prophecies of Lugard and others that evacuation would result in a massacre, though he thought them exaggerated, but his disposition was to oppose the extension of governmental responsibility over Uganda.[2] Harcourt was more emphatic. Under no circumstance, he insisted, should the government allow itself to be panicked by the Company's deadline into acting against sound Liberal principles. The party had been right when it had opposed the occupation of the Sudan from the north; it would be equally right in opposing extension from the south. All of the arguments advanced for the retention of Uganda – humanitarian, economic, or strategic – were either specious or exaggerated. There were no products there worth the expenditure of public funds, and as for the fear of a massacre, Lugard and his Maxim gun had probably already killed more Christians than would die on his departure. Britain must stay out of the morass of Uganda:

Similar enterprises in these regions have been disastrous failures. The Congo is bankrupt. The Germans have met with severe repulses. The Italians have not been more fortunate. Everything warns us against this ill-omened international jealousy which is at the root of all this annexing policy.[3]

Rosebery's effort to separate the occupation from the question of the railway was unacceptable to Harcourt. The one would inevitably involve the other. The backbenchers, he said, had understood the issue better than their leaders when they had voted against the railway survey; the government now should show as much sense as its followers and refrain from committing folly.[4] Gladstone dismissed the issue as no issue at all. In the pontifical terms which delighted the faithful and infuriated dissenters, Gladstone explained that since Salisbury had merely expressed regret when the Company first had announced its intention to

eventually converted. See Robinson and Gallagher, *Africa and the Victorians,* pp. 314–15.

[1] Meade to Ripon, 15 September 1892, Addtl. MSS 43556, Ripon Papers, British Museum.
[2] Secret memorandum, Ripon, 25 September 1892, CAB 37/31/27, P.R.O.
[3] Secret memorandum, Harcourt, 22 September 1892, CAB 37/31/24, P.R.O.
[4] *Ibid.*

withdraw, the Conservative government had in effect already made the decision to take no action and there was consequently no problem to be resolved. If it should be reopened, however, he would adamantly oppose any action by the government to replace the Company or any military measures in Uganda whatsoever.[1]

With such assurances, Harcourt was convinced that he had won the battle. 'I have saved the situation as regards the Uganda annexation,' he wrote his son at the end of September.[2]

Harcourt's exultation was premature, for Rosebery had one argument to offer that caused his colleagues to hesitate – he might resign on the Uganda issue and his resignation could produce convulsions in the Liberal party which might drive the government from office, for there was no question that he was supported by a strong tide of public feeling. This issue the cabinet, so long in the wilderness of opposition, preferred not to face, and they agreed to a 'compromise' suggested by Harcourt by which the Company would receive a subsidy to extend its tenure in Uganda to the end of March 1893.[3]

This decision was not simply an act of expediency to defer a fight in the hope that conditions might somehow change sufficiently to reconcile Rosebery to the majority position. There were alternatives to outright evacuation which in the opinion of Harcourt and others merited consideration. They did not even reject a cryptic suggestion of Leopold hinting that he might be willing to assume the administration of Uganda as an agent of the Queen, but agreed to write the King a 'dilatory reply' which would give him the opportunity to make a more detailed proposal.[4] Ripon was attracted by an idea suggested by his Colonial Office staff that Uganda should be bartered to Germany for south-west Africa and German New Guinea, thus at the same time eliminating the 'Uganda problem' and a source of vexation to Cape Colony and the Australian colonies.[5] Ripon reluctantly dropped the idea because of the coolness of Rosebery, who pointed out that if the

---

[1] Memorandum on Uganda, Gladstone, 24 September 1892, CAB 37/31/29, P.R.O.

[2] A. G. Gardiner, *Sir William Harcourt* (2 vols., London, 1923), II, 193.

[3] Harcourt to his son, 3 October, 1892, in Gardiner, *Sir William Harcourt*, II, 197.

[4] Cabinet notes, 30 September 1892, Addtl. MSS 44648, Gladstone Papers, British Museum; Cabinet Minutes, 30 September 1892, CAB 41/22/12, P.R.O.

[5] This idea is discussed in Meade to Ripon, 4 October 1892, Addtl. MSS 43556; Buxton to Ripon, 4 October 1892, Addtl. MSS 43553, both in Ripon Papers, British Museum.

Germans wanted Uganda and Britain decided to evacuate, they could take the territory without any exchange at all.[1] But the great hope of several members of the cabinet was Cecil Rhodes, whose record as an empire-builder by private agency they saw in such glittering contrast to the sorry performance of the East Africa Company. Rhodes did not ask for subsidies from government; he gave them. He had built railroads and telegraphs and opened up central Africa to settlement and economic development while Mackinnon had done nothing constructive. So circulated the myth; that it did not entirely accord with the facts was of little consequence. Rhodes represented power devoted to a noble ideal, the expansion of Britain without governmental risk or expense. Rhodes and some members of the British South Africa Company's London board, notably George Cawston, had expressed the desire to save Uganda for Britain and perhaps even to buy out the East Africa Company's rights altogether. With the telegraph to the north already at Lake Nyasa, the future of Uganda was an immediate question for Rhodes as well as for the Imperial government. During a visit to London in November 1892 he assured Harcourt of his willingness to administer Uganda purely as a manifestation of his commitment to Empire, for a subsidy of only £25,000 a year. Harcourt, though he had rejected out of hand the suggestion of continuing assistance to the East Africa Company, was excited by the prospect of a bargain with Rhodes.[2]

The offer of Rhodes came to nothing, partly because Rosebery had committed himself to work for direct governmental rule in Uganda,[3] partly because Rhodes himself was already heavily involved in the financing of the British South Africa Company, but Rosebery was given the opportunity to delay a decision which would almost certainly have been negative. As a result the government was exposed to a continuing agitation by the press and the pro-Uganda missionary and other imperialist pressure groups. Mackinnon, who continued to hope that the reversal of the cabinet's decision to abandon Uganda would mean a new lease of

---

[1] Rosebery to Ripon, most confidential, 17 October 1892, Addtl. MSS 43516, Ripon Papers, British Museum. Rosebery argued that Uganda's being in the British sphere would not be an impediment to Germany, which would manufacture disturbances on the frontier with German East Africa and occupy Uganda to 'restore order'.

[2] An account of a discussion between Rhodes and Harcourt is contained in Wilfrid S. Blunt, *My Diaries* (New York, 1921), 4 November 1892, pp. 100–1.

[3] Robinson and Gallagher, *Africa and the Victorians*, p. 319.

life for his Company, was elated. He wrote to Salisbury, enjoying his respite from responsibility in his French chalet, that now 'public opinion will certainly compel Mr Gladstone to abandon his opposition to the retention of Uganda'.[1]

Mackinnon's assessment of the effect of public pressure proved right; his hopes regarding the result for his Company proved illusory. The alternatives Rosebery was considering did not include the Company. He had not declined to deal with Rhodes in order to negotiate with Mackinnon. For a time Rosebery contemplated circumventing the objections of the anti-imperialists by assigning administration of Uganda to Zanzibar to be represented, of course, by a British officer, with a subsidy from the imperial government,[2] but he soon discarded this deception in favor of a different approach. In November he succeeded in inducing the cabinet to accept appointment of a commissioner to visit Uganda and to report his findings. Though Gladstone, Harcourt, and John Morley balked at giving the officer administrative authority and all references to such powers were struck from the draft instructions, Rosebery had scored a great coup, and the appointment of Portal confirmed the triumph. Portal's opinion that Britain must retain Uganda was well known, and his recommendations were a foregone conclusion. Yet none of the cabinet seems to have objected to a nomination which involved a repudiation of the avowed positions of the majority. It was a remarkable capitulation to domestic political expediency – Rosebery remained in the cabinet, free to pursue a foreign policy repugnant to the majority of his party.[3]

The appointment of Portal meant no reprieve for the East Africa Company. Portal's contempt for the Company was almost as well known as his support for British rule in Uganda. Both Rosebery and Portal were committed to the elimination of the Company as a factor in east Africa. Before his appointment as commissioner, Portal had proposed that the Company cease to perform all administrative functions and that the imperial government should assign to Zanzibar the administration of the coastal belt either for a specified number of years or indefinitely.[4]

[1] Mackinnon to Salisbury, 5 November 1892, File E, Salisbury Papers.
[2] This idea is discussed in Portal to Rosebery, confidential, 3 November 1892, CAB 37/32/43, P.R.O.
[3] For a detailed discussion, see Robinson and Gallagher, *Africa and the Victorians*, pp. 319 ff.
[4] Portal to Rosebery, 3 November 1892, Portal Papers, s.106, Rhodes House, copy in CAB 37/32/43, P.R.O.

So far as Rosebery was concerned, the only remaining value of the Company was to act as a stop-gap government in Uganda until Portal could complete his mission and his report could be acted upon. To that end, he proposed to the directors that the Company agree to stay in Uganda until the end of 1893 with a government subsidy. This brought Mackinnon to Whitehall in a state of great agitation. He had thought of Rosebery as a possible ally, but the one-year extension he recognized as a mere stay of execution for the Company. He pleaded with the Foreign Secretary to extend the term to two years – even Harcourt, he said, had been willing to grant four years – but received no encouragement. When he tested Rosebery on the question of the railway, he was shocked to receive a response as icy as that of the most dedicated Little Englander. Rosebery was not prepared to recommend any expenditure. The railway, he had decided, would be far too costly for the traffic it would bear and for the foreseeable future transportation would continue to be by road. Mackinnon's pleas and threats of outraged public opinion left Rosebery unmoved. The interview was among the most shattering experiences of Mackinnon's life. His spirits had been buoyed up by the assumption that the success of the campaign for the retention of Uganda meant continuation of his Company, and he now saw that he had deluded himself. The fire had gone out of him. He would be 70 on 31 March, the date fixed for evacuation. The coincidence was appropriate, he told Rosebery, for his work was done, and the Company's services were at an end. All that remained was the settlement of the compensation to be paid the Company on its liquidation.[1]

Immediately after his interview with Rosebery, Mackinnon proceeded to the Company's boardroom to report the results, but he was too ill to remain for the entire meeting. The board made a show of resoluteness against Rosebery's proposal of a one-year extension by insisting upon three years as a minimum, with a subsidy of approximately £50,000 per year.[2] This tactic was no more successful than had been Mackinnon's. Rosebery interpreted the response as a rejection[3] and he informed Mackinnon that the cabinet had 'decided not to interfere with the evacuation by the Company. This will relieve you of any further anxiety in the

[1] Memorandum, Rosebery, 17 November 1892, F.O. 84/2263, P.R.O.
[2] Mackinnon to Rosebery, 18 November 1892; Mackinnon to Currie, 18 November 1892, both in F.O. 84/2264, P.R.O.
[3] Rosebery to Mackinnon, 19 November 1892, F.O. 84/2264, P.R.O.

matter.'[1] Rosebery's treatment of Mackinnon showed no concern for the sensitivity of an infirm old man who had invested so much of his energy and money in a cause which he believed had served the national interest. Perhaps such sensitivity was a luxury which a statesman could not afford. But Stanley, who was present when Mackinnon received Rosebery's dismissal of the Company, observed the trembling hands with which he tore open the letter and the sadness with which he received the news.[2] Mackinnon lived on until June 1893, but his involvement with the East Africa Company was over. He took no part in the negotiations for the liquidation of the Company. He resigned as chairman of the board in April, but he had in fact withdrawn earlier. His Company officially survived him by almost two and a half years, but it had died in Uganda and the *coup de grâce* had been delivered by the Earl of Rosebery.

1 Rosebery to Mackinnon, private, 23 November 1892, F.O. 84/2264, P.R.O.
2 Stanley, *Autobiography*, p. 448, cited in de Kiewiet, 'History of the Imperial British East Africa Company', pp. 300–1.

9

The end of the Company

The East Africa Company was an aberration among chartered companies. No critic ever accused Rhodes or Goldie or even Dent of being an unworldly philanthropist, as Mackinnon and his board were labelled. The appellation was not a compliment even when used by professed humanitarians for it was associated with ineffectuality. The Company had been created to trade and to govern and it had failed in both, as even members of the board agreed. There was disagreement as to the causes of this failure; there was almost none as to the fact. Whatever deficiencies Goldie might have, the Royal Niger Company paid dividends. Rhodes might be overly aggressive in the eyes of some but he 'got things done'. But Mackinnon had done nothing to develop his estate. This was a serious indictment, for even the most fervent anti-slaver did not question the idea that Africa should contribute to the welfare of Europe. One writer, more candid than most, wrote in early 1894:

Divested of all philanthropic shams, the real mission of Europe is to turn that continent to profitable account, for the benefit, not of the natives but of their taskmasters. The natives lead a self-indulgent, idle, and dissolute life; and it does not seem fair to the economy of Nature, that they should be allowed to enjoy luxurious idleness, whilst we Westerns, with a higher civilisation, have to toil and moil for our daily bread. Our civilisation demands that subject and inferior races should be treated with justice and leniency; and it is to our interest that they should be taught the gospel of labour and of brotherly love. The *crux* of the whole problem is, however, that the native African infinitely prefers his own indolent life to the *Sturm und Drang* of Western civilisation, even in their attenuated forms in the Tropics.

....

In East Africa . . . the Chartered Company has failed because, under the guise of philanthropy and on the plea of exceptional political responsibilities, it has exceeded its resources and become all but bankrupt. For this the Company is alone to blame, though it may well plead the extenuating circumstances caused by the bad faith of her Majesty's Government. It has played its stake and lost. The shareholders must suffer.[1]

This 'one horse Company', as Rosebery described it,[2] had become an embarrassment to the government; the only issue so far as the Foreign Secretary was concerned, was the mode of its dissolution. By his selection of Portal to report on the condition of east Africa, Rosebery ensured that the evaluation of the Company's record would be damning, for Portal's contempt for the Company was well known. The chief commissioner did not disappoint Rosebery. Though the account of his mission published post-humously was circumspect in its comments on the Company,[3] Portal's private communications were unrelievedly condemnatory. From Kibwesi, about two hundred miles inland from Mombasa, he wrote to Lloyd Mathews:

Not a day has passed without some deep and bitter curses being called down upon that utter fraud of a Company. The much-talked-of road, the stations, the administration and control of the interior – all these are simply inventions and fabrications for the delusion of the shareholders.[4]

The 'Mackinnon road' Portal described as an overgrown path, blocked by thornbushes, vines, and trees,[5] and the Company administration was virtually non-existent. The Company's maps which showed the route dotted with 'stations' and 'posts' were a farce. Many stations had been abandoned and in those which continued to exist either the force available was inadequate or the conduct of the officer in charge had alienated the surrounding peoples.[6] In Kikuyu territory he found the Company station practically besieged despite the presence of 150 Zanzibari soldiers who had arrived with the advance guard of his caravan.[7] The Company, he wrote Percy Anderson, had grossly deceived the government; it had done worse than nothing for the country between the coast and the interior, and Buganda was in a 'more unsatisfactory, unsettled, and unhappy state' than it had been before the Company's advent.[8]

---

[1] Arthur Silva White, 'Chartered Government in Africa', *Nineteenth Century*, xxxv (January 1894), 128, 130.
[2] Rosebery to Portal, 1 December 1892, quoted in Low, 'British Public Opinion', p. 98.
[3] Gerald Portal, *The British Mission to Uganda in 1893* (London, 1894).
[4] Extract, Portal to Mathews, 18 January 1893, CAB 37/33/8, P.R.O.
[5] *Ibid.*
[6] Portal to Rosebery, 24 January 1893, in *ibid.*
[7] Portal to Rosebery, confidential, 31 January 1893, CAB 37/33/9, P.R.O.
[8] Portal to Anderson, 22 February 1893, Rhodes Papers, s.109, Rhodes House.

Portal judged the Company by standards of administrative effectiveness which no chartered company could have met. No company, German or British, had the capital to establish a governmental system over the vast areas over which it was assigned jurisdiction. Goldie's Royal Niger Company was unable to extend its administration much beyond the river system,[1] and even the vaunted South Africa Company which could offer inducements in booty not available to its contemporaries could not provide adequate resources for effective administration beyond Matabeleland and Mashonaland. One officer who was administrator in North-Western Rhodesia for four years wrote later:

In Matabeleland and Mashonaland I was one of many, in Barotseland and North-Western Rhodesia I was the boss of a few... There is, alas, no-one to testify to our Homeric battles for four years against the odds in that wide and unfriendly country – in nine months we got only one mail from the south.[2]

Portal was correct in his assertion that the resources employed to keep open the interior route were pitifully inadequate. J. Scott Keltie estimated that only about ten shillings worth of capital was available for each square mile under the Company's jurisdiction.[3] Outside of Buganda there were less than fifty European employees, about half of whom were stationed in Mombasa.[4]

The paucity of manpower and resources meant that the Company's ability to assert its power against the African societies along the caravan route was tenuous at best. The Company maintained only two permanent bases which merited the title – at Machakos, in the Kamba country, and at Fort Smith. The Machakos station, established in 1889 as the Company's first inland station, prospered with the cooperation of the Kamba, who traded their goods for the European commodities supplied by the Company, helped to protect the station, and provided laborers and runners.[5] Fort

---

[1] Perham, *Lugard*, p. 704.
[2] Coryndon to Fox, 26 November 1907, quoted in T. O. Ranger, 'African Reactions to the Imposition of Colonial Rule in East and Central Africa', in Gann and Duignan, *Colonialism in Africa*, 1, 294.
[3] J. Scott Keltie, *The Partition of Africa* (London, 1893), ch. 18, cited in Gann and Duignan, *Colonialism in Africa*, p. 294.
[4] Reports from administrator to directors, various dates, in Mackinnon Papers, cited by de Kiewiet, 'History of the Imperial British East Africa Company', p. 226.
[5] Marie de Kiewiet Hemphill. 'The British Sphere, 1884–1894', in Oliver and Mathew, *History of East Africa*, pp. 414–15. Ainsworth's reports on the prosperity of the country attracted attention in Europe. The International

Smith,[1] in the Kikuyu country, on the other hand, was confronted with a hostile population. The Kikuyu for decades had refused to allow Arab caravans to enter their territories[2] and had resisted European penetration as well. The experiences in the 1880s of caravans led by the German explorer, G. A. Fisher, and the Hungarian Count, Samuel Teleki, had caused subsequent expeditions on the way to the Lakes to avoid Kikuyu country. Lugard, however, was not deterred by the reputation of the Kikuyu, and, on his trek to Buganda in 1890, he established the station which was to become Fort Smith. Lugard's experience with the Kikuyu belied the reports he had received of them. He 'was more favourably impressed by them than by any other tribe I had as yet met in Africa . . . they were extremely intelligent, good-mannered, and *most* friendly'.[3] But the tranquility which he observed did not last long. His successors had to contend with ambushes and on occasions sieges of the fort itself. Lugard blamed 'vacillation and indecision' which 'cause in the end a vastly greater amount of bloodshed than the strong hand and the personality which commands obedience'.[4] But a contributory factor was certainly a change in Company policy. In 1892, to lighten the load of expenditures, the directors ordered that the two bases of Fort Smith and Machakos should be self-supporting. The Company's officers had attempted to seize the Kikuyu's grain and it was these actions which had produced the siege which was in progress at the time of Portal's arrival.[5]

Outside of Buganda, therefore, the Company's influence had barely touched the African societies of the interior except for contacts through the depots and stations on the caravan routes. The withdrawal of the Company would thus have no significant effect in the territories between Buganda and the coast. The delay in the dissolution of the Company related not to any problem of the transfer of power, for there was none, but to the issue of the

Freeland Association, which sought land for a communal settlement, expressed interest in establishing a colony which might flourish among the industrious Kamba. See F.O. 2/73, F.O. 83/1240, P.R.O.

[1] Fort Smith was originally named Kikuyu but the name was changed when the station was rebuilt in 1891.
[2] Edward A. Alpers, 'The Nineteenth Century: Prelude to Colonialism', in Ogot and Kieran, *Zamani*, pp. 247–8.
[3] Lugard, *Rise of Our East African Empire*, I, 327.
[4] *Ibid.* p. 537.
[5] Hemphill, 'The British Sphere', in Oliver and Mathew, *History of East Africa*, p. 417.

amount of compensation – the principle that the Company was entitled to some payment was never questioned.

During the months in which the dreary negotiations dragged on, the uncertainty of transition produced a virtual vacuum in administration. The Company was not inclined to spend more money, and the government was not prepared to accept any responsibility. So protracted was the haggling that some critics suspected the government of continuing the contretemps merely to avoid assuming the burdens of administration. *The Times* commented:

> The truth is that the Government are only too glad to find an excuse for doing nothing, consequently they grasp at the unsettled claim of the Company. We are at least entitled to know what is the difference which thus stands in the way of a policy obviously dictated by regard for the national interests. The British East Africa Company may for anything we know be making exorbitant demands, but it is much more probable that it could easily be dealt with on reasonable terms if there were any real desire to settle the matter.[1]

The Times pointed to one consideration which undoubtedly affected government policy. But there was another and perhaps more important factor. Not only did the government wish to avoid responsibility and expense after the transfer of power; it also was determined to avoid expense in effecting that transfer. The government's position was that Parliament must not be asked to vote funds to compensate the Company; the uproar if such a proposal were made was predictable. The obvious alternative was to impose the load on Zanzibar. Let the Sultan resume responsibility on the mainland, with British guidance, of course, and pay the Company a fair sum for the loss of its rights. In the definition of 'fair', however, the Company and the government were far apart. The directors argued that compensation should include not only the transfer of the Zanzibar concession but recompense for the occupation of Zanzibar and for the great services the Company had performed on behalf of the British people. Fowell Buxton argued that the government had used the Company to suppress the slave trade and to preserve a British sphere against European rivals and that the Company should now receive its just reward and at least be repaid the money it had spent, approximately £425,000.[2]

---

[1] *The Times*, 21 August 1894, quoted in McDermott, *British East Africa*, pp. 369–70.

[2] Report of fourth annual meeting, 31 July 1893, F.O. 2/59; report of special general meeting, 8 March 1894, F.O. 2/73, both in P.R.O.

Mackinnon had talked of taking his dividends in philanthropy; Buxton and his fellow-directors now seemed to be asking for the conversion of philanthropy into dividends; and the government was not prepared to pay either for philanthropy or for Uganda. The disposition of the Foreign Office was to use time to moderate the Company's demands.

When the Company in January 1894 reminded the Foreign Office that a year and a half had passed since the proposal to sell the Company's interests had been referred to Portal for comment, the response was that Portal was ill and unable to confer[1] – he died on 26 January, one month after his return to England from his Uganda mission. The annual report to the shareholders for 1894 was consequently a dreary recital of the correspondence with the government and expressed an unconvincing hope that the frustration must soon end:

The present position of affairs is intolerable; and the Directors believe it to be impossible that the decision of Her Majesty's Government upon the proposals of the Company can be much longer delayed.[2]

The directors' growing urgency was interpreted by the Foreign Office as an indication that the policy of delay was having an effect. There were signs of a split between the 'greedy' who were unwilling to lower their demands and the 'moderates' who were anxious to settle for what they could get. The majority of the board, including all the 'City' men as well as Kirk and Buxton, belonged to the first group; but two influential directors, Mackenzie and Sir Donald Stewart, by March 1894, advocated an immediate agreement on 'reasonable' terms. The rigid majority through their employment of T. Scott Keltie, the prominent commentator on Africa, were able to get sympathetic attention in *The Times*[3] but they were not able to mount a campaign which could force the government to deal with them. The policy of attrition therefore continued.

This strategy seemed to be vindicated when Mackenzie in mid-April 1894 proposed on behalf of the board that the compensation to the Company be fixed at £276,000, or approximately 10/6 for each pound of capital which had been spent.[4] This was a

[1] Note, n.d., on Kemball to F.O., 16 January 1894, F.O. 2/73, P.R.O.
[2] Report of Court of Directors to shareholders, 15 February 1894, F.O. 2/73, P.R.O.
[3] Note, Anderson, 25 March 1894, on report of special meeting, 8 March 1894, F.O. 2/73, P.R.O.
[4] Memorandum, Anderson, 16 April 1894, F.O. 83/1311, P.R.O.

substantial reduction from the previous position of the majority of the directors, but the government was not yet prepared to make a settlement. The result was that the Company with the unanimous support of the shareholders broke off negotiations and announced its intention to resume operations under the charter.[1] The threat was ineffectual; by September, the directors were again pleading for an early decision. Anderson noted with satisfaction, 'the tone of this letter is more appealing and less aggressive than that of former letters. The Company's position must be getting almost desperate'.[2] The time seemed to have arrived to impose terms.

In November the Foreign Office with the approval of Rosebery, now prime minister, indicated that it was prepared to recommend to the Sultan that he pay £150,000 for the concession on the coast and to ask Parliament to vote an additional £50,000 for the extinction of its chartered rights, in recognition of the work done by the Company in the interior on behalf of imperial interests. The Company would also be allowed to retain its 'private' property exclusive of some 200 miles of telegraph which would be transferred to the government.[3] This offer was based upon a recommendation by E. J. Berkeley, former acting administrator of the Company, who had joined Portal's Uganda mission as an assistant commissioner. Berkeley had acted as an intermediary between the government and Kemball and Mackenzie. The arrangement had the great merit that the Sultan would pay the bulk of the compensation, and Berkeley assured the Foreign Office that the transaction would actually be advantageous to the Sultan. He would pay the Company in consols which returned only three per cent, and he would now receive over £4,000 per year from customs revenue, which would rise as the coast developed. Furthermore, his dignity would be increased by the return of his 'authority' to the mainland.[4] The acquiescence of the Sultan in such a transaction was taken for granted; it was considered unnecessary to consult him. Well might Kimberley, the new Foreign Secretary, exclaim, 'What a model potentate.'[5]

[1] Kemball to F.O., 8 May 1894; report of special meeting, I.B.E.A., 8 May 1894, both in F.O. 2/79, P.R.O.
[2] Note, Anderson, 7 September 1894, on Kemball to F.O., 6 September 1894, F.O. 2/75, P.R.O.
[3] F.O. to I.B.E.A., 14 November 1894, in *Correspondence Respecting the Retirement of the Imperial British East Africa Company*, c. 7646, 1895.
[4] Memoranda, Anderson, 5 July 1894, 4 October 1894, in F.O. 83/1313, F.O. 2/75 respectively, both in P.R.O.
[5] Memorandum, Anderson, 5 July 1894, F.O. 83/1313, P.R.O.

Q

The directors made one last effort to secure a more favorable arrangement. At the urging of Lord Brassey, they proposed that Zanzibar pay £200,000 in consols and the Exchequer, £100,000. To avoid the necessity of an immediate cash outlay, Brassey proposed that the Treasury's £100,000 be held 'in trust' for the Sultan, which would make available to him £300,000 in consols, yielding a yearly income of £7,500. The deficit of £1,500 could then without strain be provided from the general revenues of the Sultan.[1] The scheme was worthy of the brilliant financier who proposed it; but the suggestion that Zanzibar be burdened with a £450,000 debt, even at two per cent interest, was too blatant a sacrifice of the protectorate for the imperial government to accept, and the Brassey maneuver was rejected. The government finally agreed on behalf of the Sultan to raise the payment by Zanzibar to £200,000 which would include the purchase of the Company's private assets in the concession for £50,000; the total payment, including the vote by Parliament of an additional £50,000, would thus be £250,000.[2] After several weeks of protest at shabby treatment, the board finally surrendered. A shareholders' revolt failed and at a special meeting on 27 March 1895 the directors' motion to accept was approved. In what Kirk described as a 'pious wish', the meeting passed a further resolution asking the directors to continue to urge the Company's moral claim to compensation for the occupation of Uganda,[3] but the battle was over, and the Company soon went into liquidation.[4] The European employees of the Company in Africa were given three months' notice, or alternatively free passages back to England if they left the country within one month of their notice of discharge.[5] Many of them were offered and accepted employment by the government on the transfer of power to the protectorate on 1 July 1895.[6]

The shareholders who had been forced to accept terms which they considered grossly inadequate probably derived a sense of perverse pleasure with the news that the incoming British administration had to contend with a rebellion of elements of the

[1] Memorandum of deputation to Kimberley, n.d. [4 December 1894?], F.O. 2/75, P.R.O.
[2] McDermott, *British East Africa*, p. 382.
[3] Kemball to F.O., 27 March 1895, F.O. 2/97, P.R.O.
[4] It was officially dissolved in May 1897. See B.T. 34/927/38949, P.R.O. This file contains a list of shareholders and their holdings.
[5] Kemball to Anderson, 23 February 1895, F.O. 2/96, P.R.O.
[6] Anderson to Kemball, 4 March 1895, F.O. 2/97, P.R.O.

Mazrui led by Mbaruk. The revolt was put down only after nine months of severe fighting in which the British had to bring in troops from India. But the outbreak was in a sense a result of the ineffectuality of the Company. During the seven years it had been responsible for the east African coast the Company had done little to establish an administrative system but had relied on existing indigenous government. This policy was essentially based on the recognition that the line of least resistance was the cheapest rather than on a sensitive understanding of the characteristics of the coastal society. The rebellion had its immediate origin in the decision of the Company's representative at Malindi to pass over the claims of the candidate who by Muslim law had a better right to the governorship in favor of one who professed to be more favorably disposed to the British. The magnitude of the uprising was increased by the fears of the Mazrui that the new rulers would be more intrusive on their lives than the Company's officials had been.[1]

Post mortems on the Company also reflected the general opinion that its greatest sin had been its feebleness. Mackinnon and the other directors were portrayed as men imbued with high idealism unfortunately not matched by drive and organizational ability. Sir Gerald Portal acknowledged that the Company had performed a public service:

To the founders of the Company belongs the sole credit of the acquisition for the benefit of British commerce of this great potential market for British goods. It should moreover be remembered, in justice to them, that in face of many initial difficulties they succeeded in marked contrast to the neighbouring European colonies in establishing their influence without bloodshed and by their own unaided efforts.[2]

Even that inveterate scourge of chartered companies, Labouchere's *Truth*, gave them credit for being well-meaning:

The East Africa Chartered Company was not, like the South Africa Chartered Company, a Stock Exchange Speculation. Its promoters would not probably have been averse to making money, but in the main they were influenced by a perverted idea of patriotism.[3]

The directors themselves admitted that the Company had done little to develop its territories, though their explanation placed the

---

[1] Bethwell A. Ogot, 'Kenya under the British, 1895 to 1963', in Ogot and Kieran, *Zamani*, pp. 256–7.
[2] Quoted in Mackenzie to F.O., 11 April 1894, F.O. 2/73, P.R.O.
[3] *Truth*, 9 July 1896.

primary responsibility on the government. In their final report to
the shareholders in July 1895 they indicted the Liberal government:

Had the co-operation of the Government been continued to the Company
as originally contemplated, had the proposals entertained by Lord
Salisbury in July, 1892, been acquiesced in by his successors, and had the
arrangement which was made at the suggestion of Her Majesty's Government in 1891 for the maintenance of the Company's influence in Uganda
by means of a subsidy to the King been adopted by the late Government
and the construction of the railway taken in hand, then the development
and administration of the territory would have proceeded at a great
ultimate saving to the Treasury.[1]

The failure of the Imperial British East Africa Company can be
seen in retrospect as inherent in the conditions of its creation.
Mackinnon was imbued, as *Truth* suggested, with a patriotic zeal
which overrode commercial considerations. He knew that, given
limitations on customs revenue and on taxation imposed by
commercial treaties, little profit could be made from administering
the coast. From the beginning he looked to the interior, in particular the Lakes area and Buganda, as the area from which most of
the Company's sustenance must come. But the plan to consolidate
the Company's position on the coast and to proceed cautiously into
the interior was wrecked by the fear of a German coup in Buganda.
The precipitate rush into Buganda, though it was encouraged by
the government, was dictated by Mackinnon's obsession with the
German peril. The result was a commitment of capital without
hope of immediate return, and the early ruination of the Company.

Even if the original plan had been executed, however, the
Company could not have flourished. Its employees could not
compete in trade with the Indian merchants on the coast, and the
surplus available from customs revenue was grossly inadequate to
support even a rudimentary government. Contemporaries and
some subsequent observers placed the onus for the failure upon the
personal deficiencies of the Company's employees. The onus was
misplaced. Given the nature of east Africa's resources, no chartered
company, however ably led, could have succeeded. There was no
gold to lure the unwary investor, little wild rubber to be harvested,
no great waterway to carry the ivory from the interior to the coast.
The potentialities were there for agricultural development but only
after the construction of a railway, which was beyond the resources

[1] Report to shareholders, I.B.E.A., 17 July 1895, F.O. 2/97, P.R.O.

of the Company. Even if Parliament had been willing to underwrite such a railway, the time span before the Company could have benefited by agricultural development was too great. The government which succeeded the Company in 1895 was not much more impressive in the early years in the development of the territory. Before the completion of the railway in 1901, much the same criticisms could have been made of the new regime as had been levelled at the Company. But a government did not depend on profits for its survival.

Judged by the standards of a business enterprise, the East Africa Company was sadly deficient. It entered into operations with the vaguest of ideas as to the economic base on which it would build. The directors through Kirk and others knew that there was little prospect of profit on the coast. The combination of limitations on revenue, paucity of resources, and strength of competition, particularly from Indian merchants, made it almost certain that the Company would not be successful in trade with the coastal peoples. In fact, the Company made little effort to engage in commerce on the coast. From reports of travellers and from the Company's own reconnoitering expeditions, the board knew that the lands between the coast and the Lakes possessed little in resources which could be immediately exploited. This territory was a barrier imposing hazards and expense. Before the construction of a railway, transportation must be costly both in porters and in the forces necessary to protect them. But a railway could not be built without large capital outlay, and capital would not be forthcoming without prospects of immediate returns of profits to investors. The known resources of Buganda and the Lakes area, however, in ivory, salt and other commodities were not valuable enough to attract investors unless the government was willing to give assistance in the form of subsidies and guarantees. The conclusion of the investing public was that the Company was a poor risk, as the response to the effort to raise more capital in August 1889 made manifest. Yet a group of men, most of whom had made their fortunes through shrewd business judgments, invested substantial amounts of their own money in this hopeless cause. Lord Brassey subscribed £10,000, the Morgans, respected in the City, many thousands more. James F. Hutton, who in west Africa showed outstanding business acumen, invested £5,000 in east Africa in a company with shabby prospects and a ramshackle organization. The successful Scottish brewer, H. J. Younger, appeared to be the victim of his product by his investment of £5,000 in the east Africa enterprise. The commitment of capital by these and other prominent businessmen seems incongruous in the light of their earlier business careers.

A partial explanation for their collective aberration is in the commitment of the greatest aberrant of them all, Sir William Mackinnon. Mackinnon contributed by far the greatest capital not only in his own name but in those of members of his family, and he backed his original commitment by further purchases of shares thereafter. At the time of liquidation, the estate of Mackinnon had 42,940 shares of £1 each. John Mackinnon had 5,000 with an additional 12,000 held jointly with another subscriber, and Duncan Mackinnon had 5,400 shares. In addition, Mackinnon's close friends and business associates contributed substantial amounts – George S. Mackenzie, Sir Edwyn Dawes, and James Hall each held 5,000 shares.[1] The Company was thus backed from its beginning by the Mackinnon group with substantial funds which demonstrated their belief in its future, and this commitment contributed to the commitment of others.

This explanation, however, leaves much unanswered. Brassey, the Morgans, and others did not usually invest simply on the basis of confidence in the judgment of others, even as successful a businessman as Mackinnon. They usually made their own independent appraisals. The question remains why they suspended their usual criteria in this instance. The answer, if an answer can be given, must vary with individual cases. Most of the original investors seem to have been motivated by the belief that they were serving a high national purpose in committing their resources to a chartered company. They hoped to make money or at least not to lose it, but profit was not their sole, or in many cases, their primary objective. They had confidence in Mackinnon whose money provided the nucleus and whose leadership they accepted. One index of the character of the Company is the nature of the correspondence among its leadership, and until the phase of imminent liquidation was reached, the bulk of these communications related to the public purposes the Company had been organized to serve. The conclusion seems inescapable that the directors believed that in investing their money they were acting not primarily as businessmen but as imperialists and that the greatest dividends would not

[1] The original £20 shares were divided into twenty £1 shares in 1894; B.T. 31/5594/38949, P.R.O.

be in personal profit but in securing to Britain territories which could be valuable economically and strategically.

These were certainly the impulses which stirred Mackinnon himself. In the last years of his life he manifested all the attributes of a convert to the religion of imperialism. Like Rhodes he was a far more ardent imperialist than the cautious politicians of Whitehall; like Rhodes he attempted by private means to accomplish great public ends. But though their objectives were similar, the environments within which they sought to accomplish them were utterly different. Where Rhodes contended with feeble Portugal, Mackinnon was confronted with the power of Germany. Rhodes could appeal to the cupidity of European investors for the reputed mineral wealth of Matabeleland; Mackinnon could offer only ivory from Buganda. Rhodes with the combined power of De Beers and the Cape prime ministership could attract capital for railway development; Mackinnon with no comparable resources could not. Sir John Kirk, when the Company was in liquidation, expressed deep regret that Rhodes had not absorbed the East Africa Company into his 'Cape regime'. Rhodes, he maintained, had made a 'great mistake'.[1] In this conclusion Kirk implied the judgment that the dynamic Rhodes would have 'succeeded' where the ineffectual Mackinnon had failed. But there is no basis for the supposition that Rhodes or any other of his contemporaries could have soon made a commercial success of east Africa by reliance on private means. Kirk in his life-long identification with east Africa had developed a distorted judgment of its importance, and when the causes of Mackinnon's miscalculation are assessed, the role of Kirk should not be underestimated. The maintenance of British influence in east Africa was of cardinal importance to Kirk. He had watched with dismay as Lord Salisbury bargained away the British position as a concession to Germany, and he had identified himself with the East Africa Company as the best hope of preserving what was left. This was also the basis for Mackinnon's commitment, and Kirk's comment to Lugard when the Company was wound up would have been endorsed by its founder as well:

With all its failings, it has been an honest concern, not a money-making one, and but for its work we should not now possess a footing in East Africa.[2]

[1] Kirk to Cawston, 29 January 1895, BSAC Misc. v, Rhodes House.
[2] Coupland, *East Africa and Its Invaders*, p. 486.

Select bibliography

MANUSCRIPT SOURCES

Public Record Office
The most important series for this study was F.O. 84 – Slave Trade. In addition the following were consulted: F.O. 2 and 83 on Africa, the appropriate series for diplomatic correspondence with Germany and Belgium, and the CAB series on cabinet papers. The Board of Trade documents on I.B.E.A. (BT 34) were also of value. The following private collections deposited in the P.R.O. were useful:
    Granville Papers
    Malet Papers
British Museum
    Dilke Papers
    Gladstone Papers
    Ripon Papers
Christ Church, Oxford
    Salisbury Papers
National Archives of Rhodesia
    Johnston's Diary of Kilimanjaro Expedition (Jo 1/2/6)
Rhodes House
    Kirk Papers
    Portal Papers
    Rhodes Papers
    Waller Papers
Royal Commonwealth Society
    Johnston Papers
School of Oriental and African Studies, University of London
    Mackinnon Papers
University of Durham
    Papers of 4th Earl Grey

UNPUBLISHED THESES

Bair, Henry M., 'Carl Peters and German Colonialism', Stanford Doctoral Dissertation, 1968.
De Kiewiet, Marie, 'History of the Imperial British East Africa Company, 1876–1895', University of London Doctoral Dissertation, 1955.

BOOKS

Aldcroft, Derek H. (ed.), *The Development of British Industry and Foreign Competition, 1875–1914.* London, 1968.

Alpers, Edward A., *The East African Slave Trade.* Nairobi, 1967.

Anstey, Roger, *Britain and the Congo in the Nineteenth Century.* Oxford, 1962.

King Leopold's Legacy: the Congo under Belgian Rule, 1908–1960. London, 1966.

Ascherson, Neal, *The King Incorporated.* London, 1963.

Ashe, R. P., *Chronicles of Uganda.* London, 1894.

Aydelotte, William O., *Bismarck and British Colonial Policy: the Problem of South West Africa, 1883–85.* Philadelphia, 1937.

Blunt, Wilfrid Scawen, *My Diaries.* 2 vols., London, 1919.

Brady, C. T., *Commerce and Conquest in East Africa.* Salem, 1950.

Brunschwig, Henri, *Mythes et réalitiés de l'impérialism colonial français, 1871–1914.* Paris, 1960.

Buckle, George E., *The Letters of Queen Victoria.* Second series, 3 vols., London, 1926–8. Third series, 3 vols., London, 1930–2

Butler, Jeffrey, *The Liberal Party and the Jameson Raid.* Oxford, 1968.

Cairns, H. Alan C., *The Clash of Cultures.* New York, 1965.

Cameron, Verney Lovett, *Across Africa.* 2 vols., 4th ed., London, 1877.

Carton de Wiart, Edmond, *Les grandes compagnies coloniales anglaises du XIXe siècle.* Paris, 1899.

Cecil, Gwendolen Gascoyne, *Life of Robert, Marquis of Salisbury.* 4 vols., London, 1921–32.

Cecil, Lord Edward, *The Leisure of an Egyptian Official.* London, 1921.

Collins, Robert O., *King Leopold, England, and the Upper Nile, 1899–1909.* New Haven, 1968.

The Southern Sudan, 1883–1898: A Struggle for Control. New Haven, 1962.

Coupland, Sir Reginald, *East Africa and Its Invaders, from the Earliest Times to the Death of Seyyid Said in 1856.* Oxford, 1938.

The Exploitation of East Africa, 1856–1890: The Slave Trade and the Scramble. London, 1939.

Crowe, S. E., *The Berlin West Africa Conference, 1884–1885.* London, 1942.

Curtin, Philip D., *The Image of Africa.* Madison, 1964.

Dilke, Charles W., *Problems of Greater Britain.* 2 vols., London, 1890.

The Present Position of European Politics, or, Europe in 1887. London, 1887.

Dugdale, E. T. S. (ed.), *German Diplomatic Documents, 1871–1914.* 4 vols., London, 1928–31.

Eliot, Sir Charles, *The East Africa Protectorate.* London, 1905.

Escott, Thomas Hay Sweet, *Personal Forces of the Period.* London, 1898.

Fitzmaurice, Lord Edmond, *Life of Earl Granville.* 2 vols., London, 1905.

Frankel, S. H., *Capital Investment in Africa.* London, 1938.

Gann, L. H., and Duignan, Peter (eds.), *Colonialism in Africa, 1870–1960.* 1, Cambridge, 1969.

Gardiner, A. G., *The Life of Sir William Harcourt.* 2 vols., London, 1923.

R

Gifford, Prosser, and Louis, W. Roger, *Britain and Germany in Africa*. New Haven, 1967.

Gray, John Milner, *History of Zanzibar*. London, 1962.

Gray, Richard, and Birmingham, David (eds.), *Pre-colonial African Trade*. London, 1970.

Greaves, R. L., *Persia and the Defense of India 1884–1892*. London, 1959.

Grenville, J. A. S., *Lord Salisbury and Foreign Policy. The Close of the Nineteenth Century*. London, 1964.

Gwynn, Stephen Lucius, and Tuckwell, Gertude M., *The Life of the Rt. Hon. Sir Charles W. Dilke*. 2 vols., London, 1917.

Hanna, Alexander John, *The Beginnings of Nyasaland and North-eastern Rhodesia, 1859–95*. Oxford, 1956.

Henderson, William O., *Studies in German Colonial History*. London, 1962.

Hertslet, Edward, *The Map of Africa by Treaty*. 3 vols., 3rd ed., London, 1967.

Hess, Robert L., *Italian Colonialism in Somalia*. Chicago, 1967.

Hill, George Birkbeck, *Colonel Gordon in Central Africa, 1874–1879*. London, 1881.

Hobley, Charles William, *Kenya, from Chartered Company to Crown Colony*. London, 1929.

Hollingsworth, L. W., *Zanzibar under the Foreign Office, 1890–1913*. London, 1953.

Ingham, Kenneth, *A History of East Africa*. rev. ed., New York, 1965.

Jackson, Frederick John, *Early Days in East Africa*. London, 1930.

Jackson, W. Turrentine, *The Enterprising Scot: Investors in the American West After 1873*. Edinburgh, 1968.

Johnston, Alex, *The Life and Letters of Sir Harry Johnston*. New York, 1929.

Johnston, H. H., *The Story of My Life*. Indianapolis, 1923.

The Uganda Protectorate. 2 vols., London, 1904.

George Grenfell and the Congo. 2 vols., London, 1908.

Keltie, J. Scott, *The Partition of Africa*. London, 1893.

Kennedy, A. L., *Salisbury 1830–1903*. London, 1953.

Langer, William Leonard, *The Diplomacy of Imperialism, 1890–1902*. 2 vols., New York, 1935.

Low, D. A., *Buganda in Modern History*. Berkeley, 1971.

Lowe, C. J., *The Reluctant Imperialists: British Foreign Policy 1878–1902*. 2 vols., London, 1967.

Lugard, Frederick D., *The Rise of Our East African Empire*. Edinburgh, 1893.

Lyne, Robert Nunez, *An Apostle of Empire: Being the Life of Sir Lloyd William Mathews*. London, 1936.

McDermott, P. L., *British East Africa or IBEA*. New ed., London, 1895.

Macdonald, A. J., *Trade, Politics and Christianity in Africa and the East*. London, 1916.

Mangat, J. S., *A History of the Asians in East Africa*. Oxford, 1969.

Middleton, Dorothy (ed.), *The Diary of A. J. Mounteney Jephson: Emin Pasha Relief Expedition, 1887–1889.* Cambridge, 1969.

Ogot, B. A., and Kieran, J. A. (eds.), *Zamani: A Survey of East African History.* Nairobi, 1969.

Oliver, Roland, *The Missionary Factor in East Africa.* London, 1952.

Sir Harry Johnston and the Scramble for Africa. London, 1957.

Palamenghi-Crispi, Thommaso, *The Memoirs of Francesco Crispi.* 3 vols., London, 1912–14.

Perham, Margery Freda, *Lugard*, I: *The Years of Adventure, 1858–1898;* II: *The Years of Authority, 1898–1945.* London, 1956–60.

The Diaries of Lord Lugard. 4 vols., Evanston, 1959–63.

Peters, Carl, *Emin-Pascha Expedition.* Munich, 1891.

Platt, D. C. M., *Finance, Trade and Politics in British Foreign Policy, 1815–1914.* Oxford, 1968.

Portal, Gerard Herbert, *The British Mission to Uganda in 1893.* London, 1894.

Ramm, Agatha (ed.), *The Political Correspondence of Mr Gladstone and Lord Granville, 1876–1882.* 2 vols., London, 1962.

Robinson, Ronald, and John Gallagher with Alice Denny, *Africa and the Victorians: The Official Mind of Imperialism.* London, 1961.

Roeykens, A., *Léopold II et l'Afrique, 1855–1880.* Brussels, 1957.

Rose, John Holland, *The Development of the European Nations, 1870–1900.* London, 1905.

Sanderson, G. N., *England, Europe and the Upper Nile 1882–1899.* Edinburgh, 1965.

Shibeika, Mekki, *British Policy in the Sudan, 1882–1902.* London, 1952.

Smith, Mackenzie and Co. Ltd., *The History of Smith, Mackenzie and Company Ltd.* London, 1938.

Stanley, Dorothy (ed.), *The Autobiography of Sir Henry Morton Stanley.* London, 1909.

Stanley, Henry Morton, *The Rescue of Emin Pasha and Our March Athwart Darkest Africa.* London, 1890.

Stansky, Peter, *Ambitions and Strategies: the Struggle for the Leadership of the Liberal Party in the 1890s.* Oxford, 1964.

Steiner, Zara S., *The Foreign Office and Foreign Policy, 1898–1914.* Cambridge, 1969.

Stokes, Eric, and Brown, Richard (eds.), *The Zambesian Past: Studies in Central African History.* Manchester, 1966.

Taylor, A. J. P., *Bismarck, the Man and the Statesman.* London. 1955.

Germany's First Bid for Colonies, 1884–1885. London, 1938.

Thomson, R. S., *Fondation de l'état indépendent du Congo.* Brussels, 1933.

Tilley, Sir John, and Gaselle, Stephen, *The Foreign Office.* London, 1933.

Tregonning, Kennedy G., *Under Chartered Company Rule: North Borneo, 1881–1946.* Singapore, 1958.

Verbeken, A., *Msiri, Roi de Garenganze.* Brussels, 1956.

Ward, A. W., and Gooch, G. P. (eds.), *The Cambridge History of British Foreign Policy, 1783–1919.* 3 vols., Cambridge, 1923.

Windelband, Wolfgang, *Bismarck und die europaïschen grossmächte, 1879–1885.* Essen, 1942.

GOVERNMENT PUBLICATIONS

Great Britain, *Parliamentary Debates*, 1882–93.

ARTICLES

Anonymous, 'England's Outlook in East Africa', *Fortnightly Review*, new series, XLVII (May 1890), 761–76.
'The Present Position of European Politics', *Fortnightly Review*, new series, XLI (January 1887), 1–31.
Anstey, Roger T., 'Capitalism and Slavery: A Critique', *Economic History Review*, 2nd series, XXI, 2 (August 1968), 307–20.
Baden-Powell, George, 'Fifty Years of Colonial Development', *Fortnightly Review*, new series, XLI (June 1887), 928–38.
Beckett, Ernest W., 'England and Germany in Africa', III, *Fortnightly Review*, new series, XLVIII (July 1890), 144–64.
Bridges, R. C., 'The R.G.S. and the African Exploration Fund, 1876–80', *The Geographical Journal* CXXIX, 1 (1963), 25–35.
Dicey, Edward, 'Is Central Africa Worth Having?' *Nineteenth Century* CLXIII (September 1890), 488–500.
Dilke, C. W., 'The Conservative Foreign Policy', *Fortnightly Review*, new series, LI (January 1892), 1–9.
Farler, J. P., 'England and Germany in East Africa', *Fortnightly Review*, new series, XLV (February 1889), 157–65.
Felkin, Robert W., 'The Position of Dr Emin Bey', *The Scottish Geographical Magazine* II, 12 (December 1886), 705–19.
Galbraith, John S., 'Italy, the British East Africa Company, and the Benadir Coast, 1888–1893', *Journal of Modern History* XLII, 4 (December 1970), 549–63.
'The Chartering of the British North Borneo Company', *Journal of British Studies* IV, 2 (May 1965), 102–26.
Gillard, D. R., 'Salisbury's African Policy and the Heligoland Offer of 1890', *English Historical Review* LXXV, 297 (October 1960), 631–53.
'Salisbury's Heligoland Offer: The Case Against the "Witu Thesis"', *English Historical Review* LXXX, 316 (July 1965), 538–52.
Gladstone, W. E., 'England's Mission', *Nineteenth Century* IV, 19 (September 1878), 560–84.
Hammond, Richard J., 'Economic Imperialism: Sidelights on a Stereotype', *Journal of Economic History* XXI (December 1961), 582–98.
Helly, Dorothy O., ' "Informed" Opinion on Tropical Africa in Great Britain, 1860–1890', *African Affairs* LXVIII, 272 (July 1969), 195–217.
Henderson, William O., 'British Economic Activity in the German Colonies, 1884–1914', *Economic History Review* XV (1945), 56–66.
Hennessy, John Pope, 'Is Central Africa Worth Having?' *Nineteenth Century* XXVIII (September 1890), 478–87.
'The African Bubble', *Nineteenth Century* XXVIII (July 1890), 1–4.
Hornik, M. P., 'The Anglo-Belgian Agreement of 12 May 1894', *English Historical Review* LVII, 226 (April 1942), 227–43.
Johnson, Douglas and Baxendale, A. S., 'Uganda and Great Britain', *University of Birmingham Historical Journal* VIII, 2 (1962), 162–88.

Johnston, H. H., 'The Value of Africa. A Reply to Sir John Pope Hennessy, *Nineteenth Century* XXXVIII (August 1890), 169–75.

'England and Germany in Africa', *Fortnightly Review*, new series, XLVIII (July, 1890), 119–27.

Kanya-Forstner, A. S., 'French African Policy and the Anglo-French Agreement of 5 August 1890', *Historical Journal* XII, 4 (1969), 628–50.

Keltie, J. Scott, 'Mr Stanley's Expedition: Its Conduct and Results', *Fortnightly Review*, new series, XLVIII (July 1890), 66–81.

Landes, D. S., 'Some Thoughts on the Nature of Economic Imperialism', *Journal of Economic History* XXI, 4 (1961), 496–512.

Lorne, Marquis of, 'Chartered Companies', *Nineteenth Century* XXXIX (March 1896), 375–80.

Louis, William Roger, 'Sir Percy Anderson's Grand African Strategy', *English Historical Review*, 81 (1966), 292–314.

'Great Britain and the Stokes Case', *Uganda Journal*, 28 (1964), 135–49.

Low, Anthony, 'British Public Opinion and the Uganda Question: October-December 1892', *Uganda Journal* XVIII, 2 (September 1954), 81–100.

Lowe, C. J., 'Anglo-Italian Differences over East Africa, 1892–1895, and their Effects upon the Mediterranean Entente', *English Historical Review* CCCXIX (April 1966), 315–36.

Lugard, F. D., 'The Extension of British Influence (and Trade) in Africa', *Proceedings of the Royal Colonial Institute* XXVII (1895–96), 4–40.

Mackenzie, George S., 'British East Africa and the Mombasa Railway', *Fortnightly Review*, new series, CCCIV (April 1892), 566–79.

'British East Africa', *Proceedings of the Royal Colonial Institute* XXII (November 1890), 3–21.

Ramm, Agatha, 'Great Britain and the Planting of Italian Power in the Red Sea, 1868–1885', *English Historical Review* LIX, 234 (May 1944), 211–36.

Rowe, John A., 'The Purge of Christians at Mwanga's Court', *Journal of African History* V, 1 (1964), 55–72.

Sanderson, G. N., 'England, Italy, the Nile Valley and the European Balance, 1890–91', *Historical Journal* VII, 1 (1964), 94–119.

'The Anglo-German Agreement of 1890 and the Upper Nile', *English Historical Review* LXXVIII, 306 (January 1963), 48–72.

Stokes, Eric, 'Late Nineteenth-Century Colonial Expansion and the Attack on the Theory of Economic Imperialism: A Case of Mistaken Identity?' *Historical Journal* XII, 2 (1969), 285–301.

'Great Britain and Africa: the Myth of Imperialism', *History Today*, X (August 1960), 554–63.

Taylor, A. J. P., 'Prelude to Fashoda: The Question of the Upper Nile, 1894–5', *English Historical Review* LXV, 254 (January 1950), 52–80.

Temple, Richard, 'A Parliamentary View of the Victorian Nyangza Railway', *Fortnightly Review*, new series, LI 305 (May 1892), 705–15.

Turton, E. R., 'Kirk and the Egyptian Invasion of East Africa in 1875: A Reassessment', *Journal of African History* XI, 3 (1970), 355–70.

Waller, Horace, 'Livingstone's Discoveries in Connection with the Resources of East Africa', *Journal of the Society of Arts* XXIII, 1,164 (12 March 1875), 360–7.

Wehler, Hans-Ulrich, 'Bismarck's Imperialism 1862–1890', *Past and Present*, No. 48 (August 1970), 119–55.

White, Arthur Silva, 'Chartered Government in Africa', *Nineteenth Century* CCIII (January 1894), 126–31.

De Winton, Francis, 'England and Germany in East Africa', *Nineteenth Century* CLIX (May 1890) 721–6.

PERIODICALS

The Economist, 1891–3.
Financial News, 1891–3.
Pall Mall Gazette, 1890–3.
Proceedings of the Royal Geographical Society, 1875–6.
The Times, 1876–95.
Truth, 1889–94.

Index

Aberdare, Lord, 97

Abushiri uprising, 136, 150, 160, 163

Africa: myths regarding its riches, 4, 5–7; ivory trade, 6–7; motives for 'scramble', 8–11; and humanitarian movement, 13–15

Africa, east: trade routes, 17–19; European trade with, 20; early schemes to open communications to Lakes, 43–7; difficulties of porterage, 76; Belgian expeditions (1878–9), 76–7; use of elephants, 76–7; first German interest, 83; Britain considers protectorate (1884), 85–9; entry of Germany (1884), 89; German influence extended (1885), 91; delimitation commission (1885–6), 101–6; Anglo-German boundary (1890), 181–8

African Lakes Company, 156–7

Ahmed Fumoluti, 146

Aitchison, Sir Charles, backs Mackinnon concession, 60

Alcock, Sir Rutherford, proposes African stations, 43–4, 45–6

Ampthill, Lord, 84

Anderson, Sir Percy, 102, 127, 182, 193; alleged pro-German bias, 98; and German east Africa claims, 99–100; supports Mackinnon's company, 134

Anglo-French treaty (1862), 84

Anglo-German treaty (1890), 181–8

Angra Pequena, 85

Badger, G. P., 60, 74–5, 131; role in Mackinnon concession (1877–8), 65–6, 68–9

Baker, Samuel, assessment of east Africa, 4

Barghash, Sultan, 71, 107; attempted coup, 23; dependence on Britain, 23–4; offers Britain guardianship for sons, 27–8; offers concession 47–9; declines Mackinnon concession (1877–8), 66–7; refuses Mackinnon concession (1879), 81–2; feels betrayed by Britain, 124; offers Mackinnon concession (1887), 127; transfers mainland rights to East African Association (1887), 131; death, 144

Baring, Sir Evelyn, opposes Sudanese soldiers for I.B.E.A., 163

Berkeley, E. J., 233

Bismarck, Herbert, 106, 145

Bismarck, Otto von, 1; and imperialism, 9–10, 85

Board of Trade, see Great Britain

Brassey, Lord, proposal for I.B.E.A. liquidation, 234

Bright, Jacob, 98

British India Steam Navigation Company, 101–2; seeks mail subsidy, 161; problems of asserting authority, 135–6

British North Borneo Company, 1, 38

British South Africa Company, 1; ambitions of founders, 156

Broadhurst, Henry, 98

Bruce, Alexander L., 157, 187; director of I.B.E.A., 139, 141

Brussels Anti-Slavery Conference, endorses African railway construction, 201–2

Brussels Conference (1876): and east Africa, 43–5; British delegation, 43, 45; Prince of Wales declines chairmanship of National Committee, 45, 46

Buchanan, J. W.: expedition to Taveta, 107; acting administrator I.B.E.A., 159

247

DATE DUE

GAYLORD			PRINTED IN U.S.A